SERGEI O. PROKOFIEFF (1954–2014) studied Fine Arts and Painting at the Moscow School of Art. He encountered the work of Rudolf Steiner in his youth, and quickly decided to devote his life to it. He became active as an author and lecturer in 1982, and helped found the Anthroposophical Society in his native Russia in 1991. In Easter 2001, he was appointed as a member of the Executive Council of the General Anthroposophical Society in Dornach, Switzerland, a position he held until his death. A popular speaker, he wrote numerous books and articles that are published in many languages.

Books by Sergei O. Prokofieff from Temple Lodge Publishing:

Anthroposophy and The Philosophy of Freedom
The Appearance of Christ in the Etheric
Crisis in the Anthroposophical Society and Pathways to the Future (with Peter Selg)
The Cycle of the Seasons and the Seven Liberal Arts
The Cycle of the Year as a Path of Initiation
The East in the Light of the West, Parts One to Three
The Encounter with Evil and its Overcoming through Spiritual Science
The Esoteric Significance of Spiritual Work in Anthroposophical Groups
Eternal Individuality, Towards a Karmic Biography of Novalis
The Foundation Stone Meditation
The Guardian of the Threshold and The Philosophy of Freedom
The Heavenly Sophia and the Living Being Anthroposophia
May Human Beings Hear It!, The Mystery of the Christmas Conference
The Mystery of John the Baptist and John the Evangelist
The Mystery of the Resurrection in the Light of Anthroposophy
The Occult Significance of Forgiveness
Prophecy of the Russian Epic
Relating to Rudolf Steiner
Riddle of the Human 'I'
Rudolf Steiner and the Founding of the New Mysteries
Rudolf Steiner's Path of Initiation
Rudolf Steiner's Research into Karma
Rudolf Steiner's Sculptural Group
The Spiritual Origins of Eastern Europe and the Future Mysteries of the Holy Grail
The Twelve Holy Nights and the Spiritual Hierarchies
What is Anthroposophy?
The Whitsun Impulse
Why Become a Member of the Anthroposophical Society?
Why Become a Member of the School of Spiritual Science?

The Case of Valentin Tomberg
Valentin Tomberg, Rudolf Steiner and Anthroposophy

The Mystery of the Resurrection
in the Light of Anthroposophy

The countenance of the Representative of Humanity that Rudolf Steiner painted in 1917, from the central motif of the small cupula of the first Goetheanum

The Mystery of the Resurrection in the Light of Anthroposophy

SERGEI O. PROKOFIEFF

TEMPLE LODGE

Translated from German by Simon Blaxland-de Lange

Temple Lodge Publishing
Hillside House, The Square
Forest Row, RH18 5ES

www.templelodge.com

Published by Temple Lodge 2010

This translation © Temple Lodge Publishing 2010

Originally published in German under the title *Das Mysterium der Auferstehung im Lichte der Anthroposophie* by Verlag Freies Geistesleben, Stuttgart, in 2009

© Verlag Freies Geisteleben 2008
This translation © Temple Lodge Publishing 2010

The moral right of the author has been asserted under the Copyright, Designs and Patents Act, 1988

All rights reserved. No part of this publication may be reproduced, stored in a retrieval system, or transmitted, in any form or by any means, electronic, mechanical, photocopying or otherwise, without the prior permission of the publishers

A catalogue record for this book is available from the British Library

ISBN 978 1 906999 12 4

Cover by Andrew Morgan Design incorporating the painting *Easter (Three Crosses)* by Rudolf Steiner (April 1924)
Typeset by DP Photosetting, Neath, West Glamorgan
Printed and bound in the United Kingdom by 4edge Limited

Contents

Preface   1

1. The Mystery of Golgotha and Spiritual Communion   3
   Various Kinds of Communion   40

2. Easter, Ascension and Whitsun in the Light of Anthroposophy   47
   The Inner Relationship between Easter, Ascension and Whitsun   88

3. The Resurrection and the Interior of the Earth   91
   Regarding the Relationship of the Earth Spirit to the Interior of the Earth   123

Appendix: The Forces of the Phantom and Stigmatization   133

Afterword   169

Addendum: Responses to Questions   171

Notes   185

Bibliography   211

Preface

The content of this book may serve to illustrate the depths of understanding that one can attain of the events of the Turning Point of Time through Rudolf Steiner's spiritual research. In order truly to understand these events, one needs the whole of anthroposophy. Or, to put it another way, only through the fundamental results of Rudolf Steiner's spiritual research is such an understanding as befits the consciousness soul inherently possible. For the events of the Turning Point of Time are thereby endowed with the cosmically human perspective that is appropriate to their nature.

Of course, the content of this book should merely be regarded as an attempt to approach the mysteries of the Turning Point of Time. Such an attempt needs to be made today in order to demonstrate the inexhaustible fecundity of anthroposophy. For even a century after its founding, its wellsprings are just as enlivening and inspiring as they were originally—as can be experienced by anyone who takes it up with an appropriate meditative mood and the necessary intensity and seeks to unite it in a fructifying and enlivening way with the best creative powers of his soul.

One will then approach the substance of anthroposophy with a constantly growing astonishment and an ever greater reverence. For only these soul-forces are capable today of opening up to man a path that is appropriate to modern times to the Christ Being, in whom alone the meaning of life on Earth is grounded.

The present book would therefore seek to express the deepest gratitude to Rudolf Steiner, the founder of anthroposophy and the great Christian Master of the West.

Sergei O. Prokofieff
Dornach, Whitsun 2008

1. The Mystery of Golgotha and Spiritual Communion

The Mystery of Golgotha is the central event of human evolution. The festival of Michaelmas stands opposite to its commemoration at Eastertide in the course of the year. Whereas the Easter festival has to do with remembering the deeds of a divine Being on the Earth, the festival of Michaelmas will arise out of purely human impulses. Rudolf Steiner calls its future establishment 'human anthroposophy' (GA 224, 23 May 1923).

The Mystery of Golgotha consists of two great steps: the death and Resurrection of Christ. The Resurrection forces have been an inherent part of His Being from the beginning of times; for He comes from the realm of eternal resurrection and bears its forces in Himself. Out of a free resolve, however, He decides to share together with human beings what has from the outset belonged not to His destiny but to that of human beings. For all people are mortal. Christ, for His part, seeks voluntarily to unite Himself with this death in order to overcome it on behalf of all human individuals for ever.

In order to resolve this twofold problem, the physical body had to be borne up into the spiritual world in its new, supersensible form in order subsequently to form there the foundation for the human ego-consciousness which was created at Christ's Resurrection. Hence Rudolf Steiner says that we must regard 'the Mystery of Golgotha as something real, as something that took place and had to take place in the evolution of the Earth; for it signifies literally the rescuing of the human ego' (GA 131, 11 October 1911). This rescue came about through the fashioning of the Resurrection body, that is, through Christ's transforming the body (or, to use the Biblical word, the 'flesh') of Jesus of Nazareth at the Mystery of Golgotha *into the Word*, in order that He might live in the spiritual world in this body that has become the Word. Since that time every human individual can himself gain access to this ego-rescuing reality of the Resurrection out of his own freedom. This happens in our time on the path of the new revelation of Michael.

Rudolf Steiner gives a kind of motto for the two festivals of Easter and Michaelmas: 'Easter festival, first death, then resurrection; Michaelmas festival, first resurrection of the soul, then death' (GA 223, 1 October 1923). Resurrection belongs to Christ, death is inseparably associated with the destiny of human beings on Earth. But through the deed on Golgotha man can become a participant in Christ's Resurrection forces and thereby encounter the forces of death without succumbing to them. This is the modern Michaelic path to Christ. Rudolf Steiner formulates it as follows: '... so that through the Resurrection of Christ man would find the power to die in Christ, that is, taking the risen Christ into one's soul during earthly life so as to be able to die in Him, which is to say, to be able to die not at death but when one is living' (GA 223, 2 April 1923)—thus passing through a modern initiation. He also speaks in this connection of 'that resurrection which man celebrates within himself' (GA 223, 1 October 1923), whereby he himself develops the possibility of encountering the forces of death in a new way so as to be able to fulfil his tasks amidst present-day civilization. For this civilization is increasingly permeated by death forces, which man can conquer in his soul only with the Resurrection impulse. He would otherwise run the danger of sooner or later being overwhelmed by these forces, which would have the consequence that the Earth would not attain the object of its development. The Michaelmas festival of the future should have a determining influence in ensuring that this eventuality does not occur.

The path towards establishing the Michael festival lies—as befits the Michael impulse—in a real spiritual-scientific understanding of the Mystery of Golgotha. For the true rescuing of the ego—and thus of the entirety of man's being—lies in a conscious inner relationship with what stands at its focal point, the Resurrection body of Christ. Without such a relationship to the Resurrection body, the human ego lies open to a dual danger: either a life characterized by a strong development of the individual ego, but which is bereft of immortality and comes to a final end with death (Western path), or the attainment of immortality at the cost of the individual ego, which on entering the spiritual world, that is—in this context—on entering Nirvana, dissolves like a drop in the ocean in a constant state of ecstasy (Eastern path).[1]

Rudolf Steiner speaks in this connection of two great Michael revelations. The first is to be found in the prologue of St John's Gospel with the central message: 'And the Word became flesh and dwelt among us' (John 1:14). The second Michael revelation, which is valid for our time and right to the end of earthly evolution, is formulated thus: 'And the flesh of man must again become spiritualized, so that it may be able to dwell in the kingdom of the Word in order to behold the divine mysteries. The Word becoming flesh is the first Michael revelation; the flesh becoming spirit must be the second Michael revelation' (GA 194, 22 November 1919). But only a Being who has in His development Himself become pure Word can live in the kingdom of the cosmic Word. And the mystery of the Resurrection body forms a particularly important part of the 'divine mysteries' which can be beheld by human beings in the light of spirit-knowledge. For only a conscious connection with it leads today to the realization of the second Michael revelation.

This must stand at the centre of a future Michael festival. For the task associated with this festival lies, according to Rudolf Steiner, in understanding the Mystery of Golgotha out of the present Michael impulse. 'And the great difference in all the teachings and all the wisdom that have streamed into the evolution of the Earth since the Mystery of Golgotha is that through the coming of the Michael spirit to the Earth [with the beginning of his present epoch] mankind could, through his inspiration, gradually begin to understand all that the Christ impulse, all that the Mystery of Golgotha, signifies' (GA 152, 2 May 1913). By 'understand' here is meant not only the acquiring of new knowledge but the beginning of the path whereby man can, in a free and conscious manner, attain a cognitive experience of the reality of the Resurrection. Inner work with the Foundation Stone Meditation prepares the way for this.

One of the greatest discoveries that one can make in the realm of Rudolf Steiner's spiritual science is that the Foundation Stone Meditation, which he gave at the Christmas Conference, describes the nature of the Resurrection body with great precision and thereby gives access to its essential being. This is shown most especially by the special 'rhythm' in which Rudolf Steiner spoke this meditation for the first time on 25 December 1923. First he read the three microcosmic sections of the first three parts, which bring to expression the threefold nature of man. Then came the fourth part, which refers to the preparation for the Turning Point of Time by the various mystery streams and to the Mystery of Golgotha as the radiating of the spiritual Christ Sun within earthly evolution. It therefore has to do with the main consequence of this event: the uniting of man with the spirituality of the entire universe. Then Rudolf Steiner again read the microcosmic sections of the first three parts, though now in connection with their three macrocosmic sections. (It was for this reason that, in another context, I referred to this rhythm as that of the Mystery of Golgotha, for it brings its innermost essence to manifestation.)[2]

Let us consider the Foundation Stone Meditation itself more clearly from this point of view. On 25 December 1923 Rudolf Steiner said at the laying of the Foundation Stone that the discovery of the threefold nature of the physical body was one of the most important results of his spiritual-scientific research. His research on this theme had been pursued for over 30 years before he was able in 1917, in the supplementary note to his book *The Riddles of the Soul* (GA 21), to speak about the results in public for the first time. (See also GA 28, ch. 5.) This achievement by Rudolf Steiner can surely be regarded as epoch-making, to be compared only with the greatest scientific discoveries of recent centuries. Carl Unger wrote in this connection: 'A debt of honour is owed here to Rudolf Steiner, for in this domain he has made a discovery which is just as significant as Harvey's discovery of the circulation of the blood. It is the discovery of the threefold nature of man's being.'[3] What is at issue here is the fact that the human body consists of three systems: the head, nerve and sense system located mainly in the brain and nerves; the rhythmic system, which—while permeating the entire body—has its focus above all in the heart and lungs; and the limb system, which includes both the metabolic processes and also the muscles and bone structure. Only on the basis of this discovery could the final step of the anthroposophical impulse to incarnation in the physical realm of the senses be taken.

The spiritual starting point of anthroposophy must be seen in Rudolf Steiner's experience of the Christ at the turn of the century, that is, in his Christ-imbued ego. The cognitive foundations of anthroposophy were, as a result of this, created through Rudolf Steiner's reading in the astral light.[4] He himself subsequently described its development in three seven-year periods, beginning in 1902 with the founding of the German Section of the Theosophical Society. Thus the first seven-year period witnessed above all the engendering of the research that was to be presented in written form in the book *An Outline of Occult Science*. In the second seven-year period, when there was a development out of the etheric forces, three realms came especially to the fore. These were the renewal of the arts, the development of anthroposophical Christology and the proclaiming of the Etheric Christ. The discovery of the three systems of the physical body coincided with the transition to the third seven-year period, when anthroposophy proved its worth through the establishing of various practical initiatives in the physical world.[5]

With the discovery referred to above, not merely was the phenomenon of the human body described in a Goethean sense—thus achieving the decisive step in the scientific discovery of its threefoldness—but the foundation was laid for the understanding of the mystery of the Resurrection. For in the Resurrection, Christ inseparably united the entire spirituality of the world with the three systems of the body of Jesus.

In the three macrocosmic sections of the Foundation Stone Meditation this circumstance is summarized and related to the birth, death and Resurrection of Christ Jesus in the sense of the threefold Rosicrucian dictum. The world spirituality that is in question here consists, in the sense of the Foundation Stone Meditation, of the forces of the Holy Trinity, which exerts its influence through the ninefold hierarchic cosmos and is perceived or heard by the elemental spirits as a consequence of Christ's union with the Earth.

One can also say that the three microcosmic sections of the first three parts of the Foundation Stone Meditation describe the life of Jesus of Nazareth before the Baptism in the Jordan together with the complex preparation of his earthly bodily nature, of which Rudolf Steiner spoke above all in the lectures on the Fifth Gospel.[6] This preparation brought it about that for the first time a human being came to the Earth who as regards his body could 'truly live in the World-Being of Man', as regards his soul could 'truly feel in the Soul-Weaving of Man' and as regards his spirit could 'truly think in the Spirit-Foundations of Man'. For only such a human being, who bore within himself a perfect harmony of body, soul and spirit, could become the earthly bearer of the cosmic Christ Being.

Whereas the three microcosmic sections of the first three parts of the Foundation Stone Meditation thereby refer to man's elevation to the stage where he can become a true bearer of Christ or a Christophorus, the macrocosmic sections point towards the great path of Christ to the Earth: from the (for us) inconceivable heights of the divine-spiritual Trinity through the ranks of all nine hierarchies, from the Seraphim to the Angels, in order there to unite with the body of Jesus of Nazareth which had been prepared for Him. In this way, after the best earthly forces had exerted their influence for 30 years on the body of Jesus, the cosmic forces of the Christ were added to it in the three years that followed the Baptism in the Jordan.

These cosmic forces transformed the three systems of the physical body—the head system in the first year, the rhythmic system in the second and the limbs in the third—so that they could serve the Resurrection process that followed. Rudolf Steiner indicates that above all the last stage has an altogether unique significance for the further evolution of mankind. For before the life of Christ Jesus on the Earth it was impossible for any initiate to win spiritual power over the bone system. (See GA 112, 3 July 1909.) Only after this three-year preparation could the mystery of the Resurrection take place, where after the death of Jesus the uniting of the three systems of his body with the highest spirituality of the world was accomplished by Christ.

In the sense of the Foundation Stone Meditation, one can characterize the Resurrection body which thereby came into being in the following way. *The Resurrection body is the human body in whose head system the forces of the Holy Spirit are active through the mediation of the Third Hierarchy (the*

Archai, Archangeloi and Angeloi), in whose rhythmic system the forces of the Christ as the divine Son achieve their development through the mediation of the Second or Sun Hierarchy (the Kyriotetes, Dynamis and Exusiai), and in whose limb system the forces of the Father become manifest through the mediation of the highest, First Hierarchy (the Seraphim, Cherubim and Thrones).

Thus Rudolf Steiner was the first in the development of Christianity to give a modern, spiritual-scientific description of the nature of the Resurrection, and, hence, of the essential core of the Mystery of Golgotha, which makes the Resurrection accessible to man's free powers of cognition.

We can see the full consequences of this event from the fact that in the thirteenth century Thomas Aquinas was still convinced that man could fathom with his cognitive powers only the existence of God but not the mystery of the Resurrection. In the present epoch, however, when the evolution of mankind is oriented above all towards a cognitive relationship to the world, the future of Christianity depends on whether access to its focal point, the Mystery of Golgotha, can also be extended to the cognitive powers. The achieving of this goal was Rudolf Steiner's most important earthly task. He himself once indicated why these truths must become apparent to human beings precisely in our time. He gave the reason for this in a brief, though highly meaningful sentence which characterizes the situation of Christianity in the modern human context from the spiritual aspect: 'Christianity has become *I*' (GA 109/111, 15 February 1909; the italics are Rudolf Steiner's).

In His 'farewell discourses' from St John's Gospel (14–17) Christ refers as though prophetically to this new relationship. There He says to His disciples after He has alluded to the coming Mystery of Golgotha: 'No longer do I call you servants, for the servant does not know what his master is doing; but I have called you friends, for all I have heard from my Father I have *made known* to you' (John 15:15). This is an indication of the central significance of knowledge for the future of Christianity. For only through knowledge will man rise from being a servant of the law to being a friend of God, of Christ, so as to become His conscious colleague, one who is able to act out of freedom—out of a full knowledge of His Being and His deeds—for the whole future evolution of the Earth and humanity.[7]

In these words of Christ the whole purpose of anthroposophy in our time lies concealed. For it has been given to present-day humanity so that human beings can come to a conscious collaboration with Christ on the path of knowledge. Thus anthroposophy works out of the source of the 'Spirit of truth' of whom Christ spoke in His farewell discourses.[8] For He will come to reveal to human beings an understanding of the Mystery of Golgotha and to show the path to the reality of the Resurrection.

In this respect it is of decisive importance that Rudolf Steiner imparted his discoveries about the Resurrection body not as a general description but in the form of a *meditation*, that is, as an inner path whereby the reality of the Resurrection body, and thus the nature of the Resurrection itself, can be experienced by the human soul as an inner experience. In this way the path towards the rescuing of the human ego was opened up and the foundation laid for a future Michael festival at whose focal point will stand the 'Resurrection, which man celebrates in his own inner being'.

What was brought about by Christ through the Mystery of Golgotha can henceforth enter into man's full and clear consciousness, thus enabling him to work already on the Earth on what Rudolf Steiner designates as a 'religion of the Gods' in the spiritual world. This consists in man's fully developed spiritual *and* physical attributes, that is, in the full spiritualization of the physical body out of the human ego. 'Before the Gods there hovers, as the goal of their creation, the ideal human being, which does not find expression in what physical human beings are now but is a state of development where the highest aspects of the human soul and spirit manifest themselves in the fully developed attributes of this physical human nature' (GA 153, 10 April 1914). The phrase 'the highest aspects of the human soul and spirit' here refers to the fully developed power of the individual ego and the 'fully developed attributes' of 'this *physical* human nature' to man's spiritualized physical body. Both are, however, the direct consequence of the Mystery of Golgotha, when this 'world-aim of the Gods' (ibid.) was accomplished *on the Earth itself* through the creation of the Resurrection body by Christ.

Rudolf Steiner then continues: 'Thus the Gods have before them an image of humanity as a goal, as their highest ideal, as their religion. And as though on the far shore of divine existence there shimmers for the Gods *the temple* which is their highest artistic achievement, representing *a reflection of divine Being in the image of man*' (ibid.). The World Ego of Christ—not as a 'reflection' but as the 'divine Being' itself—has been revealed in the image of man, that is, in the phantom or the 'true form' of the physical body (GA 131, 10 October 1911). Hence Rudolf Steiner speaks again and again of how the Mystery of Golgotha was not only a human but also a divine opportunity, that is to say, an opportunity of the higher hierarchies: 'The initiation principle in the Mystery of Golgotha stands clearly before the whole of humanity; this event is at once of a sensory nature on the physical plane ... and also supersensible, a real opportunity of the Gods' (GA 143, 17 April 1912). Thus with His

Resurrection Christ has shown the hierarchies that from this moment the aim of their heavenly religion, this high ideal of humanity, indeed became attainable on the Earth and can thenceforth gradually be achieved by every person of good will who in freedom seeks a conscious relationship to Christ's Resurrection body. In this way a significant degree of hope was given to all the hierarchies in the fulfilling of this aim of the evolution of humanity on Earth.

The apostle Paul describes this process in the following words: 'For this perishable nature [the mortal body] must put on the imperishable [the Resurrection body], and this mortal nature must put on immortality' (1 Corinthians 15:53). And in another context Paul puts this transformation of the body in more concrete terms when he indicates that Christ Jesus 'will transfigure[9] our lowly body so that it become similar to His transfigured [resurrected] body, by the power[10] which enables Him to make all things subject to Himself' (Philippians 3:21). The cognitive aspect also plays a decisive role in this whole process. Paul says in this connection: '... seeing that you have put off the old nature with its practices and have put on the new nature, which is being renewed in full knowledge after the image of its Creator' (Colossians 3:9–10). Jon Madsen's English translation, which has considerable affinity with the German version by Emil Bock, renders the last part of this sentence as follows: '... the New Man who grows with his renewed being *into knowledge and insight* according to the image of the One who created him' (italics added by the author in quoting the Emil Bock version).

It follows from what has been said that a relationship to the Resurrection body will only be achieved through 'knowledge and insight', a knowledge which is, however, not of a sense-perceptible nature but of *spiritual* origin. The third part of the Foundation Stone Meditation also refers to this. If we recall at this point that the Resurrection body is the fulfilment of the religion of the Gods, that is to say, at the same time the attainment of the 'eternal aims of Gods', we can also understand the deeper meaning of the words:

> Practise Spirit-beholding
> In stillness of thought
> Where the eternal aims of Gods
> World-Being's Light
> On thine own I
> Bestow
> For thy free Willing
>
> (GA 260, 25 December 1923)

What is being indicated here is that the 'World-Being's Light' of Christ is sent by the 'eternal aims of Gods' to man, so that he can find a conscious relationship to the Resurrection body, which guarantees to the individual ('own') ego freedom of the will not only on Earth but above all also in the spiritual world. The words 'Spirit-beholding' make it clear that the Resurrection body itself can only be beheld in a *purely spiritual* (sense-free) *way* or, in other words, in the sense of pure, body-free thinking, as described in *The Philosophy of Freedom*. For nothing that is still in whatever way associated with sense-perceptions can and *may* approach the reality of the Resurrection (the Resurrection body).

Similarly, it is of particular significance that Rudolf Steiner calls this 'religion of the Gods' or 'world-aim of the Gods' (GA 153, 10 April 1914) a *spiritual temple*, which every human being otherwise only beholds in the supersensible world before his incarnation as the purpose of his development on the Earth. The attainment of this goal is, however, possible for him only through forming a connection with the Resurrection body of Christ. He Himself refers to this in the following words: 'Destroy this temple, and in three days I will raise it up.' The Evangelist then makes the clarifying comment: 'But He spoke of the temple of His body' (John 2:19 and 21). And because Christ calls His physical body a temple, the apostle Paul could refer to the body of every human being as a temple: 'Do you not know that your body is a temple of the Holy Spirit within you, which you have from God? You are not your own' (Corinthians 6:19). For after Christ's Resurrection every human being bears within himself the potential of a connection with His Resurrection body. With the Foundation Stone Meditation this connection can be fashioned in full consciousness and through the practice of its meditation the inner building of the spiritual temple can be experienced right into man's physical body.

★

At this point consideration needs to be given to the difference between what Rudolf Steiner refers to in the cycle *From Jesus to Christ* as the phantom and the Resurrection body, which is to be understood here in the sense of the Foundation Stone Meditation.[11] Rudolf Steiner says throughout this cycle that the phantom is the restoration of the original spiritual form of the physical body that was corrupted by the Fall of man. This supersensible form arose on Old Saturn through the sacrifice of the Thrones and was thereafter developed further by the various hierarchies in the aeons of Old Sun, Old Moon and since the beginning of the earthly aeon. It follows from this that the restoration of the phantom has enabled man to be reconnected with the cosmic source of his evolution on Old Saturn and, hence, also with the ultimate source of his ego. For it is only possible to gain insight into the true relationship of the ego to the physical body, and thus also the riddle of ego consciousness, if one traces world evolution back to Old Saturn, in that 'anyone who wants to come to know the ego in its world context must be able to imagine a world similar to Old Saturn' (GA 132, 31 October 1911). In this way the reality of the Resurrection reaches back to Old Saturn or to what in the Book of Revelation is called the Alpha of world evolution.

The Resurrection also has its future aspect, which extends to the eventual Vulcan condition by way of the evolutionary stages of Jupiter and Venus and is designated as the Omega of world evolution. The two aspects together encompass the full significance of the words, 'I am the Alpha and the Omega, the beginning and the end' (Revelation 1:8). That is to say, the Mystery of Golgotha, as the shining forth of the highest 'I am' principle within earthly evolution, embraces the whole of world evolution, from Old Saturn (Alpha) to the future Vulcan (Omega).

Rudolf Steiner spoke about these words in a later lecture, after the Christmas Conference: 'By saying "I am the Alpha and the Omega" in the way the Book of Revelation does we have designated *what man will be at the end of the Vulcan condition*. At the end of the Vulcan condition man, too, will be permitted to say: I am the Alpha and the Omega.' However, the Mystery of Golgotha stands at the centre of this cosmic evolution. With this in mind, Rudolf Steiner continues: 'Let us look from the perspective of what we have imagined to ourselves as the beginning, middle and end of the evolution of humanity at the Mystery of Golgotha. In the Being who incarnated in Jesus through the Mystery of Golgotha we have—roughly at the mid-point of human evolution [between Saturn and Vulcan]—a Being in the world who is already at the stage in world evolution that man will have reached at the end of the Vulcan condition. We have a Being as a God such as man will be as a human being at the end of the Vulcan condition' (GA 346, 7 September 1924).[12] It is not only the *phantom*—whose existence goes back to Old Saturn—that is being referred to but above all the *Resurrection body*, which represents the future Vulcan condition. What is under consideration here is not this Vulcan aeon as such but, rather, its 'end', that is, the transition to further stages of evolution which cannot as yet be characterized in words of human language but to which Christ will lead human beings.[13]

Rudolf Steiner characterizes the Vulcan condition itself in the same lecture: 'By gradually taking into himself everything that is world and uniting his whole being with it, to the point where on Vulcan he has united with himself the whole content of the world, this great All to which he belongs, man will be what he was at the beginning of Saturn evolution *plus* the whole world. He will be Alpha and Omega, man who unites in himself everything that is world' (italics Rudolf Steiner). And then he adds that, in the Vulcan condition, man 'contains the whole *divine* world within himself' (ibid.). This means that on Vulcan man will take the whole cosmos into his own being, into the three systems of his transformed physical body which was laid down on Old Saturn, but also and above all 'the whole divine world', that is, the world of all nine hierarchies and of the forces of the Holy Trinity that work through them. Thus again we come in contact with the content of the Foundation Stone Meditation, where the essential nature of the Resurrection body is brought to expression.

Both the difference and also the degree of correspondence between the phantom and the Resurrection body (depending on the point of view from which one regards them) are clearly in evidence here; for both refer to the same reality, while the phantom is associated with its past aspect on Old Saturn and the Resurrection body with its future aspect, extending to Vulcan and even beyond it.[14]

Rudolf Steiner refers to this future aspect also in the cycle *From Jesus to Christ*: 'For the important thing is not what Christ Jesus taught but what He gave to mankind. His Resurrection is the *coming to birth* of a new member of human nature: an imperishable body' (GA 131, 11 October 1911). Thus the Mystery of Golgotha had to do not only with the restoration of the phantom but above all with the creation or birth of something altogether new, which Rudolf Steiner designates here as an 'imperishable body'. Rudolf Steiner says regarding the phantom in this connection: 'The body that was really intended for man by the rulers [hierarchies] of [Old] Saturn, [Old] Sun and [Old] Moon—the pure phantom of the physical body with all the attributes of the physical body—this it was that rose from the grave' (ibid.). This is clearly a reference to the past aspect of the phantom. Then he continues in the same lecture: 'What had been taken from him [man] at that time [after the Fall] through the luciferic influence can be *given back* to him through its presence as the Resurrection body of Christ' (ibid.). From these words it follows that something that formerly existed in the ancient past in a pure form has been lost by human beings and has been 'given back' to them in its original form through the deeds of Christ (GA 131, 10 October 1911).

On the other hand, the connection of the Resurrection body with the most distant future of humanity and the Earth, with Vulcan and even with what comes afterwards, is evident from the following results of Rudolf

Steiner's spiritual research. Thus he describes the transition from Vulcan to the next world system (cosmos) in the following words: 'During the Vulcan stage, all the beings who had their origin in the small beginnings of Saturn existence will have been spiritualized to the highest degree; together they will have become not just Sun but Over-Sun. Vulcan likewise will be more than Sun, it will have reached the maturity for sacrifice, the maturity necessary for self-dissolution' (GA 110, 14 April 1909). Rudolf Steiner describes the sacrifice that will lead from Vulcan to the next stage of world evolution as follows. First the Sun, which has ascended to the stage of the 'Over-Sun', reabsorbs its planets and becomes a Vulcan. Then the whole is dissolved, and the Vulcan globe later becomes a hollow globe ... Thus the [Over-]Sun will dissolve, sacrifice itself into the universe, send forth its being ... This means that when a sun has reached the point where it could reunite itself with its planets, it becomes periphery, it becomes a [new] zodiac', which can itself 'give birth to a new solar system out of its own forces'. For the beings that have formed the new zodiac 'have risen to an exalted rank of cosmic sacrificial service' (ibid.).

At the Turning Point of Time a germinal foundation was laid for this future mighty metamorphosis, which will consist in the cosmic inversion from the point to the periphery. It came about through the cosmic Word Himself coming to the Earth in the middle of the Earth aeon ('And the Word became flesh', John 1:14). From the infinite periphery of His world-creating activity there was a concentration on one point, on the body of Jesus of Nazareth. Rudolf Steiner says in this connection in his lectures on the Fifth Gospel: 'The macrocosmic Sun Being [of Christ] shapes Himself in accordance with the form of the human microcosm, thrusts its way, narrows and contracts more and more into the human microcosm ... The Christ Being had to feel how the divine power gradually waned as He became assimilated to the body of Jesus of Nazareth. Stage by stage the God became a man' (GA 148, 3 October 1913). And Rudolf Steiner continues in the same lecture: 'Of what was Christ's earthly state the outcome? It was the outcome of the deepest suffering, transcending any suffering that the human mind can conceive.'

Rudolf Steiner's research out of the realm of the Fifth Gospel gives us an altogether different perspective on the sufferings of Christ Jesus on His path through Passiontide than is generally adopted. According to this general view, the greatest sufferings of Christ were not those of the man Jesus, such as every human being can comprehend, but those which go far beyond every dimension of what is conceivable. According to the Fifth Gospel this immense suffering was associated above all with the process of the cosmic Christ Spirit becoming a man. Rudolf Steiner describes this process as the infinite 'contracting' or 'drawing together' of His divine Being to the point where it became completely one with the body of Jesus of Nazareth, and the Christ increasingly experienced the disappearance of His divine power.

The following picture may help one to gain a better understanding: one could imagine the Sun, with all its cosmic power with which it holds the whole planetary system together, entering into the narrow space of a comparatively tiny human body. And yet even this well-nigh inconceivable picture is only approximately correct; for in Christ it was not only the spiritual Sun that was 'becoming flesh' but a Being who is infinitely greater than the entire sphere of the Sun.

However, this process was accompanied by another which for Christ became the source of much greater suffering even than this. Rudolf Steiner described this situation in the following words: 'You should not imagine that this body in which the Christ dwelt was, say, a year and a half after the Baptism by John in the Jordan like any other body. An ordinary human soul would have immediately felt this body falling away from it, because it could only be held together by the mighty macrocosmic Christ Being. It was a continuous, slow dying process that lasted for three years. And this body was on the verge of disintegration when the Mystery of Golgotha occurred' (GA 130, 9 January 1912).

Thus it is evident from the content of the Fifth Gospel that Christ in Gethsemane was not struggling with fear of the destiny that He had freely taken upon Himself, nor with the fear of death which every human being would feel before suffering a martyr's death, but *with death itself*, that is, with the ahrimanic powers in His body, which wanted to tear Him away into the spiritual world prematurely, before He had completed His task for mankind, the restoring of the phantom for all human beings. For the forces of the restored phantom had almost entirely left the material substance of the body at the time of the Passion. And now Christ Himself had to hold this material substance of His body that was no longer held together by the phantom out of His own power. He had to suffer this in unimaginable pain not only on the Cross but, more drastically, in the disintegrating vessel of His physical body and endure this until the last words from the Cross: 'It is finished' (John 19:30).

Emil Bock gives the following account of this situation: 'What still has to be suffered and completed demands so much strength from the earthly sheaths [of Jesus] that there is a real danger of premature death. Ahriman lies in wait and hopes to make use of this moment. Luke, the physician, describes with precise words what happens. It is the fault of generally accepted translations that the scene has nevertheless been falsely understood in an anthropomorphic way. Where the Lutheran Bible states, "And so it was that He was struggling with death, and He prayed more earnestly," the literal meaning of the text is: "And being in agony ..." In the clinical sense of the term, the death-struggle had already come. When St Luke adds, "and His sweat became like great drops of blood falling down to the ground", he adds exact symptoms of the agony of death' (Emil Bock, *The Three Years*, the chapter entitled 'The Events of Holy Week' and the section on Good Friday, Floris Books, 1980).

The Fifth Gospel and Rudolf Steiner's research would seek to shed light not upon the anthropomorphization of the sorrows of Christ Jesus on the path of His Passion but upon their truly superhuman dimension.[15] For only because Christ followed this unimaginable way of sorrows to its end could the restoration of the phantom on the Cross be followed by the Resurrection, when it was imbued with the forces of the Resurrection body.

Thus it was not merely a human love that was born from this superhuman suffering of Christ but the *cosmic* love of the Christ impulse, whose influence will extend to the end of the entire earthly age. 'Out of this suffering was born the all-prevailing cosmic love' (GA 148, 3 October 1913) which on the Day of Pentecost fructified the souls of the apostles. Thereafter they knew: 'The death of Jesus of Nazareth was the birth of the *all-prevailing cosmic love* within the earthly sphere' (ibid., 2 October 1913). Thus the cosmic love which, as a perpetual Whitsun event, will take hold of more and more people in order that they may understand the mysteries of the Turning Point of Time was born on the Hill of Golgotha out of the superhuman suffering of Christ.

And just as Christ's suffering on His macrocosmic path from periphery to point was infinitely deep, so will the joy and rejoicing of mankind when at the end of the Vulcan age it will accomplish the opposite metamorphosis, from point to the new world periphery, be infinitely great. That this metamorphosis will be possible at all is to be attributed to Christ's deed on Golgotha. For only through the establishing by human beings of a conscious relationship to the sacrifice of Christ Jesus and its consequence, the Resurrection body, beginning from the earthly aeon and on into the aeons of Jupiter and Venus, will they be able on Vulcan to themselves ascend to the 'great cosmic sacrificial service' that has been described. This will signify for them the highest stage of development and creative power, arising as it does out of 'cosmic love' as a new creation which sprang forth from the deepest 'powerlessness of the God who had become man' (ibid.).

Christ's Ascension appears as a prophetic premonition of what will happen at the end of the Vulcan age. After He had passed through the cosmic zero-point in the Mystery of Golgotha and had united the cosmic power of the Resurrection with the whole of earthly evolution, 'He was taken up into heaven' (what this means in spiritual-scientific terms will be explained later in this chapter), 'and sat at the right hand of God' (Mark 16:19).[16]

This is a reference to the greatest 'periphery' which encompasses the entire cosmos and is at the same time the source of all creative forces in the universe. 'For whatever He [the Father] does, that the Sun does likewise' (John 5:19).

★

Returning to the mystery of the phantom, one can now better understand why it is possible to say that it was restored already *before* the death and Resurrection of Christ. Rudolf Steiner says in this regard: 'Thus it followed that when Christ Jesus was crucified ... when this body of Jesus of Nazareth was fastened to the Cross, the phantom was perfectly intact; it existed in a spiritual bodily form, visible only to supersensible sight ... The fact is that ... the ordinary law of inertia sees to it that certain material parts continue to hold together in the form that they have been given and then crumble away after some time, so that hardly anything of them is visible.[17] So it was with the material parts of the body of Christ Jesus. When the body was taken down from the Cross the parts were still coherent, but they had no connection with the phantom; the phantom was completely free of them' (GA 131, 12 October 1911).[18] This means that already before the death of Christ Jesus and in death itself the pure form of the physical body as existed on Old Saturn had been restored in the body of Jesus as a result of the three years of His life. Thus in the first year it was above all the part of the phantom that underlies the head system of the physical body which was restored in its primordial state, when it was as yet untouched by the adversarial powers; in the second year this happened for the rhythmic system and in the third for that of the limbs.

Because of this the adversarial powers could no longer gain access to this supersensible form of the physical body, which is how this supersensible form was able to establish the foundation for receiving all the spiritual forces of the universe extending to the future Vulcan stage and to appear on Easter Sunday as the Resurrection body which bears the phantom within itself. Hence although Rudolf Steiner had previously said that the phantom had been fully restored before the death on the

Cross, he could repeatedly point out that this 'phantom ... arose from the grave of Golgotha' (GA 131, 14 October 1911).[19]

These two components of the Resurrection body, which are related, respectively, to the past and the future and thereby connect the beginning and end of the whole of cosmic evolution from Old Saturn to Vulcan, can be more clearly understood from the following point of view. In the book *An Outline of Occult Science* Rudolf Steiner describes how Christ Jesus only appeared as the teacher of humanity when everything that Lucifer had made obscure in human beings became clearly manifest in His soul. This happened directly after the Baptism in the Jordan. We know from other descriptions by Rudolf Steiner that Lucifer tries above all to darken and distort man's perception of the past. When Christ Jesus was able to survey the entire past of the Earth back to Old Saturn in a manner not bound to Lucifer, His three years' work on the restoring of the phantom of His physical body began.

When after Christ's death on the Cross the power of Ahriman—which strives continually to distort the future of evolution and to truncate human development—had been 'confined to its limits' (GA 13), the Resurrection body could be fashioned as something entirely new in the Resurrection that followed. Through it human beings who find a conscious access to it are connected with the whole future evolution of the Earth as far as Vulcan and, as we have already seen, even beyond it.

With the help of the Foundation Stone Meditation one can conceive of this path to Vulcan as follows. With the consummation of the Resurrection the World Ego of Christ imbued the head system of Jesus with the forces of the Holy Spirit, mediated by the Third Hierarchy. In this way the stage of the future Jupiter was prepared. Through the imbuing of the rhythmic system of Jesus with the forces of the Son, mediated by the Second Hierarchy, the Venus stage was laid down.[20] Finally, there ensued the permeation of the metabolic and limb system with the forces of the Father through the mediation of the First Hierarchy. By this means the stage of Vulcan was reached and the foundation was laid for the mighty metamorphosis described above, which will lead from Vulcan like a bridge to the creating of the new cosmos.

★

The fact that the phantom of the physical body had been restored to its full extent already before Christ's death on the Cross casts a decisive new light on His three years of life in the bodily sheaths of Jesus of Nazareth. For the question as to how the phantom was restored during this time has to do with what Christ did while Jesus was sleeping on the Earth. In the

Gospels there is only one reference to the sleeping Jesus, and that is the scene when He was in a boat with His disciples during the storm on the lake.[21] One may justly surmise from this that, after the Baptism in the Jordan, Jesus needed not only food but also sleep like other human beings. But what did Christ do while Jesus slept? In order to understand this, one needs to call to mind what takes place with every human being during sleep. The physical and etheric bodies remain in the bed, while the astral body and ego leave it and work unconsciously on the two bodily members that have been left behind from without, permeated by the forces of the higher hierarchies. By this means the forces of the etheric body which have been used up during the day, together with the destroyed parts of the physical body, can be built up again and renewed.

In addition to the up-building activity taking place in the sheaths that have been left behind by means of the life-processes, there is also a twofold moral influence—of which the sleeping person is deeply unconscious—that unfolds outside the physical body within his astral body and ego. In order to gain a conscious experience of the first aspect of this twofold influence, a person must have reached the stage of the Life Spirit. Then there is revealed to him what Rudolf Steiner describes as follows: 'If human beings were able to enter into the consciousness of the Life Spirit when their astral bodies are active and alive out there [in the spiritual world during the night], they would be able to speak to that which happens with their astral bodies ... For who would be speaking if human beings suddenly attained the consciousness of the Life Spirit in their sleep? ... The human astral body would be speaking as a judge of good and evil in man. So that one must actually say: in sleep the astral body becomes the judge of the soul' (GA 208, 13 November 1921).

However, Rudolf Steiner does not confine himself to this purely human aspect of the situation but extends it to something that concerns the whole of mankind: 'If the idea expressed in the words "In sleep, the astral body becomes the judge of the soul" comes from Inspiration, we find this well represented in Michelangelo's fresco *The Last Judgment*, painted in the Sistine Chapel' (ibid.). These words enable one to answer the question as to what Christ was accomplishing every night in Jesus' astral body outside the physical and etheric bodies while he was asleep: He was judging the world and was thereby preparing what will eventually take place as the future 'Last Judgment', as prophetically painted by Michelangelo in the Sistine Chapel.[22]

The second moral process, which is brought about during sleep not by the astral body but by the ego, can only be observed by an initiate out of the power of the Spirit Man. 'Were it [the human ego] to awaken to a consciousness of the Spirit Man, the ego ... would be furnished with the consciousness which is active in the physical body that it has left behind, which sends forces from above to below in this physical body' (ibid.). Rudolf Steiner characterizes what an initiate would then experience in the following sentence: 'The ego becomes its own sacrifice, the sacrifice of the spirit which is active in the body.' The highest spirit, which enters right into the material substance of the body, overpowers the forces of the ego, which at this stage of its development is not yet capable of collaborating in full consciousness in this process and thereby becomes 'its own sacrifice', that is in this case a sacrifice to its weakness. Thereby the initiate experiences the true relationship of the ego to the physical body whose phantom has not yet been restored.

In the same lecture, Rudolf Steiner extends what here relates to man also to the life of Christ on Earth, at the end of which there stands the phantom in its absolute, intact form: 'And again [he was speaking initially about Michelangelo's picture], if we look upon what appears to us as an immensely moving picture, the image of the Lamb of God, the Christ, that Christ who unites Himself with the human ego, who permeates this human ego, the thought of the ego becoming the sacrifice as it enters into the state of sleep stirs into activity in our soul as we contemplate the Lamb who sacrifices Himself; and we find how aptly this sacrificial nature of man during sleep is expressed by the image of the Lamb' (ibid.).

What concerns us here is a human ego which has been permeated with the Christ impulse. For such an ego the experience that has been described changes during sleep. The person concerned no longer beholds his ego as 'its own sacrifice' but in such a way that 'during sleep it [the ego] becomes the sacrifice of its own selfhood' (ibid.). This apparently minor difference in the formulation is, however, of decisive significance. For now the ego has found its higher being, and it can consciously begin the process of restoring the phantom of its own physical body through the power of Christ. By this means there is revealed to the human individual in question the mystery of what corresponds to this microcosmic process within himself in the macrocosm, namely, how Christ had worked during the three years of His earthly life on restoring the phantom in the body of Jesus of Nazareth.

The picture of the Lamb in Rudolf Steiner's quoted words is a reference to the testimony of John the Baptist, who after the Baptism in the Jordan proclaimed of Christ: 'Behold, the Lamb of God, who takes the sin of the world upon Himself!' (John 1:29). By the 'sin of the world' is meant primarily the consequences of the original Fall, which manifested themselves most strongly in the destruction of the phantom. Since then every earthly human being (including Jesus of Nazareth) has borne within himself this destroyed phantom. Thus when the Gospel speaks of taking the sins of mankind upon Himself through His sacrifice, it means for Christ Himself none other than, in Jesus, taking the degenerate phantom upon Himself and transforming it. And that is the spiritual activity which was being carried out every night during the three years within the physical body of Jesus while he was asleep: the restoring of the phantom.

Thus to summarize we can say: while Jesus slept Christ was judging mankind out of His astral body and rescuing it through the power of His Ego, while at the same time transforming the physical body. This enables one to understand the sense in which Christ's judgment of mankind is meant. It will consist not in a condemnation, let alone damnation, of man but in the fashioning of the purified phantom of the physical body of every human being, so that he may be able to see in the mirror of the phantom—in which the physical and moral forces form an indivisible unity—how far he himself still is from this great moral ideal. Hence Rudolf Steiner calls Christ the 'great human earthly archetype' (GA 13).

*

Returning to the main theme of this chapter, there is an important quality relating to the scars of the phantom which should not pass without mention. For according to Rudolf Steiner, the wounds of the Crucified One remained not in the phantom but in His 'condensed etheric body'.[23] For the etheric body is also the memory body. (In this case, however, memory itself is of a 'being' quality.) The so-called scars visible on the phantom, on the other hand, were of a completely different nature and significance. Rudolf Steiner speaks as follows about their origin: 'Anyone who understands the true nature of man and of humanity, and the nature of the earthly ego and its relation *to the human form* of the body ... may ask: How would this body be if the totality of egohood were to enter into it? His answer must be that it would be pierced by five wounds' (GA 139, 21 September 1912). Thus the bodily nature into which the World Ego of the Christ had entered 'had to appear ... with five wounds, which were necessary because the Christ Being, that is, the full ego of man, projected beyond the *form* of the bodily nature' (ibid.). Thus the five marks on the phantom derive not from the scars of the wounds received by the physical body of Jesus on the Cross but from the complete victory of the Christ Ego over the 'form of the bodily nature', that is, over the degenerate forces of the phantom. (That in both quotations Rudolf Steiner consistently speaks of the *form* of the body indicates a reference not to its material substance but to the phantom.) Hence the five marks of the phantom were from the outset not wounds but portals through which the Christ forces radiated out into the world.

In this connection it is particularly important to distinguish between the visibly bleeding wounds of the body on the Cross and supersensibly perceptible marks on the body of the Resurrected Christ. For the former still belong to the old world, which together with the Resurrection event ultimately belongs to the past. The marks on the phantom, on the other hand, are to become the source of an altogether new world, which had its beginning in Christ's Resurrection. In a human being who will in future take the forces of the phantom into his own being, these five marks will become new supersensible organs with which he will behold the spiritual world in perpetual association with Christ.

Rudolf Steiner referred to these five forces in a meditative verse that he composed around the end of 1912:

> The soul of the world lies outstretched
> Upon the cross of the world's body.
> In five out-bearing rays, luminously, it lives
> Through wisdom, love, and power of will,
> Through all-awareness and ego-awareness,
> Finding thus
> Within itself the Spirit of the World.
>
> (Translation by Arvia MacKaye Ege from *Truth-Wrought-Words*, AP, 1979)

These words relate initially to the picture that Plato conveyed from the old mystery knowledge in the *Timaeus*, where there is a prophetic indication of what was to become a mystical fact in the Mystery of Golgotha. Rudolf Steiner writes in this connection: 'Plato describes the macrocosmic aspect when he says that God stretched out the world-soul on the world's body *in the form of a cross*. This world-soul is the Logos; and if the Logos is to become flesh it must be through the repetition of the macrocosmic events in fleshly existence, being nailed to the Cross and rising to new life' (GA 8, the chapter entitled 'Christianity and Pagan Wisdom'; the italics are Rudolf Steiner's).

With the help of this verse, we can conceive of the radiating of moral forces from the Ego of Christ through the five portals of the Resurrection body as follows: love streams through the portal of the heart; power of will and wisdom stream though the two upper portals; and through the two lower ones there radiate the forces which simultaneously take hold of and permeate the essential nature of the ego and the world.

In order to arrive at a better understanding of the complicated reality of the Resurrection, it is necessary briefly to refer once again to something that has already been investigated at some length elsewhere.[24] After Rudolf Steiner had in October 1911, in the cycle *From Jesus to Christ*, placed so strong an emphasis on the Resurrection *in the body*, he spoke again about the mystery of the Resurrection two and a half months later, in January 1912 in Munich, though now his constant theme was no longer the Resurrection in the physical body but in the etheric body. In this lecture there is a clear reference to the apostles seeing 'an etheric body condensed into visibility' (GA 130, 9 January 1912) after the Resurrection. 'Thus the Risen Christ was enshrouded with an etheric body condensed to the point of physical visibility' (ibid.).[25] Or, in other words, the Resurrection body bore this condensed etheric body as its outward sheath. Only in this lecture, on the basis of his spiritual research, did he describe the event involving doubting Thomas, who asked to place his fingers in the wounds of the Risen One. In this connection, Rudolf Steiner gives the decisive indication that *the wounds on Christ's body did not remain in the phantom but only in the condensed etheric body*.[26]

Rudolf Steiner refers to this in the following powerful words, as though he was seeking to correct a significant error: 'Yet someone might object that the Risen One, when He appeared to the disciples, urged Thomas to touch His wounds. One might therefore think that these wounds were still there and that Christ had come to the disciples in the same body that had crumbled into dust. No!' (GA 130, 9 January 1912). For what Thomas experienced as wounds related not to the phantom of the physical body of the Risen One but to the 'condensed etheric body'. Thus Thomas actually touched the condensed places of the Risen One's *etheric body* (the etheric 'scars', as Rudolf Steiner calls them), which arose where the bodily wounds had been. The phantom itself was completely free of this.

In the same lecture, Rudolf Steiner also mentions that, in the Emmaus scene (Luke 24:30–1), the Risen Christ had eaten before the disciples not in a physical sense but in a purely etheric way: 'This [the Emmaus scene] is described in the Gospel not as an ordinary intake of nourishment, but as a dissolution of food directly though the etheric body, through Christ's power, *without the involvement of the physical body*.'[27] This intake of nourishment came about directly through the etheric body, *not* through the phantom, which also in this case remained untouched by any earthly matter. One can also say that for the Risen One any intake of nourishment became pure transubstantiation, just as He had accomplished this in an archetypal sense for the apostles at the Last Supper.[28]

With this Rudolf Steiner is referring to the important fact that, in future, when the spiritualization of his body has been advanced to a further stage through the connection with the Resurrection body, man will not cease to take in nourishment but will on the contrary raise it to another, etheric level, so that the process of the spiritualization of the Earth can be furthered.[29] In this way it is possible to resolve the apparent contradiction that, after he had indicated that the phantom needs and tolerates no food (see GA 131, 12 October 1911), Rudolf Steiner nevertheless confirmed the fact that the Risen One had eaten before His disciples. For He wanted thereby to demonstrate the further significance of human nourishment, albeit in this transformed (etherized) guise.

If we return to the context of the previous discussion, one should not immediately suppose that there is a contradiction in the descriptions given by Rudolf Steiner but must give oneself sufficient time, in order that—by carefully studying the relevant statements—one may ascertain that in this case (and also with regard to the phantom and the Resurrection body) attention needs to be focused on various aspects of a highly complicated process, which can barely be grasped in human words.

Thus Rudolf Steiner indicated subsequently that not only man's *physical* body but also his *etheric* body was objectively rescued in the Mystery of Golgotha. 'Through the Mystery of Golgotha complete provision was made for the physical-etheric nature of mankind as a whole,' for 'the deed on Golgotha was fulfilled for the physical body *and* the etheric body in the universally human sense' (GA 224, 7 May 1923).[30]

In order to understand the nature of this rescuing more clearly, one needs to bear the following in mind. Just as the inherently supersensible form of the physical body only becomes perceptible to the senses through its being filled with matter, so too does man's etheric body enter into outward manifestation through the fluids of the human body. This is substantiated above all by the fact that all the fluids in man are in constant movement; and rhythmical movement is the most important mark of the etheric body. It follows from this that the etheric body comes to manifestation primarily through the blood, because of all the fluids in the human organism it is most strongly subject to the rhythmic element.[31]

Once we have established this connection, we can understand the mystery of the events on Good Friday in a new way. For at that time not only did man but also the whole Earth as a living being receive *cosmic communion*, and indeed in the literal sense. First the Earth itself received the blood of the Crucified One[32] and, hence, also the forces of His etheric body. So long as the blood flowed from the wounds, that is, continued to remain in movement, the etheric body was connected with it. Then the

Earth also received the body of the Crucified One. As Rudolf Steiner states in the Fifth Gospel, after the death of Christ Jesus the body was taken from the Cross and laid in the tomb.[33] Through an earthquake a fissure then appeared in the Earth, into which the body was received. (See GA 148, 2 October 1913.) In this way the material substance of Jesus' body was united with the Earth.[34]

That this had to do not with the phantom but only with the material substance which had previously filled it follows from Rudolf Steiner's statement 'that after three years the whole body of Jesus of Nazareth was close to being a corpse, and was only held together by the power of the macrocosmic Christ Being' (GA 130, 9 January 1912). The condition of a corpse is that it has been abandoned by the phantom and is therefore in a process of decomposition. This separation of the phantom from the material substance with which it was imbued was, however, utterly necessary for its restoration in its original purity through the power of Christ. This happened before the death on the Cross. (See Rudolf Steiner's words on p. 17.) Because of this, no human ego would have been able to remain even for a single moment in such a body. For 'an ordinary human soul would have immediately felt this body falling away from it' (ibid.). In other words, such a person would immediately die. 'This body had reached the verge of dissolution when the Mystery of Golgotha occurred' (ibid.). After Joseph of Arimathaea and Nicodemus had anointed the body—*already without the phantom*—with special 'spices' (ibid.) and had lowered it into the grave, 'very little was needed for *this body to fall to dust in the grave*. What had been laid into the grave fell to dust' (ibid.). Then 'the earth opened up [because of an earthquake], the dust of the corpse fell into it and *united with the whole substance of the Earth* (ibid.).[35] By this is meant that not the body but only its material substance (without the phantom) was received by the Earth in a state of the finest dust (it was actually already wholly spiritualized, in that this substance had by this time virtually nothing material about it) and was thereby united with its 'whole substance'. Rudolf Steiner refers to these spiritual facts that he had discovered as the 'most recent occult researches' (ibid.).

Thus through the Earth's having taken into itself the material substance of Jesus' body, the foundation was laid for what Rudolf Steiner describes as follows: 'We shall see things in their true light only if we discern in every atom [of earthly matter] something of the Christ Spirit that has indeed imbued it since that time [the Mystery of Golgotha] ... Since the Christ Spirit has permeated it, the Earth has consisted of life, down to its every atom' (GA 112, 7 July 1909). Hence in future a true science will increasingly emphasize: 'Matter is constructed in the sense that *Christ* [since the Mystery of Golgotha] has gradually ordered it!' (GA 15, ch. 3; italics Rudolf Steiner).

Just as the material substance of the body was united with the entire Earth, so likewise was the blood of the Crucified One. Rudolf Steiner has this to say about its substance: 'When it [the blood] flowed from His wounds and streamed into the Earth, a substance was imparted to our Earth which, in uniting with it, constituted an event of the greatest possible significance for all future ages of the Earth—and it could take place only once. What became of this blood in the times that followed?... In the course of Earth evolution, this blood has been passing through a process of etherization ... *The etheric body of the Earth is permeated by what has become of the blood which flowed on Golgotha*' (GA 130, 1 October 1911). This 'etherization' of Christ's blood within the Earth became possible only because the forces of the etheric body of Christ Jesus remained connected with Him also in the future. Hence Rudolf Steiner also speaks of the 'new etheric body' in which the Christ was clothed after His Resurrection (GA 130, 9 January 1912).

Thus the *cosmic communion* which the Earth received on Good Friday consists of two parts: the material components of the body, which permeated the entire substance of the Earth, and the etherized blood, which infiltrated the Earth's etheric body.

At this point the question arises: why was it necessary for the Earth to have this twofold communion with blood and body? The answer lies rooted in the fact that at the Turning Point of Time the Earth's connection with the spiritual forces of the cosmos had been gradually waning. This was an inevitable part of establishing the foundation for human freedom. For if human beings had continued to perceive these forces throughout the natural world as directly as was the case on ancient Atlantis, they could never have become free beings. Hence the Earth had to be separated from the spiritual forces of the cosmos, those of the seven planets and the twelve aspects of the zodiac. Thus it was sundered from the forces of its origin and would, if nothing further had happened, have gradually succumbed to death. However, this death process of the Earth was to experience a reversal at the Turning Point of Time. New forces had then to flow into the Earth which ensured its renewed connection with the spiritual world of the planets and the zodiac. It was precisely this which was accomplished in a quite particular way on Good Friday through cosmic communion.

In order to understand this process still more clearly, we must turn once again to the absolute uniqueness of Christ's three years in the body of Jesus. For the fundamental difference between His life and the earthly lives of all other people was as follows. The star configuration which appears at the moment of an ordinary person's birth impresses itself upon him and continues to have an unchanging effect throughout his whole life. With Christ Jesus, on the other hand, the influence of the star configuration changed at every moment, so that He was constantly in harmony with the whole cosmos.

From the spiritual aspect this signifies the following. Every person incarnating on the Earth (including Jesus of Nazareth) forms in his pre-birth existence the spiritual seed of his later physical body out of the twelvefold forces of the zodiac, and then the seed of his etheric body out of the sevenfold forces of the planets. Hence the physical body is membered in a twelvefold way (from the Ram in the upper part of the head to the Fishes in the feet) and, like the fixed stars in the sky, maintains its fixed form in space. In contrast to this, the etheric body is regarded as being in a permanent state of rhythmical change, which has its source in the movements of the seven planets; and it can, therefore, be described as the sevenfold-membered time body of man.

When a human individual comes to the Earth at birth, during the incarnation process the configuration of the fixed stars and the planets that is manifested at this moment is imprinted into the most intricate forms of his brain and continues to be connected with him unchanged throughout the whole of his life as a memory of his cosmic existence. It is this that constitutes the nature of the human horoscope. 'And if one were to photograph a person's brain at the moment when he is born, and then also photograph the celestial region lying directly above this person's place of birth, this picture would show exactly the same features as the human brain. The way that certain parts of the brain are ordered would resemble the stars in the picture of the heavens' (GA 15, ch. 3).

That which remains unchanged until his death in the case of an ordinary human being was subjected to a constant change as regards the three years of the earthly life of Christ Jesus. As a result there arose the unique situation which Rudolf Steiner describes in the following words: 'The Christ was always under the influence of the whole cosmos; He took no step without the cosmic forces exerting their influence upon Him. What was taking place in Jesus of Nazareth *was a continual enacting of the horoscope*; for at each moment there was happening what otherwise only happens when a person is born ... He who walked the Earth as a particular being appeared like any other person. But the forces that were inwardly at work were the cosmic forces coming from the Sun and the stars; and these were directing His body' (ibid.)—'The whole *spirit of the cosmos*' (ibid.) was influencing this unique earthly life.

In this way 'the spirit of the whole cosmos' (ibid.) was constantly active in the physical and etheric bodies of Christ Jesus during His three years of life on the Earth, or, in other words, the spiritual forces of the fixed stars (above all the zodiac) and the spiritual forces of the planets. That is to say, the connection to the spiritual cosmos, which in the case of all other people breaks off after their earthly birth, continued to work on uninterrupted with Christ Jesus from the Baptism in the Jordan to the Mystery of Golgotha, and on Good Friday passed over into the Earth with the consummation of cosmic communion. Through this the Earth achieved a new relationship with the entire spiritual cosmos and at the same time with its own cosmic future. Rudolf Steiner describes this process thus: 'What in another person flows at birth into earthly existence [and then ceases] was flowing into Christ Jesus *at each moment* [of His earthly life]. And when the Mystery of Golgotha was accomplished, what had streamed forth from the cosmos passed over into the spiritual substance of the Earth' (ibid.; italics Rudolf Steiner).

In earlier lectures Rudolf Steiner portrays this process on several occasions in a mighty imagination, which gives an indication of its cosmic dimension. If a being endowed with clairvoyant powers had beheld the aura of the Earth from its most distant past until the Turning Point of Time, he would have detected that it was gradually becoming ever darker and darker. This process of darkening was the sign of its separation from the cosmic forces of its origin. But then the moment came when the whole aura of the Earth suddenly completely changed. Its descent into darkness ceased, and it was filled with a new light and wonderful colours. The first glimmerings of a new Sun radiated into it like a star. And then Rudolf Steiner indicates the precise moment when this change in the Earth's aura occurred. It was the moment when the blood from the Redeemer's wounds flowed into the Earth,[36] thus beginning its great cosmic communion.

In the lecture of 1 April 1918, Rudolf Steiner described the lighting up of this new star in a particularly striking way. After he had described the colours of the Earth's aura as the bluish-violet shining eastern Earth and the reddish-yellow glimmering western Earth, he concluded this imagination with the following words: 'As spiritually contemplated from the cosmos, the event of Golgotha was the appearance of a golden star in the blue Earth-aura of the eastern half of the Earth' (GA 181).

★

This cosmic communion also found its direct expression in the new mysteries. Thus it can be found in the last lecture that Rudolf Steiner was able to give to anthroposophical listeners in the First Goetheanum, when he spoke the words of the mantric formulation of the cosmic communion of mankind. For only a few hours after the end of this lecture the building became a sacrifice to the flames. To be precise, the fire had already been started by a criminal act before Rudolf Steiner's lecture. However, as the flames initially spread between the double walls of the building, so that the smoke was for several hours confined to the spaces between the walls and the two cupolas, the act of arson was not immediately discovered. So Rudolf Steiner was summoned to the scene of the fire from his house, the Villa Hansi.

One may gather from the course of this sequence of events that, at the time when Rudolf Steiner was concluding his lecture with the words of cosmic communion, the whole periphery of the building within the dividing walls was already completely engulfed in flames. In this way, as though at the last moment, what had not as yet been able to come about was accomplished on the scale of world history. For although the building was almost complete by this time, Rudolf Steiner kept on delaying its opening.[37] Subsequently, after the fire, he emphasized quite clearly that none of the nine major events that had taken place in the building could be regarded as the true (esoteric) opening of the building.[38]

With the fire the consecration of the building now came about in a quite particular way. Surrounded by the fire Rudolf Steiner stood there as the high priest in the midst of a cosmic ritual and, in the great hall of the First Goetheanum, spoke the words of cosmic communion, words in which 'the whole spirit of the cosmos' was actively present. He spoke to them in the great hall of the First Goetheanum, which shortly afterwards was received into the cosmos with all its forms consumed by the sea of flames. In this way Rudolf Steiner accomplished for the building what he referred to at the end of his lecture as a 'cosmic ritual', which in this moment became the 'new baptism' which John the Baptist had prophetically proclaimed as Christ's baptism with the Spirit and with fire. (See Luke 3:16.)[39]

Rudolf Steiner introduced the mantric formulation of cosmic communion with the following words: 'Surrendering himself to the supreme direction of the universe, the cosmic existence that is all around him [man], he can experience the act of transubstantiation that is carried out by him in the temple of the cosmos when he stands within it sacrificially in a purely spiritual way' (GA 219, 31 December 1922).[40] While speaking these words Rudolf Steiner was himself standing in the midst of the burning Goetheanum as a 'sacrificial being' and was, in the sense of the highest sacrificial service, performing a ritual in the temple of the cosmos.

This process was accompanied by these further words: 'The world becomes the temple, the house of God. When man as a cognitive being summons up his powers of feeling and will, he becomes a sacrificing being. His fundamental relationship to the world rises from knowledge to a world cultus, a *cosmic ritual.*' And Rudolf Steiner connects this ritual with the essential task of anthroposophy: 'The first beginning of what must come about if anthroposophy is to fulfil its mission in the world is that our whole relationship to the world as human beings comes to be recognized as a cosmic ritual.'

The entire description of cosmic ritual then culminated in the mantric words of cosmic communion, which Rudolf Steiner solemnly spoke at the end of the lecture:

> In Earth activity draws near to me,
> Given to me in substance-imaged form,
> The heavenly being of the stars:
> In willing I see them transformed with love.
>
> In watery life stream into me,
> Forming me through with power of substance force,
> The heavenly deeds of the stars:
> In feeling I see them transformed with wisdom.
>
> (Translation by Dorothy Osmond)

In his recollections Heinz Müller describes the conclusion of this lecture—at which he was himself present—in the following words: 'The solemnity and urgency of his speech grew during the course of the lecture. One had the feeling that a great initiate was here celebrating the ritual of the future, the cosmic ritual of mankind. After he had once again spoken the verses, he stepped away from the podium with the greatest modesty, and so it was taken for granted that no one should applaud, as inevitably happened at other lectures. Both verses remained visible on the two blackboards in his beautiful handwriting as we, both old and young, went out deeply moved into the starry New Year's Eve night.'[41]

In the guidance that he gave for working with these verses Rudolf Steiner particularly emphasizes the path of schooling which he inaugurated, leading through the stages of Imagination, Inspiration and Intuition. For only now does he reveal the great mystery and the ultimate destination of this path which would lead people today to a true knowledge of the spiritual world. 'Spiritual knowledge is thus a real communion, the beginning of a cosmic ritual that is appropriate for present-day humanity' (GA 219, 31 December 1922). Man is thereby called to achieve, with the consummation of cosmic communion, a new relationship to the world of the fixed stars through the solid elements of his diet and a new relationship to the spiritual forces of the planets through the liquid elements. Both are transubstantiated on the path of supersensible knowledge through love in willing and through wisdom in feeling, becoming thereby the foundation for the future spiritualization of our earthly planet. That this will be at all possible is the consequence of the great cosmic communion of the Earth on Good Friday. For only because of this are the spiritual forces of the fixed stars and the spiritual forces of the planets contained, respectively, in the solid and the liquid elements of our food.

One year later Rudolf Steiner pointed out that his last lecture in the First Goetheanum was in complete harmony with the forms of the building. (See GA 233, 31 December 1923.) With this he was referring to the mystery of an inner relationship subsisting between the mantric wording of cosmic communion and the innermost nature of the First Goetheanum. This relationship is by no means purely symbolic, for the building was erected in accordance with the principle of spiritual communion. Thus in the space of the large cupola was manifested the principle of the sevenfold planetary evolution and in the space of the smaller one the twelvefold principle of the starry world (the zodiac). In this way 'the whole spirit of the cosmos' (GA 15, ch. 3) was brought to manifestation in the double domed building. And in the great countenance in the red window, man was portrayed as the celebrant in the great temple of the cosmos.[42]

With this architectural conception of the First Goetheanum in view, Rudolf Steiner was now able to pronounce the corresponding mantric words in the last lecture within the space which was already invisibly surrounded by flames. In this way he was revealing the true destiny of this building as a reflection of the 'great temple of the cosmos', in which after its consecration and esoteric opening the 'cosmic ritual' constituting the true task of anthroposophy was to have been celebrated. In other words: the building in its entirety was to lead people in our modern era to a true spiritual communion. Rudolf Steiner himself testified to this a year later in looking back to the fire: '*On that very evening* the link was made with that to which our Goetheanum building was to be dedicated in its whole being' (GA 233, 31 December 1923).

If the First Goetheanum had been completed, the culmination of a cosmic communion would have been achieved through the visitor's inner connection with the form of the Representative of Humanity in the small cupola. This sublime form would have been like the spiritual Sun, surrounded by twelve stars, coming to meet man from the East (that is, from the spiritual world). Rudolf Steiner refers to this as follows: 'In Ephesus the statue of the goddess; here in the Goetheanum the statue of man, the statue of the Representative of Humanity, Christ Jesus, in whom—*identifying ourselves with Him*—we thought in all humility to attain to knowledge, just as formerly, in their own way ... the pupils of Ephesus attained to knowledge in Diana of Ephesus' (GA 233, 31 December 1923). The First Goetheanum was intended to lead to such an 'identification' with the highest Ideal of Humanity, which is also the ideal of cosmic communion. In other words: it had to do with an experience of the spiritual cosmos in which an encounter with Christ in one's own ego becomes possible.

This consecration of the Goetheanum as a baptism with fire and Spirit was then accepted by the spiritual world together with the essential nature of *cosmic communion*, in order that it might subsequently be received by Rudolf Steiner in a renewed form out of the far expanses of the cosmos as the path of *spiritual communion* and, at the Christmas Conference, placed at the centre of the new mysteries.

Rudolf Steiner referred to this mighty metamorphosis at the end of the Easter Conference in 1924: 'What hitherto was more or less an earthly affair, what was founded and developed as an earthly affair, was carried forth with the flames into the cosmic expanses. Precisely because this misfortune came upon us, when we recognize its consequences we may justly say: henceforth we understand that we are not merely pursuing an earthly concern but, rather, a concern of the wide ethereal universe in which the Spirit lives. For the concern of the Goetheanum is indeed a concern of the wide ether in which the spirit-filled wisdom of the world lives. It has been carried forth, and *we may fill ourselves with the Goetheanum impulses coming in towards us from the cosmos*' (GA 233a, 22 April 1924). The mantric formulation of cosmic communion was, however, carried forth with the forms of the building into the etheric expanses of the cosmos, in order then to be taken up again from this point by Rudolf Steiner as the mantric foundation for spiritual communion.

The Foundation Stone Meditation, which represents the meditative connection to the Resurrection body and, hence, forms the first element of spiritual communion, has already been spoken of above (see p. 9). But what about its second part, communion with the blood or with the forces of the resurrected etheric body? We find a clear and exhaustive answer also to this question in the accomplishing of the founding of the new mysteries at the Christmas Conference. As already mentioned, the nature of rhythm—whose source lies in the movements of the seven planets—

forms an integral part of the etheric body, which is why it likewise has a sevenfold structure. If we bear this in mind, we will understand why at the Christmas Conference Rudolf Steiner gave the members not only the Foundation Stone Meditation as a spiritual foundation of the newly founded Anthroposophical Society but also its *seven rhythms*, which esoterically filled the subsequent days of the assembly. For these rhythms form the bridge to experiencing the etheric body of the Risen One. In this way the Foundation Stone Meditation, together with its seven rhythms, offers a fully valid path of spiritual communion as a continuation and metamorphosis of the essential nature of cosmic communion, once this latter had been received in this renewed form by Rudolf Steiner out of the far expanses of the etheric cosmos.

Hence one can say: just as on Good Friday[43] the blood and the body of Christ Jesus was received by the Earth, in order then on Easter morning to appear as the Resurrection body and the etheric body—condensed to the point of earthly visibility—of the Risen One, so in the new mysteries did the mantric words of cosmic communion stream out into the widths of the cosmos and return as the path to a fully valid spiritual communion through the free, creative deed of a human being. Thus the macrocosm is reflected in the microcosm and the divine deed in the human deed, in the deed of Rudolf Steiner. The difference, however, is that, at the Turning Point of Time, between the events on Good Friday and the Resurrection on Easter Sunday the path of Christ led into the depths of the Earth;[44] whereas at the consummation of this cosmically earthly act the impulses ascended with the flames into the cosmic expanses, in order—on returning from thence—to form at the Christmas Conference the foundation of the new mysteries.

Already in the cycle *From Jesus to Christ* Rudolf Steiner had referred very clearly to the future significance of spiritual communion: 'The aim of anthroposophy[45] is to work in such a way that we shall grasp in the spirit itself something concrete, something real. By means of meditation, concentration and all that we learn as the knowledge of higher worlds, human beings become sufficiently mature in their inner being ... to permeate themselves with the element of the Spirit; and in this way they will experience communion in the Spirit'[46] (GA 131, 13 October 1911). With this Rudolf Steiner took a decisive step in the further development of Christianity on the Earth: he created the transition from the sacramental to a purely spiritual communion. What the great Christian esotericist of the twelfth century, Joachim of Fiore (1130–1202)—who taught about the historical epochs, that of the Father, that of the Son and that of the Spirit—could only point towards prophetically, namely the coming transition from the second to the third epoch, was accomplished by Rudolf Steiner with the establishing of spiritual communion on the Earth. For the foundation was thereby laid for the incipient epoch of the Spirit, when a new, purely spiritual relationship to the Christ Being will be possible. Rudolf Steiner says in this connection: 'And just as everything evolves from the physical up to the spiritual under the Christian influence, so those things which existed primarily as a bridge must develop under the Christ influence; the sacrament of Communion must rise from the physical to the spiritual plane in order that it may lead to a true union with the Christ' (GA 112, 7 July 1909).

This inner union with Christ is to be achieved on the path leading from the essential nature of cosmic communion to spiritual communion, as initiated at the Christmas Conference. For the first has the aim of spiritualizing the Earth and the second the spiritualizing of man. Both are accomplished through man's free and independent inner work. In this way, it becomes possible to realize the 'highest ideal of human evolution that is conceivable for man: *a spiritualization* which human beings achieve through their own effort' (GA 13).

If one compares in this connection the words of cosmic and spiritual communion, one discovers the mighty step taken through the fact that the mantric substance had in the meantime ascended into the heights of the cosmos. For in the wording of cosmic communion the spiritual forces of the planets and fixed stars were addressed only in general terms, whereas in spiritual communion one is concerned with the actual spiritual beings who are active *behind* these cosmic forces. These are the nine hierarchies referred to by name in the Foundation Stone Meditation and its rhythms and whose activity stands behind all the planetary spheres and the whole starry cosmos.

The modern path to spiritual communion and, hence, to the full reality of the Resurrection given by Rudolf Steiner to all people of good will in the new mysteries had been prepared centuries beforehand in the closest circles and the most strictly secret schools of esoteric Christianity. Both elements of spiritual communion were, to begin with, cultivated separately in its two principal streams. Thus what lay at the heart of the Grail mysteries was above all communion with the blood of the Risen One or with the forces of His transformed etheric body, whence the Grail knights in their cultic ceremonies derived the life-forces for their manifold tasks amongst mankind.[47]

Similarly, the Rosicrucians subsequently worked pre-eminently with the second part of spiritual communion. In what they called working with the Philosophers' Stone they sought a conscious relationship with the forces of the Resurrection body, with whose help they endeavoured to change their own being right down to its finer structure. One can compare this work with the transformation of coal into translucent diamond. For this reason the Rosicrucian dicta belong to the essential nature of the Foundation Stone Meditation.

What had been going on for centuries in a state of separation was united for the first time by Rudolf Steiner in the new mysteries and accordingly brought out of the narrow circles of the esoteric brotherhoods into the clear light of day. What made this possible, however, was the fire that consumed the First Goetheanum, the greatest tragedy of the anthroposophical movement, and the metamorphosis on a cosmically earthly scale of its nature which occurred as a result, as has been described above. Thus it passed through a kind of death and resurrection in order to make the founding of the new mysteries on the Earth *in this form* inherently possible.

★

In conclusion, the striking connection of these events within the anthroposophical movement with what happened at the Turning Point of Time should also be mentioned. Thus after the death of Christ Jesus the apostles had to live through the deeply shattering mood that prevailed in the still hours of Easter Saturday, when their entire future was as though veiled in thick clouds and full of oppressive uncertainty. Something of an echo of this mood can also be discerned among anthroposophists on 1 January 1923, the morning after the Goetheanum fire in Dornach.

Two images from this time may be presented here. As we know, on the following day Rudolf Steiner did not want any of the planned lectures or the advertised performances to be cancelled. Thus he recalled this day a year later: '... we did not allow even the flames to distract us from continuing with our work' (GA 260, 1 January 1924). Among other events a performance of the *Three Kings Play* was planned for 1 January. What happened at the beginning was described by Assya Turgeniev in the following words: '"Most reverend Worships ..." That was as far as the Angel got with her words of greeting. The Angel from the *Three Kings Play* made one more attempt, then stood speechless leaning against her staff with tears rolling down her cheeks until she found the strength to continue.'[48] In the overcrowded carpentry workshop, which was still awash with water from the night of the fire and was in a sorry state, everyone waited for a long time in total silence until the actress had finally composed herself and the performance could continue. Rudolf Steiner sat in the front row and silently watched the crying Angel, who was perhaps like a reflection of what not only these people but also the Angels in the spiritual world were feeling at this moment. A real Easter Saturday mood reigned over everywhere.

The second image relates to the events of the Turning Point of Time from a different standpoint. Out of his spiritual research in the realm of the Fifth Gospel, Rudolf Steiner spoke of how at the time of Christ Jesus' death on the Cross a 'darkness caused by thick clouds' covered the entire sky, so that around the hill of Golgotha it was for a short time as dark as night.[49]

Margarita Voloshin, who because of an entry permit problem only arrived in Dornach on 2 January, described her impression at the time: 'I was walking very close to the concrete basement and saw that the carved wooden doors were completely undamaged. So everything was all right! Then I tried to see through the mist to the second floor, but I couldn't see anything. I walked round the building. The wooden buildings close by were intact, but now—from the East—I could see clearly through the mist: looking up I could see neither cupolas nor walls, nothing was there at all.'[50]

And just as the mood of the apostles at the Turning Point of Time after the first encounter with the Risen One altered and changed into one of joy and jubilation, so was it a year after the fire with the mood at the Christmas Conference, which one can describe with the words from the Book of Revelation: 'Behold, I make all things new' (21:5). Already in his opening lecture Rudolf Steiner spoke of what he expected of the members above all for *this* conference: 'the appropriate mood of soul, more and yet more mood of soul'(GA 260, 24 December 1923). He went on to characterize this special mood as a new beginning, the building up of a future orientation filled with joy, a reaching out towards new perspectives for humanity and an uplifting feeling of collaboration in a sense of common purpose—a true Easter mood!

Behind all this, however, there stood the metamorphosis—already referred to—of the First Goetheanum, the burning of which Rudolf Steiner once described as a death. ('The Goetheanum has died a death.'[51]) After this there followed a year later the resurrection of the spirit of the Goetheanum and its appearance in the earthly sphere at the Christmas Conference. Since then it has been active amongst human beings as the spirit of the new mysteries, permeating the whole anthroposophical movement as what Rudolf Steiner called the 'new esoteric impulse'.

Rudolf Steiner also referred to this at the end of the 1924 Easter Conference: 'Then, when we can do this, we shall feel ourselves to be an important part of everything that lives in anthroposophy. And this sense is the anthroposophical Easter mood, that anthroposophical Easter mood which can never think that the spirit dies but that, if it dies through the world [what is meant here is the spirit of the Goetheanum], it will always rise again. Anthroposophy must hold on to the spirit that rises ever again out of eternal foundations' (GA 233a, 22 April 1924).

These words at the conclusion of the lecture, which was followed by a performance of the Foundation Stone Meditation in eurythmy, are like a retrospective echo of the actual mood of the Christmas Conference, which had the task of forming a foundation for the new Christian mysteries. Hence we can say: as the macrocosm constantly finds its reflection in the microcosm, so do the great events of the Turning Point of Time also have their counterpoint in the history of the anthroposophical movement. What nearly 2000 years ago changed the whole existence of the Earth and of humanity was repeated in the—as yet—small community of anthroposophists on the level of their consciousness. This gives an indication of the essential thrust of the new mysteries, namely the task of raising the events of the Turning Point of Time into human consciousness in the light of Michael in order then so to enliven this consciousness on the path of spiritual communion that it can receive into itself the reality of the Resurrection.

★

A further question belongs to the substance of this chapter, a question which has more often been posed to the author in this context: what is the difference between the creative process of what the Rosicrucians called the *Philosophers' Stone* (the stone of wisdom), which they regarded as their highest goal, and the *Stone of Love*, which Rudolf Steiner created in the spiritual world bordering upon the Earth at the Christmas Conference? This question can only be answered on the foundation of the difference established above between the phantom and the Resurrection body.

As—in his time—probably the first person to do so, F.W. Zeylmans van Emmichoven referred in his book *The Foundation Stone* to the mighty evolutionary step within esoteric Christianity that was accomplished by the transition from the Philosophers' Stone to the Stone of Love (in the chapter entitled 'From the Philosophers' Stone to the Stone of Love'[52]). The grounds for this will briefly be presented here.

By inner work with the Philosophers' Stone the Rosicrucians understood drawing upon the forces of the phantom of the Risen One, firstly in their soul, in the astral body (imaginative stage), then in the etheric body (inspirative stage) and finally in the physical body itself, though in a strictly spiritual way (intuitive stage).[53] Thus Rudolf Steiner describes the fourth stage of Rosicrucian initiation, which in the initiation of modern times corresponds to the stage of Intuition, in the following words: 'The Philosophers' Stone is the noblest thing that a human being can acquire and make out of his [physical] organism in order to come to a higher stage of development' (GA 97, 16 February 1907). And Rudolf Steiner characterizes the nature of the stone as follows: 'Man is advancing towards this goal, that of building up his body from carbon: ordinary carbon or coal is the Philosophers' Stone. It will not be black coal but carbon that is as transparent as water, when the human body has become starlike. These are not just chemical processes but, rather, high ideals. Rosicrucians are gradually achieving this, and the whole of humanity will subsequently rise to it as well' (ibid.).

By means of this inner work Rosicrucians sought a conscious connection with the phantom of Christ (or the phantom aspect of the Resurrection body), in order thereby to win through to the primordially pure spiritual form of the human body so that it again corresponds to the paradisaical state of mankind.

The first human being who attained this stage to the fullest extent was Christian Rosenkreutz in his initiation in the thirteenth century, of which Rudolf Steiner has the following to say: 'After a few days the body of the thirteenth became quite transparent, and for days he lay as though dead' (GA 130, 27 September 1911). And after his soul had encountered Christ in the spiritual world and had been directly permeated by Him, it returned to the physical body and took hold of it in such a way 'that this revival of his absolutely transparent body was beyond compare' (ibid.). If one bears in mind that where the phantom is concerned Rudolf Steiner especially emphasizes the quality of transparency, one will rightly grasp the nature of what was going on.[54] He also mentions that true Rosicrucian alchemists worked on the phantom out of this knowledge (see GA 131, 12 October 1911). For the aim of their initiation was to create 'a bond of attraction' between man's being and the phantom that was restored on the hill of Golgotha. (See GA 131, 14 October 1911.)

In the new mysteries, however, the second and future aspect of the Resurrection must be added. Or, to put it another way, the path of the Alpha of world evolution must be supplemented by the path to the Omega, so that the *full* reality of the Resurrection can appear before humanity: from Old Saturn (phantom) to the future Vulcan (Resurrection body).

We live today at a time when the full mystery of the Resurrection body can become manifest to human beings out of the inspirations of Michael, who as an Arché is already at the stage which mankind will reach only on

Vulcan. This was accomplished by Rudolf Steiner not just in a theoretical sense but also practically, and came about through the establishing of a path accessible to all human beings which leads to a union with the forces of the Resurrection body.

Hence in the mantric verse with which he concluded his 'Last Address', Rudolf Steiner added the words about 'cosmic age of Spirit Man' (GA 238, 28 September 1924). For *this* cosmic age has indeed begun today, an age when man can seek and also find a conscious relationship to the Resurrection body.

The foundation for this relationship was given through the creation of the Stone of Love at the Christmas Conference. By implanting the Foundation Stone of Love into the ground of his own heart, every human being can establish a conscious relationship to it and—through meditative work on the Foundation Stone meditation—also embark upon the path leading him to the full reality of the event of the Resurrection.

Various Kinds of Communion

Some supplementary remarks regarding the substance of the previous chapter now follow. First a brief indication as to how the author arrived at these thoughts. The stimulus for them came from the cycle on the Book of Revelation given for the priests of the Christian Community, where Rudolf Steiner makes the observation that two cosmic realms are intimately connected with one another: the nature of transubstantiation and the nature of karma.[55] In this cycle, which was given three-quarters of a year after the Christmas Conference, Rudolf Steiner made reference to the Christmas Conference and its focal point, the Foundation Stone Meditation, right at the beginning of the first lecture. He said to the priests assembled in Dornach: 'Having gathered once again at this place, we shall have important matters to address in the light and in the warmth that have come to us through the Christmas Conference as a kind of compensation for the earthly losses caused by the flames [the Goetheanum fire]' (ibid., 5 September 1924).

These words, referring to the light coming from the spirit-world and warmth deriving from it, also point towards the fourth part of the Foundation Stone Meditation, where these qualities are directly spoken of and given to all anthroposophists as a meditative exercise. During the laying of the Foundation Stone itself Rudolf Steiner spoke in this regard: 'We can best bring strength to that warmth of soul and that light of soul which we need, if we enliven them with the warmth and the light that shone forth at the Turning Point of Time as the light of Christ in the darkness of the universe' (GA 260, 25 December 1923).

From this it follows that this cycle on the Book of Revelation, which forms the culmination of the esoteric teaching given to the priests of the Christian Community, derived entirely from the substance of the Christmas Conference or from the source of the new mysteries. And if one reads there that the influence of karma and the nature of transubstantiation are closely interrelated, the task that arises from this is to bring this relationship to consciousness by finding within the new mysteries, to which the great karma revelations in the 82 karma lectures of 1924 belong, also the other element that forms a part of them, namely transubstantiation, which is the greatest mystery of any true communion. For only on this foundation can the essential nature of spiritual communion, which forms the central part of the new mysteries, be rightly understood. This research task, first given by Rudolf Steiner to the priests of the

Christian Community but of decisive importance for all anthroposophists, led after some years of working with it to the results that have been presented here.

★

Reference should also be made to a further indication of Rudolf Steiner's that is of significance here. It is a familiar fact that he spoke in many lectures about Christ's appearance in the etheric realm, which began in the 1930s. At the same time he mentioned that at the end of the twentieth century Christ will take on His new office as the Lord of Karma,[56] which will last until the end of the earthly age. Moreover, Rudolf Steiner often brings both these events into a still closer connection, so that the question arises as to the nature of their relationship.

This can be answered if one bears in mind that the present appearance of Christ in the etheric body on the astral plane, which will last for about 3000 years, will be followed by His next revelation in the astral body on Lower Devachan. After this a still higher revelation will take place, when He will make His Ego-Being accessible to human beings on Higher Devachan. (See GA 130, 4 November 1911.) From other indications by Rudolf Steiner one may gather that this sequence of revelations will come to a certain conclusion only when Christ appears out of the still higher Buddhi sphere to human beings as the Sun Word of spiritual Sun, which encompasses and guides the whole of Earth evolution from beginning to end. Seeing Christ at this height is possible today only for an initiate of the rank of a bodhisattva.[57] At the end of Earth evolution all human beings will be able to behold this revelation of Christ. At the present time this stage is accessible only during cosmic midnight in the life after death to those human beings who have trodden the modern path of initiation in their previous earthly life. For there in the heights of the cosmos the two streams of Christ's activity meet: the ongoing ascending sequence of His revelations and His activity as the Lord of Karma. At the same time there come together in this cosmic sphere also the karmic activity of Christ and the forces which bring about spiritual communion with His Resurrection body.

★

After my various lectures on this theme I have also been repeatedly asked about the relationship of spiritual to cosmic communion, on the one hand, and about the sacramental communion of the Christian Community on the other and the difference between them. In this regard one can, as an initial starting point, distinguish three criteria:

1. In cosmic and sacramental communion it is a matter in each case of the transformation of earthly substance by spiritual forces coming to man from without. In spiritual communion, on the other hand, one has to do with an inner process involving the transformation of the human body (the development of Spirit Man). No external substances are used for this in the new mysteries.
2. Spiritual communion has as its ultimate purpose the transforming of mankind into the Tenth Hierarchy. Thus it will continue as an active influence also after the spiritualizing of the Earth, or the union with the Sun at the end of its evolution. Cosmic and sacramental communion will have fulfilled their task by then, since their remit lies with the transformation of earthly substances, which will no longer exist at that time.
3. Sacramental communion is not solely associated with the event of Easter but also with the Last Supper on Maundy Thursday, that is, with the event that preceded the Mystery of Golgotha. One can also say: the path of sacramental communion to the reality of the Resurrection leads through the events of the Last Supper and stands even today in the spiritual stream of its rightful continuation. Hence the words, 'Do this in remembrance of me'[58] in the Act of Consecration of Man are wholly valid.

With cosmic communion, too, there is an unmistakable relationship to the events that preceded the Resurrection. Its origin lies on the Hill of Golgotha in the events of Good Friday, through which its further path leads to the reality of the Resurrection.

Spiritual communion, in contrast, has no direct relationship to the events on Maundy Thursday or Good Friday. It is related directly to the event on Easter Sunday and is, therefore, connected solely with the essential nature of the Resurrection.

★

In the following section, some indications will be given as to how the theme of communion runs through the whole of Rudolf Steiner's life and work. When he was only 26, he wrote out of his innermost experience in the second volume of *Introductions to Goethe's Scientific Writings*: '*Becoming aware of the idea in reality is the true communion of man*' (GA 1, ch. 6, 'Goethe's Approach to Knowledge'; italics Rudolf Steiner). With this epoch-making sentence the essential nature of communion is associated for all time with true, modern knowledge. For in the above words we have the beginning of the path whereby the world of ideas becomes a world of perception for a transformed thinking. As in this case thinking itself and the world of ideas apprehended by it are of the same 'substance', this form of knowledge is similar to a true communion. Already at the turn of the century Rudolf Steiner, in continuing to follow this path in the spiritual world, had arrived at a supersensible encounter with Christ by 'standing in spirit before the Mystery of Golgotha in the most inward, most earnest celebration of *knowledge*' (GA 28, ch. 26).

In the book *Occult Science* Rudolf Steiner describes how the spirit-pupil can reach the stage of modern initiation at which an encounter with Christ in Intuition takes place and thereby—because Intuition leads to knowledge of the physical world of the senses—experiences the whole cosmic and earthly significance of the Mystery of Golgotha for earthly evolution (GA 13). From this stage onwards all supersensible knowledge leads such a pupil of the spirit to an intimate connection with the object of his perception or to a true *spiritual communion*. In this way there arises within him an altogether new supersensible faculty, which we find developed in an exemplary way in Rudolf Steiner.[59] Thus it was possible for him independently to research on an ongoing basis all spheres of the spiritual world, including its highest regions, and from thence also the earthly events of the Turning Point of Time, while fully maintaining his ego-consciousness.

In the last quotation cited, the word 'knowledge' refers to the consistency of Rudolf Steiner's inner path, which led from intellectual communion through the spiritual witnessing of the Mystery of Golgotha to spiritual communion and, hence, from his so-called early philosophical work to anthroposophy. At the same time these quoted words refer to the source out of which Rudolf Steiner received his full spiritual power and creative potential also to renew, or even newly establish, the other forms of communion on the Earth. These are the sacramental communion of the Christian Community, the cosmic communion already described in this book, then the communion in the 'Festival of Offering' (Offering Service) of the Waldorf school, which—as a communion through the word—is a unique phenomenon in the entire history of Christianity until now. For the 'Festival of Offering' is in its essential nature linked directly to Christ's 'Farewell Discourses' from the Gospel of St John (chapters 14–17) and to the 'High Priestly Prayer' (chapter 17), where communion with the word was brought about for the first time by the incarnated Logos. And finally—as the culmination of the whole sequence—we have spiritual communion as the central focus of the new mysteries.[60]

Thus in all one can speak of five different kinds of communion. Rudolf Steiner achieved the first already in his youth. It also formed the basis upon which he himself experienced *spiritual communion* in his initiation around the turn of the century. It consisted in the Ego of Christ being received into the ego of a human being. Rudolf Steiner thereby became the bearer of the Christ consciousness out of which he was able to develop the whole of anthroposophy. Only at the end of his life, at the Christmas Conference, did he reveal to his pupils the inner path to it.

At the beginning of the 1920s Rudolf Steiner established the three further forms out of the source of spiritual communion: sacramental communion, cosmic communion and communion through the word. Then, as the culmination of the entire evolutionary journey, with the founding of the new mysteries at the Christmas Conference he placed the principle of spiritual communion at its centre. From this point the path to it lies open for all human beings.

The whole picture can be summarized in the following way:

By its very nature, spiritual communion has from the outset also been inseparably connected with knowledge of the karma[61] which every human being bears in the depths of his will or, from a physiological point of view, in the spiritual forces of his limb system (walking). In the diagram the small triangle links walking with the other two basic human faculties of thinking and speaking, which are associated with intellectual communion and communion through the word. These three faculties of walking, speaking and thinking are directly associated with Christ's activity within man. (See GA 15, ch. 1.) Hence Rudolf Steiner says that true sacramentalism must first take hold of a person's whole life, beginning with the areas of education and knowledge, which must both gradually become a real '[divine] service' (GA 172, 27 November 1916). From this the individual must learn 'in all [life's] tasks to fulfil a divine service and bring sacramentalism into everything' (ibid.). For 'it is in this direction that the Christianizing of man must move forward' (ibid.).

The necessity for the two other kinds of communion, where earthly substances are directly transformed, derives from this. Thus in the diagram the large triangle shows the arising of the establishment, or renewal, of cosmic and sacramental communion out of the experience of spiritual communion. In this context Rudolf Steiner could say to the priests of the Christian Community in September 1924 that the movement for religious renewal can become 'the bearer of an important part of the new mysteries' (GA 346, 7 September 1924).

In summary, the following relationship can be discerned between the four kinds of communion and the events of the Turning Point of Time. *Sacramental communion* has its origin in the Last Supper on Maundy Thursday, as described in the three synoptic Gospels. *Cosmic communion* relates to the events on Good Friday (the receiving of the blood and body by the earthly planet). *Communion through the word* in the 'Festival of Offering' is in its essential nature connected with the 'Farewell Discourses' from St John's Gospel (chapters 14–17). At the Last Supper John experienced these sayings of Christ in full consciousness, and received pure communion through the Logos into his own being as these words were being spoken so strongly that he does not even mention the communion with bread and wine that took place beforehand in his account of the Last Supper.

Of course, all three of these forms of communion acquired their full power and significance only after Easter morning out of the source of the Resurrection. Nevertheless, they all seek access to this central mystery by taking into account those events which took place before the Resurrection. Only *spiritual communion* has a direct and original connection with the innermost essence of the Resurrection.

Intellectual communion, on the other hand, whence the young Rudolf Steiner had embarked upon his path towards experiencing the Mystery of Golgotha in Intuition at the turn of the century (towards 'standing in spirit before the Mystery of Golgotha'), has no model and no origin in the events of the Turning Point of Time and is a free, *purely human deed* on the part of Rudolf Steiner, which, however, subsequently granted him access to all the other forms of communion. Only through this unique deed out of his own forces did he become the greatest agent of renewal for Christianity in our time.

2. Easter, Ascension and Whitsun in the Light of Anthroposophy

The event of the Ascension has an important place among the great Christian festivals, of whose spiritual significance Rudolf Steiner spoke on numerous occasions out of the source of his spiritual research. Although in comparison to other festivals he said relatively little about it, these few remarks nevertheless reveal a deep connection with the development of anthroposophy on the Earth.

At the centre of anthroposophical Christology, and at the same time representing its culmination, are the fruits of Rudolf Steiner's research in the domain of the Fifth Gospel. This research tells of the events of the Turning Point of Time not from documents written by human hands but from what has been inscribed with indelible letters in the Akashic Record in the higher worlds. In the third lecture on this theme in Christiania (GA 148), the event of the Ascension is mentioned in a quite particular connection. Rudolf Steiner begins by comparing the most important points of Christ's earthly life with the cycle of a human incarnation and makes the comparison that, in the case of the unique life of Christ on Earth, His union with Jesus at the Baptism in the Jordan corresponds to a conception in an ordinary human life. This is also confirmed by the original words of St Luke's Gospel, where it is stated that a voice from heaven proclaimed at Jesus' Baptism: 'Thou art my beloved Son; today I have begotten thee' (Luke 3:22: quoted in accordance with GA 114, 21 September 1909). The ensuing three years of Christ's presence in the physical body of Jesus are comparable with the embryonic state of an incarnating human being. Then in the Mystery of Golgotha, with which this time was concluded, there follows Christ's actual birth in the earthly sphere. 'The Mystery of Golgotha itself is to be understood as the earthly birth—that is to say, the death of Jesus is to be understood as the earthly birth of the Christ' (GA 148, 3 October 1913). Only after the Resurrection does His actual earthly life begin, lasting altogether only 40 days. In the Acts of the Apostles it is stated that at this time Christ was together with the eleven disciples in order to reveal to them the mysteries of the heavenly world (Acts 1:3). Then Rudolf Steiner refers to the Ascension as that event which corresponds in an ordinary human being to death together with the ensuing ascent into the spiritual world. For Christ, however, this signifies by no means a departure from the earthly sphere but the exact opposite: instead of ascending into the heights of the spiritual world He brings the forces of the spirit-land down into the earthly realm, a unique deed which, ten days later, could be received at Whitsun also into the consciousness of the apostles. Rudolf Steiner describes the whole event in the following words: 'From the event of Whitsun onwards, the Christ Being passed through experiences which signified for Him what the transition into the spirit-land signifies for the human individual: they signified His entry into the sphere of the Earth. For instead of passing—as does a human being—into Devachan, into a spiritual domain, after death, the Christ Being made the sacrifice of establishing, of seeking His heaven on the Earth' (GA 148, 3 October 1913).

Although Rudolf Steiner does not specifically mention the Ascension in this description, it is absolutely clear from the whole context that the great sacrifice made by Christ of bringing Devachan to the Earth was accomplished in the ten days between Ascension and Whitsun. For shortly before he says: 'The further life of Christ in the earthly sphere *after the Ascension* or after Whitsun is to be compared with what the human soul experiences in Devachan, in the spirit-land' (ibid.).

Such a complicated process has various aspects. Rudolf Steiner shows us one of these in a much later lecture in connection with what happens with the human etheric body after death (GA 224, 7 May 1923). Because the etheric body is, in the case of every human being, formed before his incarnation mainly out of the etheric forces of the Sun, it retains the constant tendency also during earthly life to unite with its heavenly home, that is, with the world-encompassing Sun sphere which was the cosmic dwelling-place of the Christ Being before the Mystery of Golgotha. However, man's etheric body can pursue this inherent tendency to a full extent only after death. This happens during the first three days after the physical body is discarded, when the etheric body expands more and more until finally it completely dissolves and unites with the Sun sphere (see ibid.). In this way there also comes about the union of the etheric body with the forces of that spiritual realm of which the Sun is the great entrance gate and where its content is imprinted upon the Akashic Record.

Rudolf Steiner goes on to draw attention to the fact that through the hardening of physical bodies—which had strongly increased especially by the Turning Point of Time—there arose the very real danger that etheric bodies would unite to an ever-decreasing degree with human beings and would completely withdraw from them as a result of the force of attraction of the Sun sphere, which would eventually have brought human life on Earth to an end.

In order to avert this danger and hence to rescue humanity, Christ united Himself with this tendency of human etheric bodies to aspire towards the Sun. As, however, they cannot exist on Earth without a connection with Sun forces, Christ imbued them with the entire fullness of His Sun substance already on the Earth, so that they might remain connected to the Earth for the duration of human life. Since this time the etheric body of each human being has had full access to what it could formerly only receive through its connection with the Sun after death or through initiation in the old mysteries.

The apostles beheld this rescuing deed of Christ in the mighty event of the Ascension, in which was also revealed to them the most important consequence of what has already been described as Christ's deed of bringing the forces of Devachan down to the Earth. For from then onwards the goal towards which man's etheric body had previously been striving was to be found no longer in the realm of the Sun but directly on the Earth in its new spiritual focal point, in Christ Himself. The reversal of direction referred to took place because Christ was now no longer connected with the Sun but with the Earth. Rudolf Steiner describes what happened in the following words: 'As man's etheric body strives towards the Sun, it is striving towards Christ. Now picture to yourselves the scene on the day of the Ascension: in spiritual vision the disciples see Christ rising heavenwards. That is to say, a vision is conjured up before them [the disciples] of how man's etheric nature, which strives upwards, unites itself with the power, the impulse of Christ; thus of how at the time of the Mystery of Golgotha man facing the danger of his etheric body being drawn towards the Sun like a cloud, but how, in its sunward streaming, it is being held together by Christ' (ibid.). After man's physical body had been rescued in the Mystery of Golgotha, his etheric body now also experienced a rescue, in that a completely new connection with the earthly realm arose for it.

In order to gain a better understanding of the significance of what is meant by this, it is necessary that one calls to mind what would have happened on the Earth if this sacrificial deed of Christ had not taken place. The relationship of man's etheric body to the Sun was a familiar factor in the old mysteries and was used again and again as a bridge to the spiritual world. Rudolf Steiner describes in many places how the culmination of the old initiation consisted in a three-day period of deathlike sleep: where not only was the connection of astral body and ego to the physical body loosened, as also occurs in sleep, but—and herein lay the dangerous aspect of such initiations—also that between the physical body and the etheric body. In order that this relationship might not be completely broken (which would have led to the immediate death of the person being initiated), twelve hierophants had to be gathered around him in the mysteries. For only under the constant scrutiny of the twelve could the etheric body of the thirteenth for a short while pursue its tendency towards the Sun unhindered. In association with this tendency of the etheric body, the person's astral body and ego could also gain entry to the Sun sphere—or the all-encompassing cosmic realm of Christ—in the spiritual world outside the physical body. And on the way back the experiences that had been gathered by the astral body and ego in the Sun sphere could, with the help of the twelve hierophants, be imprinted upon the etheric body, which had the consequence that the individual concerned could remember the supersensible experiences in the cosmic Sun sphere after his awakening and tell other people about them.

In the lectures on the Fifth Gospel, immediately after referring to the Ascension Rudolf Steiner describes the seven stages of the old Persian initiation. He characterizes its sixth degree in the following words: 'During his initiation the Sun Hero lived in communion with the whole solar system; the Sun was his dwelling-place, in the same way as an ordinary person lives on the Earth as his own planet ... The Sun Hero had to be transported to the Sun during his initiation. In the old mysteries, this could be achieved only outside the body' (GA 148, 3 October 1913). Thus the Sun Hero was able to ascend in the old mysteries to the cosmic Sun Kingdom of Christ in order from thence to bring the impulses needed by the whole of mankind in a particular epoch for its further development. The 'vehicle' for this spiritual Sun journey was, however, the tendency of the etheric body that has been described.[1]

Likewise in later times, albeit in ever more problematic ways, this quality of the etheric body was used in various Eastern practices. A person left his body, which for this time was put in a trancelike state, and experienced in a state of the highest ecstasy the dissolving of his etheric body in the Sun sphere, which, however, could only happen at the cost of individual ego-consciousness. On the yoga path this state of highest ecstasy is called 'Nirvikalpa samadhi', and in Buddhism it is the ascent into the state of Nirvana. In both cases the last individual sensation was clothed in the picture that the human individuality dissolves like a drop in the infinite ocean of the world-light. In contrast to the old mysteries, however, such yogis were unable to bring back any concrete memories of these states. Their recollections extended only to the lower spheres of the spiritual world, which one could experience until the moment of the dissolving of the ego. From this it becomes apparent that a human individual who does not consciously seek the Sun forces of Christ, which have been present in his etheric body since the Ascension, is condemned after leaving his body inevitably to follow the cosmic tendencies of his etheric body and, hence, to an ever-increasing degree to lose his individual ego. As we shall see later, it is therefore the case that true human freedom cannot be established out of the spiritual memories of Eastern initiation.

On the other hand, becoming conscious of the presence of the Christ forces in the etheric body, or raising it into full ego-consciousness, represents the true Whitsun experience of present-day humanity—an experience which guarantees man true freedom not only on Earth but also in the spiritual world. Furthermore, there lies within it the possibility of coming to know while still on Earth in the physical body what an initiate in the old mysteries only experienced outside the body in the high Sun sphere.

Thus Rudolf Steiner relates of the apostles that after the event of Pentecost they had attained that state of consciousness which in the old mysteries was reached only at the sixth stage of initiation. 'And the apostles had in a certain way become souls of such a kind that they bore within themselves that inner substance that the old Sun Heroes had had in their souls. The spiritual power of the Sun had poured forth over the souls of these men and continued thereafter to exert its influence in human evolution' (ibid.).

What has been said here casts a completely new light upon the whole evolution of humanity, above all from the standpoint of the polarity between East and West. In the first chapter it has already been indicated that from both these sides a decisive question could be raised. If the worth of the ego were to be recognized in the East, the question would be: How does one achieve immortality in the spiritual world without losing one's individual ego in ecstasy? And the possible question in the West would then be this: How can one achieve for the individual ego-consciousness that has been attained the immortality which alone gives it full significance?[2] In the light of the above one can also characterize this twofold demand as follows. Eastern humanity still lives—as did the whole of mankind in earlier times—in the conviction that everything that is spiritual and morally valid comes not from Christ but from the Sun. (Likewise in the West in antiquity Plato was convinced that the highest good derives from the Sun.) In tracing such moral impulses back to their cosmic origin, one finds that man's individual ego completely dissolves. One becomes a king to be sure, but does not really know anything about it. Conscious kingliness, on the other hand, where man understands himself as the culmination of all creation, comes about in the West through the full development of the individual ego. However, this ego remains separated from the cosmic Sun forces in ordinary consciousness and thereby becomes mortal. A human being cannot take the most precious thing that he has acquired on the Earth with him into the spiritual world (above all after death). Thus this kingly realm that he has built for himself, a realm of which one is so proud in the West, is constructed only on sand.

This question with regard to the physical body—and hence also concerning the individual ego—found its solution through Christ's Resurrection in the Mystery of Golgotha, as described in the previous chapter. Both these questions must now be looked into from the standpoint of man's etheric body. Something quite decisive emerges from this, especially for the spiritual development of the West. For what happens if Western man aspires to develop his individuality, that is his ego, without reference to the Christ forces present in his etheric body as a result of the Ascension? Ego-consciousness, which in an earthly human being is embodied above all in thinking, is then confronted by two possibilities: either it unites with the etheric body without Christ and is then taken hold of by Samadhi (ecstasy), in which all thinking ceases and the ego completely dissolves in the realm of the Sun, or it distances itself from its own etheric forces in the face of this danger and, in order absolutely to maintain ego-consciousness and its principal instrument, thinking, transfers the activity of the etheric body wholly to the physical body, that is, man is restricted to thinking with the mortal brain.

How far this thinking restricted exclusively to the brain can nevertheless lead human beings is exemplified by Rudolf Steiner in the case of the great philosopher Georg Wilhelm Friedrich Hegel, who did indeed achieve the highest that is possible in the domain of thinking but could take hardly anything of his clever philosophical system with him into the life after death. 'This is Hegelian thinking! It is pure thought, but only thought in so far as it can be grasped with the instrument of the physical body [with the brain] and which dies with death. Hegel thought at the deepest level that is possible in earthly life, but the configuration of these thoughts was such that they perished with death. Hegel's tragedy was that he did not notice that he had understood the spirit in logic, in nature, in the life of the soul, but only that spirit which exists in the form of thought and which does not accompany us when we pass through the gate of death' (GA 161, 10 January 1915). This was also the case with Hegel's two greatest contemporaries, fully with Fichte and somewhat less with Schelling. The latter turned around the middle of his life to Jakob Boehme's writings and thereby took the step from a purely intellectual philosophy to a kind of mystical, theosophical world-conception.

Rudolf Steiner ended the lecture containing the quoted words about Hegel with the allusion to the poet and anthroposophist Christian Morgenstern who had died a year before and of whom he said that in this man there lived a soul 'who in his deepest inner nature knows himself to be at one with our anthroposophy, not merely as with something that gives us knowledge about this or that but as something which enlivens us' (ibid.). As we shall see very shortly, the mentioning of Christian Morgenstern at this point is of particular significance. But first we must pursue the train of thought that we have begun a little further.

The dilemma referred to between the ecstatic dissolving of thinking in the cosmic forces of the etheric body on the one hand and its total bondage to the physical brain on the other can be resolved solely by man's forming a conscious link with the Christ forces in his own etheric body, which have been present there since the Ascension. At this point, if not before, one feels that the problem indicated here as perhaps the most important in the whole evolution of humanity in modern times—in so far as this unfolds on the unshakeable foundation of thinking—exactly corresponds to, and is depicted in artistic form in, the nature and entire composition of the sculptural Group of the Representative of Humanity between the adversarial powers of Lucifer and Ahriman.[3]

On the level of thinking and, hence, within the whole ego-development of mankind,[4] this dilemma was in an archetypal sense resolved in Rudolf Steiner's early work. One can find this solution above all in his books *Truth and Knowledge* as a prelude to *The Philosophy of Freedom* and in *The Philosophy of Freedom* itself. Pure thinking is most exhaustively considered in the latter book. If the reader practises this systematically, it shifts entirely from the brain to the etheric body and is protected there from being dissolved in ecstasy by the Ascension forces of Christ. Hence man is in the position of thinking outside his physical body (or brain) without losing his ego-consciousness.

It follows from what has been said that, although the mystery of the Ascension is not directly addressed anywhere in the books referred to, they could be written by Rudolf Steiner pre-eminently because the body-free thinking out of which they were written is indicative that he was imbued with the Ascension power of Christ.

Another path—though leading to the same goal—described by Rudolf Steiner is the study of the content of spiritual science whereby one can reach the stage of pure, that is, sense-free or body-free, thinking. Hence he repeatedly stressed that the study of spiritual science is the first and indispensable stage of modern initiation.[5]

Christian Morgenstern is an excellent example of this latter aspect from Rudolf Steiner's closest circle of pupils; for he, less through his study of Rudolf Steiner's early work than through his intensive study of anthroposophy itself, was indeed able to rise to the heights of sense-free thinking and thereby acquired a living thinking in the realm of supersensible knowledge. There was also the fact that, through his—it is fair to say—unique connection with the depths of anthroposophical Christology, he was able quite considerably to strengthen the Ascension forces of Christ in his etheric body. 'What had opened up to him was that which appears to us as the highest point of anthroposophical research, speaking from his tender, intimate and yet so strong soul: a deep relationship with the Christ.'[6] And in another context: 'The Christ Being flowed into him together with the [anthroposophical] teaching. The Christ, as He lives in our movement, likewise merged into his soul' (GA 155, 14 July 1914). Because of this, the spiritual knowledge that he received had a particularly strong and vitalizing influence upon his soul. Thus Rudolf Steiner emphasizes in the above quotation probably not without reason that Christian Morgenstern's relationship to anthroposophy was not merely to a form of knowledge but to an enlivening force, that is, he was in his study of it able to penetrate to the life-forces of his etheric body. As a result, he was—through the bridge created by his enhanced Ascension forces—in a position to take the whole of his individualized, deeply experienced and felt knowledge unscathed after death into the spiritual world.[7] He entered the spiritual world 'with a consciousness that was illuminated and spiritually imbued by spiritual science'.[8]

As already mentioned, the anthroposophical knowledge of the Christ Being stood at the centre of Christian Morgenstern's soul-life. Hence he knew better than virtually any of the other esoteric pupils of Rudolf Steiner that the answer to the question as to what man is in reality was given in the context of world history in the Mystery of Golgotha. ' "Christ gives me my humanity"—that will be the fundamental feeling which will well up in the soul and pervade it' (GA 26, p. 94). These words of Rudolf Steiner's, written ten years after Christian Morgenstern's death, can be felt as a leitmotif for his entire inner life. He took this experience with him after death as a key to his all-encompassing understanding of the spiritual world. Equipped with this key and the whole richness of anthroposophical knowledge about man's spiritual origin which he had taken into his living thinking on Earth and continued to cherish in his existence after death, Christian Morgenstern encountered individualities such as Fichte, Schelling and Hegel in the spirit-land shortly after death. He revealed to these individualities—who had lost all orientation in the spiritual world (probably for the reasons outlined)—what they had the greatest need of there. 'Like a bright star'[9] he brought them the long-awaited answer 'to the great significant question: "What *is* man, the living human being in the spirit-land?"' (ibid., italics Rudolf Steiner).

For these great individualities were—despite all their philosophical achievements on Earth—unable to recognize the essential nature of man so as to find their further path in the spirit-land. Only now, through the encounter with the entelechy of Christian Morgenstern, who was wholly imbued with an anthroposophy that was grasped in living thinking, could above all 'Hegel and Fichte' say to themselves, not out of an abstract knowledge but through the appearance of this individuality: 'We tried to fathom on Earth what explains its mysteries. But in the entire range of concepts that we have developed out of an earthly understanding, out of the deep layers of a certainty derived from earthly knowledge, there was no answer to the question that is posed to us here: What is man? What, in truth, is man in the context of the whole cosmos? Then this human being, this human star comes and explains to us *through what he is*, through what he brings to us, through what he has already prepared on Earth for the heavens!' (ibid.). It was for the Earth that Fichte, Schelling and Hegel erected their proud philosophical constructions out of an earthly reasoning power developed to its highest potential, while it was for the heavenly world that Christian Morgenstern, though still living on the Earth, had in his etheric reasoning power united and inwardly experienced with his soul the wisdom of anthroposophy. In this way he was able to open up new perspectives to these great nineteenth-century spirits and guide them on their further path in their life after death.

As already mentioned, this was possible only because he had with his whole being become a living witness for the cosmically earthly influence of the Ascension forces in the spiritual world. These forces enabled him to bear his all-embracing knowledge of anthroposophy fully consciously in his soul without losing his ego in a state of ecstasy. Not merely was he able to present the knowledge of man to souls in spirit-land, but it was this knowledge itself that filled his entire being and streamed from him into the spiritual world. In the following words Rudolf Steiner speaks of one of the 'deepest' things that he was himself allowed to experience in the spiritual world: 'Indeed, this soul was well prepared to bring into the spiritual worlds what it was able to receive here in the earthly world [as anthroposophy] in so full a way. And so Christian Morgenstern's *spirit-body* also appears to me in such a way that his spiritual raiment after death was interwoven with the cosmic truths and mysteries from our spiritual movement which he had received here on Earth. This is now, in a sense, his body, and it is one of the deepest things that I have experienced in the spiritual worlds: to find what I have striven for in this earthly incarnation in the spiritual worlds, *to see it spread out everywhere in the higher worlds* as in an artistic painting, to see it interwoven with Christian Morgenstern's spiritual raiment.'[10] 'To see it [anthroposophy itself] spread out everywhere in the higher worlds'—this was the consequence of the connection of Christian Morgenstern's etheric body with the Ascension forces of Christ.[11]

Completely filled with the Christ-permeated 'consciousness of his humanity', Christian Morgenstern was able directly to impart this after his death also to many other beings, purely by appearing before them. Hence the words which Rudolf Steiner was to speak later (on the evening before the Christmas Conference) apply to no other anthroposophist in the way they do to Christian Morgenstern, the 'archetype' of the 'best anthroposophist' (ibid.): 'Anthroposophy should actually be none other than that Sophia, that is to say, that content of consciousness, that inner human experience, which endows a human being with his full humanity. The right interpretation of the word anthroposophy is not "wisdom of man" but rather "the consciousness of one's humanity"' (GA 257, 13 February 1923).

Through this almost unique connection of Christian Morgenstern to the Ascension forces of Christ, his entry into the world after death was distinctively 'an event for these spiritual worlds'. Moreover, it even marked an 'epoch in these spiritual worlds' (ibid.).[12] And just as the consequences of the Mystery of Golgotha were made manifest to the entire spiritual world through the Ascension, so did Christian Morgenstern after his death show countless human souls what it means to take the forces of the Mystery of Golgotha into oneself through spiritual science, in order to accomplish what Rudolf Steiner, as the summation of everything that he had said about Christian Morgenstern's life after death, observed: 'Christian Morgenstern is for us the victory of life over death' (ibid.).

What Christian Morgenstern could in this way receive only through anthroposophy Rudolf Steiner had already created in his early work out of the source of the Ascension mystery. Only in one single place in his entire output did he refer to this in a few words: this was when he mentioned that the source of the mortal element which in pre-Christian times was sought by all initiates on the Sun was now, after the events of the Turning Point of Time, to be found on the Earth as the source of moral intuitions, so that since then every human being has been able to create it out of himself. Rudolf Steiner said of the old initiates: 'They pictured the Sun in the first instance as a Spirit Being' (GA 202, 18 December 1920). This Spirit Being was the Christ Himself before His descent from the Sun to the Earth. And then he continues: 'The initiates conceived of this Spirit Being as the source of all morality' (ibid.). And now comes the decisive sentence: 'In my *Philosophy of Freedom* I have said that moral intuitions are derived from *this* source, but [now] derived from the earthly world; for moral intuitions shine forth from human beings, from what can live in human beings as moral enthusiasm' (ibid.).

This is what is most important: what formerly came from the Sun as an incentive to moral activity can today be found in the earthly world and, indeed, in man himself, whence it shines forth as moral intuitions for the whole cosmos. The reason why the source of all morality can no longer be found on the Sun but within man himself as the wellspring of his moral intuitions *is the Ascension of Christ*. This is owing to the fact that He brought His Devachan, His great cosmic Sun kingdom, down to the Earth and united it with the depths of the human etheric body. And because this had happened as a 'mystical fact' of world history and Rudolf Steiner discovered these forces in his own etheric body, he was able to write his *Philosophy of Freedom* out of these forces. This happened from two sides: in the first part of the book the nature of pure thinking was established, a thinking that is rooted in the etheric body and ensures that man does not obscure his ego-consciousness outside his body in ecstasy; and in the second part of the book the new source of moral intuitions was revealed, intuitions which lead *within man* to free deeds out of the forces of the Sun.[13]

Further distinctive qualities of *The Philosophy of Freedom* become understandable from this. That the free deeds of man can be implemented only 'out of love for the object' (GA 4, ch. 9) is likewise a reference to the essential nature of the etheric body, which is pre-eminently the bearer of the forces of love within man. 'For love is a living force that stimulates something deep in our being, keeping it awake and alive ... For the etheric body is the same as the body of love' (GA 130, 2 December 1911). And when Rudolf Steiner adds in one of the sections added to the second edition of his book in 1918 that the penetration of thinking into the phenomena of the world 'is brought about by a power flowing through the activity of thinking itself—the power of love in its spiritual form' (ch. 8), what is meant by this is a body-free, etheric thinking taking place in the human etheric body as a body of love.[14]

If we consider not only *The Philosophy of Freedom* but the whole of

Rudolf Steiner's early work from the point of view that has been adopted, and recall that the basic concept of his 'freedom philosophy' was already in his mind in 1881,[15] we can understand the whole of the young Rudolf Steiner's path of development in a new and intensified way.

In his 'Tale of the Rockspring Wonder' from the second Mystery Play (GA 14) Rudolf Steiner allowed some of his childhood experiences to shine forth in artistic form. Something is communicated there in poetic images from his inner life in Pottschach that is associated with the awakening of his clairvoyant faculties, through which he was able to perceive the elemental world of nature. In the tale itself this supersensible gift is firmly referred to as a Moon gift. The three Moon women who appear to the boy at the waterfall during a moonlit night give him a cup, which they had previously filled with moonlight. This gift is largely of a moonlike character, because it derives from the boy's previous incarnations and was not achieved through his conscious efforts in this life. However, after he has received it in a renewed form in the present life without any effort on his part as though through the grace of destiny, it lies thereafter entirely in his freedom to transform its Moon character deriving from the past into the Sun quality of a future impulse through the strength of his own ego.

The astonishing thing about Rudolf Steiner's life is that he set himself this task already as an eight-year-old, after his family's move to Neudörfl, and at this same age took the first steps towards implementing it. As is well known, this happened through his first encounter with geometry. At the end of his life Rudolf Steiner described that already then and constantly thereafter he was aware of the feeling: 'In my relation to geometry I must perceive the first germination of a conception which later gradually evolved within me. This lived within me more or less unconsciously during my childhood, and around my twentieth year took on a definite and fully conscious form.' Around this time there also lived in Rudolf Steiner's soul a fully rounded conception of his freedom philosophy. And then he puts it more clearly: 'Naturally, I did not as a child say this to myself distinctly, but I felt that one must carry knowledge of the spiritual world within oneself after the manner of geometry' (GA 28, ch. 1).

Thus the way was open for—to express it pictorially—the Moon cup of clairvoyant forces sent to Rudolf Steiner as though through the grace of destiny to be filled with the substance of pure thinking. In this imagination of the cup one can also recognize a clear reference to what he established after the turn of the century as a 'science of the Grail' (GA 13). Thus it was on this path that Rudolf Steiner shortly afterwards arrived at the insights about the Christ Being and the Mystery of Golgotha which in

1886 he was able to present in the conversation with the Cistercian priest Wilhelm Neumann in Vienna. In the lecture of 18 July 1924 he summarized this conversation in the following words: 'We were going away from a gathering, and speaking about the Christ problem. I propounded my ideas which were essentially the same as those I give in my lectures' (GA 240); and with regard to the substance of this conversation Rudolf Steiner referred to the corresponding place in his autobiography, *The Course of My Life*. There we read in this connection: 'I expressed my view to the effect that Jesus of Nazareth received the Christ into himself as a result of an influence from beyond the Earth, and that Christ, as a spiritual Being, has been involved with human evolution since the Mystery of Golgotha' (GA 28, ch. 7).

It has already been observed by various biographers of Rudolf Steiner that although he had come to this 'purely anthroposophical' knowledge of the Christ Being in his Viennese period he hardly mentioned anything about it before the turn of the century and above all during his time in Berlin. Moreover, at this time he made remarks which placed him alongside freethinkers such as Nietzsche who stood far removed from official religion. In this connection Rudolf Steiner concerned himself only with denominations with deep-rooted traditions. He himself later recalled: 'Before this [before the turn of the century], the Christian content to which I referred had always been that found in the existing denominations. This Nietzsche also did' (GA 28, ch. 26). And Friedrich Rittelmeyer recounted a conversation where Rudolf Steiner expressed himself as follows about Rittelmeyer's question about this time in his life: '"Did you always think of Christ as you think today, even in your scientific days?" I asked him. "I remember that in a conversation in the middle of my twenties [probably with Wilhelm Neumann] I spoke of Christ like this," he answered. "But then of course it fell temporarily into the background. I had to pass through all those other phases. It was a karmic necessity."'[16]

Above all the words 'But then of course it fell temporarily into the background' refer to something important in this connection. For the knowledge of Christ that Rudolf Steiner acquired initially had to fall into the background for a certain time in his life, since it was attained not wholly from within—solely from the strength of his own ego and after difficult spiritual trials—but lit up in his soul as though generated from without. The extreme difficulties of the Berlin years—which brought Rudolf Steiner to the edge of his spiritual and even physical existence—had to be endured if it was to be experienced in a new, deepened and internalized form as purely spiritual knowledge. It was the deepest crisis of his life, whence, however, he emerged victorious, succeeding in 'standing in spirit before the Mystery of Golgotha' in the 'celebration of knowledge' that has been already mentioned.[17]

After the knowledge of Christ had been won in Vienna and the Moon cup of the bestowed clairvoyance had been filled to the brim with Sun substance during the following period in Weimar (which was proclaimed in 1893 by the arising of *The Philosophy of Freedom*), there followed the third section in the form of the very difficult Berlin years, which concluded the great Sun period in Rudolf Steiner's life.[18] Then his spiritual path led through the abyss where all his previous knowledge (including that of Christ) had to fall into the background, in order to forge a path forward into cosmic solitude.

Rudolf Steiner only had a single thread to hold on to. And this led him from the lack of assumptions or prerequisites that had characterized *Truth and Knowledge* through the 'state of emergency' of *The Philosophy of Freedom* to the true ego and the shining forth of the new Christ consciousness in man that is associated with it. In a state of inner struggle and filled with great anguish, of a kind that an ordinary person can barely conceive of, Rudolf Steiner had now to find the only possible way out through the strength of his own ego.

In the chapter of his autobiography where in a few words he comes to speak about this central trial in the culmination of his own initiation, he also mentions—though without referring to the person concerned by name—the conversation with the priest of the Cistercian order, Wilhelm Neumann. 'In an earlier passage in this biography, I described a conversation about Christ which I had with the learned Cistercian who was a professor in the faculty of Catholic theology in Vienna. I was in the presence of a sceptical mood. The Christianity which I had to seek I did not find anywhere in the various denominations. After the time of testing had subjected me to stern battles of the soul, I had to submerge myself in Christianity and, indeed, in that world where it is spoken of directly by the spirit' (GA 28, ch. 26). That is to say, everything that had formerly lived in Rudolf Steiner either intellectually or as a spiritual imagination with regard to the Christ Being, including the knowledge that he had acquired thereby, had to recede into the background, just as on the path of schooling all imaginations that have been formed have to be dissolved at the transition to the next stage, that of Inspiration. In this way man's consciousness of the spirit initially falls into a total emptiness, in order thereafter to enter into a deepened relationship to the spiritual world.

Still more difficult, however, is the transition to the world of Intuition, where the person being initiated stands not merely before an inner emptiness but before the objective world-abyss, where everything—even his own being—can be destroyed. Now everything that has gone before is silent, for he must now himself create a new relationship across the abyss not only with the spiritual but with the *super-spiritual* world. At this world-abyss Rudolf Steiner also had to forget all his previously acquired knowledge about Christ. In leaping over the abyss it was a question for him of taking hold of the innermost core of his being in full consciousness and thus intuitively grasping the presence of Christ as the starting point for the new Christ consciousness. For this new Christ consciousness does not extinguish individual ego-consciousness but endows it with the wholly new capacity of maintaining the uprightness of the ego at all levels of world-existence and, hence, of bringing forth spiritual research to the extent that Rudolf Steiner conducted it in anthroposophy. In other words, it was a question here of fully making the words 'Not I, but Christ in me' (Galatians 2:20) a reality.

In a later lecture Rudolf Steiner describes in the following words this experience through which man takes hold of his true ego in full consciousness on the other side of the world-abyss: 'But one is standing wholly rightly in a true manner at the abyss of existence if one makes the resolve to extinguish, to forget oneself through free inner will, through an energetic deed of will. Actually, all these things are also evident in man's being in a factual sense; but he knows nothing about it. Every night he must unconsciously extinguish himself in this way. But it is quite a different matter to commit with full consciousness one's memory-ego to destruction, to forgetfulness, to the abyss, to stand for a definite period in the spiritual world at the abyss of existence experiencing nothingness as nothing. It is the most shattering experience that one can have, and one must embark upon this experience with great trust. If one is to go towards the abyss as nothing, it is necessary that one has the trust that one's true ego will be brought to meet one out of the world. And this happens ... Thus the ascent to the super-spiritual world, the experience of a completely new world at the abyss of existence and the receiving of the true ego out of this super-spiritual world at the abyss of existence, is an inner experience' (GA 147, 30 August 1913). What is happening here, what is bestowed upon a human being as the true ego across the abyss of existence, is the Ego of Christ itself or—in the sense of spiritual economy—the reflection of Christ's Ego, which at this stage a person receives into his own ego.[19] Herein lies the source of the new Christ consciousness achieved by Rudolf Steiner at the turn of the century, out of which he founded the whole of anthroposophy in the years that followed.

He himself described this process later in a completely objective form, as it will be accessible to all human beings in the future (which is to say, from our time onwards): 'If souls can become truly accustomed to such an understanding, they will become sufficiently mature on seeing that holy chalice to get to know the mystery of the Christ Ego—the eternal Ego into which every human ego can be transformed. This mystery *is* a reality. All that people have to do is to follow the call by spiritual science to understand this mystery as a fact, so that they can receive Christ's Ego at the mere sight of the Holy Grail. For this to be so, it is necessary only that one understand and accept these happenings as fact' (GA 109, 11 April 1909; the italics are Rudolf Steiner's).[20]

Just as Christian Rosenkreutz rose to this stage in the sixteenth century[21] and was therefore able to receive the authority to send his 'most intimate pupil and friend' (GA 130, 18 December 1912), Gautama Buddha, to the spiritual sphere of Mars, so it was Rudolf Steiner who attained the same stage of initiation as the first Rosicrucian in the Michael epoch that has now dawned. Through this he revealed the path to this goal for our time *to all human beings*. For what Christian Rosenkreutz attained on a hidden path, as though in the background of human history, Rudolf Steiner has now accomplished in full public view; and by establishing spiritual science on Earth he has given the prospect of a new possibility for the further development of mankind. 'It is part of the inner mission of the spiritual world-stream [of anthroposophy] to prepare human beings to become so mature in soul that an ever-increasing number of them will be able to receive a copy of the Ego Being of Christ Jesus ... And now you see from what depths the spiritual-scientific world-stream exerts its influence' (GA 109, 7 March 1909).

If one really tries to understand this path that Rudolf Steiner followed into the abyss but also out of it again, a path which made it possible for the modern 'science of the grail' to be founded, one can only contemplate it with the greatest reverence. The immense significance of the breakthrough that was achieved here for the first time in the history of humanity will only gradually become apparent over the coming centuries. For the path that Rudolf Steiner was the first to take *in this form* is of the kind that will in future become the general path of mankind into the spiritual world and, hence, for a conscious experience of Christ.

If in our time we look for an archetype at the Turning Point of Time for Rudolf Steiner's Berlin period, so often argued about among anthroposophists but—in the sense of what has been presented earlier—nevertheless very clear in its aims, we may come to the following picture. For nearly three years the apostles had accompanied Christ in the physical body and therefore with their ordinary earthly consciousness. After the

Resurrection they followed Him in His Resurrection body with their imaginative consciousness and heard the words in which He revealed to them the mysteries of the heavenly sphere whence He had come (Acts 1:3). With this they reached the stage of Inspiration. Then the Ascension took place, Christ disappeared from their clairvoyant gaze and they could no longer hear His inspiring words. From now on He was no longer accessible either to their imaginative or to their inspirative forces. With this came the most difficult time for the apostles; for everything that they had previously had was taken away from them. The experience of this loss was even more painful than the time from Easter Saturday to Easter morning. For then they at least had a memory of Christ's promise that after His death the Resurrection and, hence, the opportunity to see Him again—even though in a different form—would be possible. But now Christ disappeared without their having understood His promise for the future. From this time the apostles felt totally abandoned. Only ten days after this most difficult trial of their lives, when their ego-consciousness was as though immersed in a deep sleep,[22] they received the Christ anew, though now no longer from without in the physical body as during the three years, nor in His spiritual manifestation, which they had perceived during the 40 days also as though from without, but in the baptism with fire and spirit on Whitsun morning from within their own inner being, from the deepest depths of their ego as a consequence of the experience of loss which they had suffered.

Rudolf Steiner describes this process as follows from his spiritual research: 'There was a point in the lives of the disciples of Christ Jesus when they said among themselves: We have seen Him, but we see Him no longer. He came down from heaven to us on Earth. Where has he gone?

'The point of time when the disciples believed that they again lost the presence of Christ is commemorated in the Christian festival of the Ascension, which preserves a memory of the clear awareness that the sublime Sun Being who had walked the earth in the man Jesus of Nazareth had vanished from the disciples' sight. When Christ's disciples had had this experience, there came upon them a sorrow such as cannot be compared with any other sorrow on Earth. When the Sun ritual was celebrated in the ancient mysteries, and the image of the god was laid in the grave and lifted out only after some days, the souls of those participating in the ceremony were filled with sorrow at the death of the god. But this sorrow was not to be compared in magnitude with the sorrow that filled the hearts of Christ's disciples.

'All knowledge that can truly be called great is born from pain, from inner travail. When through the means for the attainment of knowledge described in anthroposophical spiritual science one tries to tread the path into the higher worlds, a goal can be reached only by experiencing pain. Without having suffered, suffered intensely and thereby having become free from the oppression of pain, one cannot come to know the spiritual world.

'During the ten days following the Ascension, the suffering of Christ's disciples was beyond all telling, because Christ had vanished from their sight. And out of this pain, out of this infinite sorrow, there sprang what we call the Whitsun mystery. Having lost sight of Christ in their instinctive, outward clairvoyant vision, the disciples of Christ found it again in their inmost being, in their feelings, in inner experience through sorrow, through pain' (GA 226, 17 May 1923).

The personal knowledge of Christ that Rudolf Steiner had had access to from his youth onwards had to yield its place, in order that he could master it out of his own individual power—though now for the whole of mankind. In this way he accomplished in his own spiritual biography the transition from Ascension to Whitsun,[23] or, if one traces the thematic development of his work, from his early epistemological writings to his anthroposophical work after the turn of the century. Hence he could describe the anthroposophy which he founded as the beginning of a new epoch in the history of mankind.[24]

*

At the end of the lecture quoted earlier, which is devoted to the Ascension, Rudolf Steiner refers to a further consequence of the Ascension of Christ. This is that every person today who after death beholds the dissolving of his etheric body during the three days (Rudolf Steiner calls such a process of dissolution the union of the etheric body with the Sun) experiences in this process at the same time a reflection of the Ascension: 'Since the Mystery of Golgotha, man has beheld in this etheric body which is departing from him the Christ, who has become its saviour in future Earth-existence; so that since the Mystery of Golgotha there has stood before the soul of every human being who dies the Ascension picture which the disciples saw that day because of their particular state of soul' (GA 224, 7 May 1923).

Rudolf Steiner adds, as a further element in this fruit of his spiritual research, that the effect that this picture has on the soul of the dead person depends on whether or not it has developed an understanding for the Mystery of Golgotha already during earthly life. In the former case such a soul derives from the picture of the Ascension the 'very great comfort' which consists in that it is now absolutely certain that Christ has since the

Mystery of Golgotha become the saviour of the whole of earthly evolution. The comfort that the human soul is able to derive from beholding the picture of the Ascension lies above all in that it sees from it directly that the human ego can already on Earth be in full possession of the spiritual forces of the Sun and, hence, of its immortality, in order thereby to fulfil its human destiny. If, however, it has not acquired the knowledge in question, this picture becomes a great reproach and at the same time a serious exhortation to cultivate the appropriate knowledge about the Mystery of Golgotha in the next earthly life.

However, all this is possible only if human beings on Earth form a conscious connection with the Whitsun impulse, that is, with the influence of the Spirit which entered into humanity through the event of Whitsun. 'The Mystery of Golgotha was fulfilled for all human beings, in respect of the physical and etheric bodies only. The sending of the Holy Spirit, the Whitsun mystery, signifies that the soul and spirit of man can partake of the fruits of the Mystery of Golgotha only if he rises to a real recognition of the essence of the Mystery of Golgotha' (GA 224, 7 May 1923). 'The soul and spirit' are in this case man's astral body and ego. It is with them that present-day humanity must, through modern spiritual science, make a direct connection with the Whitsun event at the Turning Point of Time. That is to say, he must gain a new understanding for the Mystery of Golgotha and the associated events of the Ascension and Whitsun out of their forces. 'It follows that the truth of the Whitsun festival can be grasped only when people realize that the sending out of the Holy Spirit is the challenge to humanity gradually to achieve spirit-knowledge. For only through spirit-knowledge can the Mystery of Golgotha be understood' (ibid.). From this arises the whole significance of anthroposophy for the present and future evolution of mankind. Herein, too, lies the reason why Rudolf Steiner has described spiritual science as a modern Whitsun message or a message of the Spirit to mankind.

What had been accomplished by Christ in the Mystery of Golgotha and then in the revelation of the Ascension as something of *universal* validity is taken further in the event of Whitsun as a call to each *individual* human being to understand the impulse of the Mystery of Golgotha and to receive it into himself in the sense of spiritual communion, as was set forth in the first chapter of this book. For what, at the Turning Point of Time, the apostles inwardly grasped on Whitsun morning as a Spirit impulse in the symbol of the fiery tongues as with a heavenly power must now, in our time, be attained out of a free resolve and through the individual efforts of every human being. It is in this sense that Rudolf Steiner's words from his Whitsun address of 1923 must be understood:

'Anthroposophy would wish its destiny to be one with the destiny of Christianity' (GA 226, 17 May 1923).

An exemplification of what is indicated here as the aim of the further development of Christianity on the Earth can be found in the life and work of Rudolf Steiner. For by crossing the threshold from his early work to anthroposophy, he accomplished in the course of his life's biography at the same time the transition from the Ascension to Whitsun on an esoteric plane or, in other words, from a body-free experiencing of the Christ forces in pure thinking in his etheric body to taking hold of them in his ego as the birth of the new Christ consciousness. However, this transition was possible only because—by experiencing the Whitsun Spirit in his own ego—he attained a direct inner relationship to the Mystery of Golgotha, with the result that the mystery of the Resurrection became the foundation of the anthroposophical method of research, so that it can truly be said of it: Its source is Rudolf Steiner's 'standing in spirit' before the Mystery of Golgotha.[25]

★

In conclusion, a brief survey needs to be made of the whole course of events at the Turning Point of Time, in so far as they are imbued with the uninterrupted influence of the Christ Spirit. At their centre stands the Mystery of Golgotha, preceded as it was by two events which were then reflected back in a new form.

At the Baptism in the Jordan the Christ Being united Himself with the body of Jesus and, hence, with earthly evolution as a whole. In the scene of the Transfiguration Christ revealed His higher Sun nature and thus also His origin from the cosmic realm of the Sun to the three chosen disciples. These two events are mirrored, in a manner transformed by the Mystery of Golgotha, in the Ascension and Whitsun.

In His Ascension Christ showed that He has connected the spiritual Sun forces which became manifest in the Transfiguration on Mount Tabor with the etheric bodies of all human beings. Since this time man has received moral intuitions no longer from without, from the cosmic Sun kingdom, but he can, rather, create them on the Earth in full freedom out of the new source that is to be found within himself. And in the event of Whitsun there shines forth a reflection of what took place as a unique event at the Baptism in the Jordan. At that time Christ took hold of the earthly sheaths of Jesus in such a way that the ego of Zarathustra, which had previously dwelt in them, had to leave the body. For in Christ there appeared on the Earth a divine Being of such power and greatness that no human ego, not even that of a high initiate as Zarathustra indeed was, could receive this Being into himself without his ego-consciousness being immediately extinguished. But this was no longer to happen in future. Christ wanted to be wholly present in the human ego without dulling it in any way at all. 'He wanted to dwell within mankind, but He did not want to dull the emerging ego-consciousness of human beings. He had done this once in Jesus, in whom from the Baptism onwards the consciousness of the Son lived in place of his ego-consciousness. But this was not to take place in people of future times, in whom the ego was to be able to rise up in full consciousness and the Christ nevertheless to dwell within them' (GA 214, 30 July 1922).

In order to bring this about, Christ had first to vanish before the direct sight of human beings in order to unite with them in a new way. The former event happened through His Ascension: 'As Christ fulfilled His Ascension, so did He become invisible' (ibid.). But then after ten days He sent His disciples the Holy Spirit, or 'that divine being who does not extinguish ego-consciousness, to whom one ascends not in contemplation but in the Spirit who cannot be beheld' (ibid.). Now Christ could also enter into human souls without extinguishing individual ego-consciousness. This happened in the event of Whitsun. For from then onwards He worked within man not directly but through the mediation of the Holy Spirit. 'Thus the Holy Spirit is that which was to be sent by Christ in order that man might be able to retain his ego-consciousness and Christ can dwell unconsciously within man' (ibid.).[26]

Thus the Ascension and Whitsun are interconnected as two direct consequences of the Mystery of Golgotha. For through His death and Resurrection Christ united Himself with the whole of earthly evolution; He became part of humanity as such through the twofold event of the Ascension and Whitsun. And so, just as we see in the Ascension the transformation of the scene of the Transfiguration, we can recognize in Whitsun the metamorphosis of the Baptism by John in the Jordan: in the one case the Baptism of Jesus with water, in the other a baptism by Christ with fire and Spirit. In this way what happened on Whitsun morning was that Christ entered into all His disciples in such a way that a departure of the ego was no longer necessary. From this point onwards, Christ could be active in all human beings just as He had formerly been active in the human being Jesus of Nazareth, without extinguishing their individual ego-consciousness.

The consequence of this is that in the further perspective of earthly evolution human beings will by its end increasingly be in a position to form a new, ego-conscious unity out of mankind, a wholly new being which will in its basic gestures be imbued by Christ as its new group-Spirit or higher group-Ego. 'Just as the higher ego is born in the individual, so the higher Ego of all mankind, the divine Ego, was born in Palestine' (GA 112, 24 June 1909).

With this the possibility is given to mankind to reach the transition to the new cosmic aeon designated by Rudolf Steiner as the future Jupiter, which appears as the imagination of the Heavenly Jerusalem at the end of the Book of Revelation. But how will this transition come about, and how can it be prepared? Rudolf Steiner said in this regard that in the second half of Earth evolution everything that has hitherto been fashioned materially, that is, the whole of outwardly physical existence, will gradually be dissolved. 'What will then be left?' he asks and, in answer to this, gives the mighty picture of how human beings can create Christ's new supersensible sheaths for His impulse through their moral deeds on the Earth: the supersensibly physical sheath from all actions springing in life from the human conscience; the etheric sheath from all deeds of love and compassion; the astral sheath from 'all that paves the way to supersensible knowledge' (GA 155, 30 May 1912) associated with the feelings of reverence and amazement. By this means mankind will be united with the Christ Being in a way that something akin to a new being, which will encompass all human beings, will arise.[27] This being will then make the transition to Jupiter as a humanity that has been permeated by Christ's Ego, after the material Earth has crumbled into cosmic dust.

Rudolf Steiner describes this new being in the following words: 'When the Earth will one day have reached its goal, when human beings will understand the right moral impulses through which all that is good is done, there will be a resolution of what flowed as an ego into the development of humanity through the Mystery of Golgotha in the form of the Christ impulse. It shall then be enveloped by an astral body which is formed through faith, through all men's deeds of wonder and amazement;[28] by something which is like an etheric body formed through deeds of love; and by something which envelops it like a physical body, formed through deeds of conscience' (ibid.).

The circle of the twelve apostles which came about on the basis of the Whitsun event formed the model for this future human community. For, as we have seen, Christ Himself at that time entered into them through the mediation of the Holy Spirit. Through this they became a new community, whose members were wholly imbued with Christ and were therefore able to bring the Christian message to the whole of mankind, that is, to the whole second half of earthly evolution. That this original Whitsun community of the apostles corresponds absolutely to the ideal of a human community referred to follows from the words with which Rudolf Steiner describes the future being of mankind in the lecture from which these quotations are being made: 'Thus people will, in the course of earthly evolution, lay the foundations for a great community, which can be permeated and made Christian through and through by the Christ impulse' (ibid.). This new humanity, then inseparably connected with Christ and, indeed, wholly permeated by Him, will accomplish the transition into the future aeon of Jupiter under His guidance and with His help.

The extent to which this great ideal of human evolution subsequently lived in particularly outstanding individuals, even though they were not fully aware of its occult antecedents (they can only be discovered through spiritual-scientific research), is shown by the example that Rudolf Steiner brings of Goethe. In a letter of 18 July 1828 to Friedrich August von Beulwitz, Goethe wrote of rational humanity as of the 'great immortal individual' (ibid.), who represents the great goal of earthly evolution.

A younger contemporary of Goethe similarly had this goal of humanity in view. In his essay *Christendom or Europe*, Novalis wrote of a great 'universal individuality', which was his way of referring to the same ideal of earthly evolution. In the same section he also called this future 'a new Golden Age', when the 'Saviour' will be present and active in all members of this 'new mankind' in the most diverse ways extending to true communion.[29]

★

The essential qualities of the Mystery of Golgotha, above all in their cosmic dimension, are by no means only associated with the aforesaid transition to Jupiter. As was shown in the first chapter, its influence embraces *the whole of world evolution*, from Old Saturn to the future Vulcan. In the Mystery of Golgotha itself the two poles of world evolution as its beginning and end are inseparably connected with one another. Only because of this could Christ say of Himself: 'I am the Alpha and the Omega, the beginning and the end' (Revelation 1:8).

Before His death on the Cross Christ had so fully restored the forces of the phantom that they corresponded wholly to their original state when created on Old Saturn. Because of this, Christ could speak about His death in such a way that it was understood that He was speaking of the divine Father.[30] The Father God was also the highest Regent of Saturn evolution.[31] Hence His forces were present wherever the impulses of Old Saturn were at work. The establishing of a direct relationship to Old Saturn was preceded in the life of Christ Jesus by two preparatory stages, when the corresponding connections to Old Sun and Old Moon were made.

If one considers from this standpoint the 33 years of Jesus of Nazareth's life at the Turning Point of Time, one can state the following: in the 30 years until the Baptism in the Jordan the whole history of mankind in the first part of earthly evolution, which came under the influence of Mars forces, was reflected. This comes to expression above all in the family tree of St Luke's Gospel, where it is stated that this Jesus was descended directly from Adam and even from the time before the Fall ('from God', 3:38).

The earthly life of Christ began with the Baptism in the Jordan, when His higher Sun Spirit was united with the lunar, hereditary stream of earthly humanity. Heredity stands under the guidance of the Moon Archangel Gabriel, who for this reason proclaimed the birth of Jesus on the Earth. The very fact that the Baptism itself took place in water points to the connection of this ritual with Old Moon, where the main formative substance was akin to water. From the spiritual side the process was accompanied by the Holy Spirit, who—proceeding from the Father—guided the whole of pre-Christian evolution. Rudolf Steiner said of it that the Holy Spirit in world evolution was the highest Regent of Old Moon. John the Baptist bore witness to the Holy Spirit's appearance during the Baptism in the following words: 'I saw the Spirit descend like a dove from heaven and remain on Him' (John 1:32). Thus at the Baptism in the Jordan the Sun Spirit of Christ was able on His path to the Earth, the last cosmic stage of which was the Moon sphere, to fill the 'Moon chalice' of His earthly bodily nature offered to Him by Jesus. Jesus was thereby a Christophorus, the living symbol of the Holy Grail: the Moon sickle as a chalice, bearing within itself the spiritual Sun. At the same time Christ established the relationship of His astral body (for after the Baptism the astral body of Jesus became His astral body) to the Old Moon, where this body had been created. In this way the astral body was led back to the original pure condition that it had possessed before the Fall.

The next scene that is described in the Gospels after the Baptism in the Jordan—the threefold temptation of Christ Jesus in the wilderness—has a connection to the previous incarnation of the Earth. For evil in the cosmos received its full independence on Old Moon. It was still the case on Old Sun that obstacles could arise only because certain hierarchies were, so to speak, 'detailed' to become spirits of hindrance. That is to say, until Old Moon evil was still wholly included in the plan of the good. On Old Moon, however, and specifically in the realm of the Angels, there came about for the first time a complete separation from the forces of the good. 'The first [in the sequence of the hierarchies] who had the possibility of becoming evil were the Angels, for this possibility only existed from the Moon evolution' (GA 110, 18 April 1909–II). Thus the nature of the adversarial powers (Lucifer and Ahriman) by whom Christ Jesus was tempted in the wilderness was in accordance with the fact that they had already left the plane where evil was still guided out of the sphere of the good on Old Moon. They were already working out of the sphere of the truly evil.[32]

We find the next stage of this development in the scene of the Transfiguration. In this scene Christ revealed His own Sun Being for the first time,[33] though at the same time also His relationship to Old Sun, where He became part of the cosmic evolution described in the temporal stream of world evolution. (See GA 137, 12 June 1912.) For this reason Rudolf Steiner calls Him the highest Regent of Old Sun.[34] Christ was therefore renewing His original connection to Old Sun and re-establishing it in His etheric body, which was created at that time.

The third stage consisted in establishing a direct relationship to Old Saturn, through which alone the rescuing or restoring of the phantom in its original radiance became possible. In preparation for this deed on the Hill of Golgotha Christ speaks—as we have already seen—of His imminent death as of the path to the Father. This theme fills His farewell discourses, which are recorded only in St John's Gospel, then follows His great prayer in Gethsemane and finally it appears in the words on the Cross.

Just as the Holy Spirit, who—proceeding originally from the Father—had from the outset prepared Christ's incarnation on the Earth, was involved in the Baptism in the Jordan, so did Christ manifest His Sun Being and at the same time His still higher Son nature at the Transfiguration. This Son nature shone forth when, on the evening before the Mystery of Golgotha, Christ for the first time really made the disciples aware of the mystery of His relationship with the divine Father. Thus in the first part of the Mystery of Golgotha there was a rekindling of the relationship to Old Saturn and, hence, to the origin of the physical body, which in its very earliest form had been created by the Father God through the First Hierarchy. Only through this could the human phantom be rescued on the Cross on the Hill of Golgotha.

After the phantom had finally been renewed on Good Friday, the second part of the Mystery of Golgotha set the scene for 'the coming to birth of a new member of human nature—an incorruptible body' (GA 131, 11 October 1911). For with the transformation of the phantom into the Resurrection body something altogether new was created in world evolution. Whereas the restoring of the phantom signified merely a reaching back to the primal source of world evolution, with the creating of the Resurrection body something entirely new was going on. It was the first creation out of nothingness in earthly evolution.

Rudolf Steiner defines the essential nature of creation out of nothingness as a creation out of 'relationships' and 'conditions'.[35] This definition does not contradict the uniqueness and originality of a new creation, on the grounds that—although for creating out of nothing the corresponding relationships are indeed necessary—the creation itself remains nonetheless absolutely original. Thus it was with the creation of the world by the Father God, which occurred out of nothing and had as its sole prerequisite the collaboration of the Son, who as the divine Word created the whole cosmos. Here the activity of the Son, the Logos, forms the necessary *conditions* whence the creation of the world becomes possible out of His *relationship* to the Father for creation out of nothingness.

In a similar way, though now on the Earth itself, for His creation out of nothingness Christ first formed the necessary *relationship* to the forces of the Father reaching back to Old Saturn. Then before His death on the Cross He established the necessary *conditions* for the unique way of creating out of nothingness which was to follow through the restoring of the phantom in its original form.

This going back to Old Saturn through the previous stages of Old Sun and Old Moon (the connection to the Mars half of Earth evolution was established out of the earthly genealogy of Jesus) also has a further significance. Rudolf Steiner says of Christ's deed on Golgotha: 'What is this greatest deed of freedom? It is that the creative and wise Word of our solar system Himself resolved to enter into a human body and to take part in Earth evolution through a deed unconnected with any previous karma' (ibid.).

That Christ, coming from the spiritual world, brought no earthly karma with Him goes without saying. However, the sheaths of Jesus of Nazareth—his astral body, etheric body and physical body—were connected with earthly forces of heredity and influenced by them; and they had a karma out of their time before the Baptism in the Jordan. How could this now be extinguished and, hence, be rendered inactive, so that Christ came to be able to accomplish His deed on Golgotha *in the sheaths of Jesus* actually free of karma?

This was possible only in *one* way. Jesus' astral body had first to be led back to the moment when it came into being on Old Moon, where—in the state of being born—it had been without karma. This was accomplished through the connection with the forces of Old Moon at the moment of the Baptism or shortly afterwards at the temptation in the wilderness. Then in the Transfiguration scene the etheric body of Jesus was led back by Christ to the origin of its forces on Old Sun and thereby made free of karma. Finally the restoration of the phantom, which enabled also the physical body to be brought to the state of complete freedom from karma, was equivalent to how it had originally been on Old Saturn at the moment when it emerged out of the womb of divine-spiritual beings. In this way the necessary 'conditions' were established to transform the phantom into the Resurrection body through one act of creating out of nothing.

The fact that Christ, in spite of incarnating in the bodily sheaths of Jesus of Nazareth, Himself lived for three years without any earthly karma, is one of the most important results of Rudolf Steiner's research out of the content of the Fifth Gospel. For had Christ been burdened with an earthly karma He would never have been able to balance out the karma of the life of Jesus (as any other human karma can be balanced out), which would, however, have been a process within the great karmic causality encompassing the whole of world evolution from Old Saturn to Vulcan.[36] In order to find a way out of this karmic causality, the bounds of karma had to be completely broken, or, in other words, it was necessary in order to bring about the Resurrection to reach the sphere of duration, of eternity, which lies beyond the sevenfold evolutionary chain of the cosmos.

Thus the essential nature of the Resurrection in its cosmic dimension can be understood only if one avails oneself of the whole of anthroposophy, and above all of what it tells us about world evolution and the working of karma. Then it gradually becomes understandable how the whole of anthroposophy is contained in one single sentence which comes in the lectures on the Fifth Gospel. This is the sentence about the three years of Christ Jesus' life, stating that this life was lived on the Earth *without karma*. This statement refers not only to the life of Christ, which was anyway without karma, but also to the *three years* of Jesus' life. Hence Rudolf Steiner could say: '*The Fifth Gospel is the anthroposophical Gospel* and reveals to us that the three years of Christ's life is the only life in a human body which was lived without karma, the only life to which the concept of karma in the human sense is not applicable' (GA 148, 3 October 1913).

These words relate both to the restoring of the phantom and the creation of the Resurrection body, though with the former it is a question of a liberation from old karma and with the latter of a new creation, which from the outset is without karma. Just as the phantom is indicative of the past and reaches back to Old Saturn, so does the Resurrection body point towards the most distant future of world evolution, towards Vulcan, where the ideal of creating out of nothing will be made a reality by human beings also in its cosmic dimension. The model for this will, however, remain the Resurrection body as the highest deed of creation out of nothing. Rudolf Steiner says regarding this: 'There was no preceding karma forcing the Christ to His resolution to enter a human body; He undertook to do it as a free deed entirely based upon foreseeing mankind's future evolution. This deed had no precedent, having its origin in Him as a thought[37] out of nothingness, out of His pre-vision' (GA 107, 17 June 1909).

What for Christ was a preview with respect to the ultimate goal of human evolution (which will be fully attained only on Vulcan)—man as a being who creates freely out of nothingness—had already become a full reality within present earthly evolution in His Resurrection. For the bringing forth of the Resurrection body as a creation out of nothingness on the foundation of its 'relationship' to the phantom occurred in such a way that the two poles of world evolution, Saturn and Vulcan, were directly connected with one another at the mid-point of the whole evolution by a unique creative act. However, this was accomplished not within the spiritual time encompassing evolution (from Old Saturn to the middle of Earth evolution) and involution (from the middle of Earth evolution to the future Vulcan) but through the forces of eternity, which preceded Saturn and will follow the condition of Vulcan. In other words: only from the standpoint of eternity, which lies before Saturn and after Vulcan, can one connect both cosmic poles directly together. It was this that happened with the transformation of the phantom (Saturn) into the Resurrection body (Vulcan), whence arose a unified being encompassing the whole of world evolution from its beginning to its end.

To summarize: Christ entered through the gates of Mars, Moon, Sun and Saturn into eternity with the restored phantom as the Son of Man and, from the other side of eternity, returned through the gates of Vulcan, Venus, Jupiter and Mercury into the stream of time with His Resurrection body, in order on this path from out of the future to meet mankind as the Son of God, who is at the same time mankind's cosmic representative.

In the bosom of the Father

Father

Son of Man .... Son .... Son of God

Holy Spirit

Connected with mankind through the Holy Spirit

Only after His Resurrection, during the 40 days of His conversations with the disciples (according to Rudolf Steiner's spiritual research), did Christ speak to them of the central mystery of His Resurrection. In the following words Rudolf Steiner summarizes what was communicated at that time to the apostles: 'Christ came to bring the element of time again to human beings. And when the human heart, the human soul, the human spirit unite themselves with Christ, they regain the stream of time that flows from eternity to eternity' (GA 236, 4 June 1924).

In the course of earthly evolution man has lost the power from the sphere of the Sun which exists in spiritual time, so that in his connection with the Earth he has almost become a being who can only perceive the realm of matter. Only after his death has man been enabled to enter into the stream of spiritual time, which in the higher worlds flows in the opposite direction. However, Christ did not only bring this time but in addition something infinitely higher, namely that which flows from 'eternity to eternity'. St John's Gospel refers to this in the following words: 'And from His fullness have we all received, grace upon grace' (1:16). For the first grace consists in the receiving of spiritual time, which flows through the seven planetary stages of evolution. The second grace, on the other hand, consists in the 'stream of time' which derives directly from eternity and bridges the cosmic abyss between Saturn and Vulcan.

If one adds to these two higher streams of time the lowest and generally familiar one, where the historical consciousness of human beings is embodied, one can bring all three to clarity by means of the diagram on p. 76.

Through the creating of the Resurrection body Christ also enables human beings in future to become participants in these forces of eternity. This future does, however, begin already in the present; and from the present epoch onwards mankind shall gradually develop the independent capacity for creating out of nothingness. For whoever creates out of time creates only for time, and what one causes to arise in this way will become nothing when time ceases. However, anyone who really creates out of nothing creates out of the forces of eternity, so that a new creation arises out of them which is subject not to the laws of time but to those of eternity. And it is to this creation that Christ seeks to lead human beings through His Resurrection.

In this way Christ added to the impulse of evolution, which has its origin in the Father God, and to the impulse of involution, which is guided by the Holy Spirit, the third, decisive element: creation out of nothing. Rudolf Steiner says of this: 'It is a difficult concept, but it will always be included in Christian esotericism, *and everything depends* on our

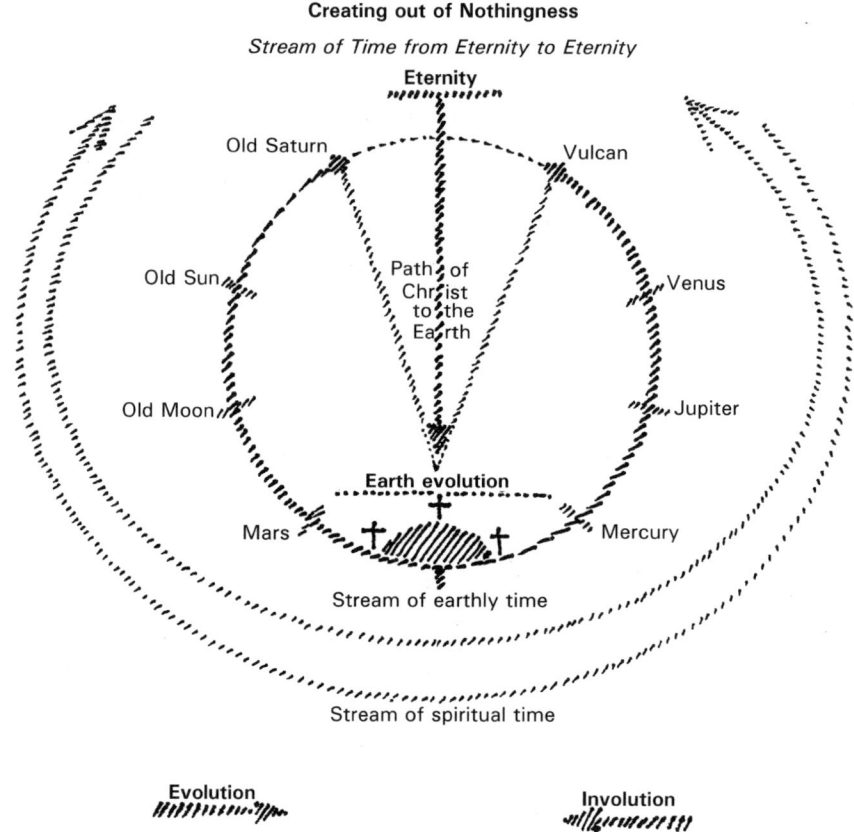

being able to add the thought of creation out of nothingness to those of evolution and involution' (GA 107, 17 June 1909). From this we can understand Rudolf Steiner's statement that the Mystery of Golgotha gave the whole of earthly evolution its highest significance. For if this had been confined to the first two elements of evolution and involution and had not been able to rise to the higher threefoldness, the world would simply be a matter of a meaningless, cyclic repetition of eternal sameness. Only through the third element, through the capacity of creating out of nothingness, which has its origin in the arising of the Resurrection body out of the phantom, does the whole receive its true meaning. 'Whoever speaks of evolution and involution only will speak of development as though everything were merely to repeat itself like a circle [this is how most Eastern religions speak about world evolution]. But such circles can never really explain world evolution. Only when we add to evolution and involution this creation out of nothingness, which adds something new to the conditions currently pertaining, do we arrive at a real understanding of the world' (ibid.).

With this 'real understanding of the world' which anthroposophy makes available today, the path associated with the new mysteries is opened up which will make man a creator out of nothing through a conscious connection with the forces of the Resurrection body. 'The anthroposophical conception of the world gives man strength, hope and confidence in life, for it shows him that he can in future have a share in working at creations which today not only lie in the womb of causality [even though this has a cosmic dimension, extending from Saturn to Vulcan] but in nothingness [in eternity]; it gives him the prospect that, in the true sense of the word, he is working his way *from being a created entity to being a creator*' (ibid.).

In the light of these words Rudolf Steiner indicates in the same lecture that, in the further progress of world evolution, man will cast off and gradually, in succession, replace through new creations out of nothingness all previous cosmic stages. 'He will have cast off all that the gods gave him during the Moon, Sun and Saturn evolutions and the first [Mars] half of Earth evolution.' This work will be concluded in the Venus aeon (ibid.), so that at the ensuing Vulcan stage man will, in creating out of nothing, not merely be replacing the old by the new but will now be engendering something absolutely new. And the model for this highest form of creation out of nothingness was added to evolution and involution (through the Mystery of Golgotha). 'After Saturn, Sun and Moon had passed away, Christ came to the Earth as the great enriching leaven which ensures that something quite new will be there on Vulcan, something not yet present on Saturn' (ibid.).

Rudolf Steiner spoke these words in 1909, and at the end of his life, in September 1924, he added: 'By gradually taking into himself everything that is world and uniting his whole being with it, to the point where on Vulcan he has united with himself the whole content of the world, this great All to which he belongs, man will be what he was at the beginning of Saturn evolution *plus* the whole world. He will be Alpha and Omega, man who unites in himself everything that is world' (GA 346, 7 September 1924; italics Rudolf Steiner).

In order that all human beings might eventually reach this stage on Vulcan, the new capacity of creating out of nothing which was born *on the Earth* in the Mystery of Golgotha had to be implanted. In other words: the Vulcan forces that were used by Christ in the creation of the Resurrection body had to be brought to human beings in the reverse spiritual stream of time flowing out of the future through all the intermediary stages of

Venus and Jupiter. Christ accomplished this through the two events which derived directly from the Mystery of Golgotha, the Ascension and Whitsun.

As already described in this chapter, the Ascension represents a reflection of the Transfiguration with respect to the Mystery of Golgotha which lies between them. Both events occur on a mountain: the Transfiguration on Mount Tabor and the Ascension on the Mount of Olives. And just as in the Transfiguration the relationship to Old Sun was established, so does the event of the Ascension have a connection with the revelation of forces from the future Venus aeon. In contrast to the Jupiter condition, in the Venus aeon the Sun will no longer be separated from the Earth. This is indicated by the fact that Christ does not leave the Earth through His Ascension but, in contrast, unites heaven and Earth in a new way. He made the sacrifice, as Rudolf Steiner puts it, of 'making the Earth His heaven' (GA 148, 3 October 1913). And this also means imbuing the Earth (to begin with only its spiritual aura) with Devachanic Sun forces.

A further aspect of the Ascension, consisting in the rescuing of the etheric body (see above in this chapter), has—in so far as it concerns above all man's life after death—to do with the future of the Life Spirit. For the Life Spirit is the etheric body that has been transformed and spiritualized out of the power of the ego and will be achieved by mankind as a whole only on the future Venus. However, already today every person is clothed after death with the sheath of the Life Spirit, which is why a conscious life in the spiritual world is at all possible. 'Our life between death and a new birth is only possible through our being enshrouded by this Life Spirit' (GA 168, 18 February 1916). For 'we have to live far more [after death] with the whole universe. The whole universe has to be for us *a great living being*, and we must live with it' (ibid.). 'It is the Life Spirit which enables us' to grow in the land of spirit together with the whole universe as a living being (ibid.). And because Christ in His Ascension brought the forces of the spirit-land to the Earth, it is also possible for a person who receives them into himself to extend his ego-consciousness after death over the entire universe without losing himself in the process. Thus Christ revealed Himself to the apostles during the 40 days of conversations that preceded His Ascension as the cosmic Life Spirit or Buddhi. Christ stood before them as the all-embracing Being of love, in possession of all the forces of the Venus aeon that is to come.

At the end of his book *An Outline of Occult Science* Rudolf Steiner writes: 'It is the sublime Sun Being, of whom we spoke when describing the evolution of the Christ, who at His revelation stands forth as the all-awakening "prototype of love"' (GA 13).

The next step led from Venus to Jupiter—or from Ascension to Whitsun. Now the forces of the Mystery of Golgotha, which had previously exercised their influence over earthly evolution only outside human beings, also entered into human consciousness. This happened through the mediation of the Holy Spirit. The Baptism of Jesus with water which had taken place in the Jordan now became a baptism by Christ with fire and spirit. The apostles were thereby furnished with the forces which will only come to their full potential on the future Jupiter, while nevertheless having to be prepared already during the Earth aeon. In his book *Theosophy* Rudolf Steiner defines the Spirit Self as follows: it is 'the spirit forming an "I" and living as the "I", or ego' (GA 9). On Whitsun morning the apostles were filled with this spirit. By this means the capacity to create out of nothing which had initially been brought objectively into earthly evolution was implanted into man's inner nature. For creating out of nothing is at the same time creating out of the Holy Spirit. 'When a person is able out of nothingness to create the right or true, the beautiful and the good, the Holy Spirit fills him with bliss. But for someone to be able to create in the sense of the Holy Spirit, he had first to be given the foundation for all creating out of nothingness. This foundation was given to him through Christ's intervening in our evolution. Through experiencing the Christ event on Earth, man became able to rise to creating in the Holy Spirit. Thus it is Christ Himself who creates the greatest, most profound foundation. If man becomes such that he stands firmly on the ground of the Christ event [the Mystery of Golgotha] ... the Christ sends him the Holy Spirit [the Whitsun event], and man becomes capable of creating the right, beautiful and good in the course of his further evolution' (GA 107, 17 June 1909).

In the sense of what has been described here, this signifies the possibility of forming a connection with the world of moral intuitions already on the Earth, as described in *The Philosophy of Freedom* as the foundation of future morality. 'And you will know the truth, and the truth will make you free' (John 8:32). These words are the leitmotif of the event of Whitsun.[38] As the Whitsun Spirit who is active individually in every person is at the same time always the same Spirit, he works in a community-building way and is the earthly instigator of the living together of free human beings.

At the Turning Point of Time, the Whitsun event was followed by the sending of the apostles out into the world, in order that the new impulse of the Spirit working within them might be brought to all human beings. This task corresponds to the second half of earthly evolution, which stands in the sign of the Mercury forces. It is the time when mankind must find

Christ both individually and socially, in order to forge a connection with its true purpose and its future.

As has already been described, the task of the first (Mars) half of earthly evolution consisted in the preparing of the bodily sheaths for Jesus of Nazareth as the future Christophorus out of the stream of heredity of mankind—beginning from Adam until the Turning Point of Time.[39] The great ideal of the Second (Mercury) half, on the other hand, consists in building up the new humanity in whose sheaths Christ's Ego can find His new dwelling-place on the Earth. It is a question here of a purely spiritual line of descent which is also linked in the social domain directly with the Christ impulse. The Whitsun impulse at the Turning Point of Time forms the inner foundation for this. Rudolf Steiner formulates it thus: 'But this Christ impulse at first finds nothing with which it can clothe itself. Therefore it has to obtain a sheath through the further evolution of the Earth; and when the Earth has reached the end of its evolution the fully developed Christ will be the final man—as Adam was the first—around whom humanity in its multiplicity has grouped itself' (GA 155, 30 May 1912). Just as Adam, as the first man, stands at the beginning of the Mars half of Earth evolution, so does Christ stand as the Representative of Humanity at the end of the Mercury half.

★

Thus the earthly life of Christ can be perused on three different levels, which at the same time correspond to the three qualities of time that have been described. Christ initially came to the Earth through the gate of the Baptism in the Jordan and so united Himself with the general stream of time of human history, which flows out of the past into the future. Christ entered into this stream of time, which is for the most part the only one known to human beings, through His Baptism. And because the three years of His life on Earth also belonged to this stream, this life became a fact of world history.

However, the inner life of Christ unfolded in another stream of time, which is accessible only to initiates who have reached the stage of the higher ego. Its nature consists in that, in addition to the ordinary stream of time, which has its origin in the past, there is in the world another, occult stream coming to meet man out of the future. Rudolf Steiner spoke in this connection of 'an upwards- and a downwards-moving double stream' of time.[40] He described it elsewhere as a 'regressive evolution, the occult-astral, which interferes with the progressing one' and whose existence is a necessary condition for a true perception of the spiritual world.[41] The

Christ Being lived on the Earth in this spiritual stream of time at an incomparably higher stage than all initiates. How this was accomplished has already been described above. With the stations of His life, preceding the actual mystery of the Resurrection, Christ lived in the reverse stream of time through the stages of the Mars half of the Earth, Old Moon, Old Sun and back to Saturn. The final restoring of the phantom took place at the moment of the Crucifixion on the Hill of Golgotha out of the spiritual forces of Old Saturn, which are at the same time those of the Father.

After His Resurrection, moreover, Christ lived in the spiritual stream of time—though now in the direction coming from the future—from Vulcan through Venus and Jupiter to a supersensible union with earthly history in the sign of Mercury, in order thus to accompany the whole evolution of mankind to the end of the Earth aeon.[42]

Still higher than the spiritual stream of time passing through the whole of evolution from Old Saturn to Vulcan is the stream that, in the words quoted above, Rudolf Steiner designated as flowing 'from eternity to eternity'. According to his spiritual research eternity consists of the combination of two elements: 'Eternity embraces both "immortality" *and* "un-bornness"' (GA 236, 18 May 1924; italics Rudolf Steiner). When related to human life this applies initially only to the 'little' eternity which a person can inwardly grasp when, on the path of modern initiation, he consciously goes beyond the portals of birth and death and experiences the spiritual world lying both before birth and after death as a unity. This unity is like a reflection of the great, real eternity, which consists of *cosmic* un-bornness and *cosmic* immortality. Cosmic un-bornness precedes Old Saturn and cosmic immortality follows the future Vulcan. When a being is capable of connecting this cosmic un-bornness and immortality in a unity, that is, of forming a bridge across the abyss of worlds directly from Old Saturn to Vulcan (not on the path of evolution through all the cosmic intermediary stages but directly), this essential nature of eternity takes hold of both shores of world existence simultaneously and is therefore able to bring that stream of time that flows from eternity to eternity to the Earth.

Through the transforming of the restored phantom into the Resurrection body in the Mystery of Golgotha, Christ achieved a direct transition from Old Saturn to the future Vulcan and, hence, brought the forces of eternity to the Earth.[43] Since then every person who has established a conscious relationship to the Mystery of Golgotha on the path of modern initiation has been able to gain access to these forces, which is an indispensable condition for creating out of nothing.

Christ's intervention was therefore decisive on all three levels of time. The Mystery of Golgotha forms the spiritual centre and point of balance of the history of mankind. Hence it is not for nothing that a new calendar begins with the birth of Jesus on Earth.[44] For spiritual time its significance lies in the transition from evolution to involution, extending to Vulcan. Thus the foundation has been laid for cosmic evolution from Old Saturn to the Earth to find its further continuation through Jupiter and Venus to Vulcan. And at the third level the following occurred: out of that stream of time that flows directly from eternity, the capacity of creating out of nothing—which goes beyond Vulcan[45]—was brought down by Christ onto the Earth and implanted within mankind in the manner already described.

In this way Christ accomplished with respect to time what the new geometry recognizes concerning space: a line which is extended in one direction to infinity returns from the opposite direction. In His Resurrection Christ has shown—not on the level of consciousness (as a scientific problem) but *on the level of world existence*—how the spiritual stream of time, traced back into the past to the point of its dissolution in eternity, reappears out of the same eternity as that stream of time which flows out of the ultimate future into the present. In other words: if one goes back from the present to Old Saturn, where time flows into eternity, one reappears from this eternity in the most distant future, namely at the end of Vulcan, in order to return from thence into the present, bearing within oneself the forces of eternity. And this was Christ's deed at the Turning Point of Time.

What has just been said can be traced particularly clearly in Rudolf Steiner's path of initiation. Like all human beings he was born with his earthly ego into the first (historical) stream of time. As a 19-year-old he had the first experience of his higher ego, as he described in a letter of 13 January 1881 to Josef Köck. He writes: 'It was the night of 10–11 January, when I did not sleep for a moment. I had concerned myself until 1 a.m. with particular philosophical problems, and then finally forced myself to go to bed; my endeavour the previous year had been to investigate whether it was true what Schelling says: "In all of us there dwells a secret, wonderful ability to withdraw from life's many changes into our innermost selves, stripped of everything that has come from without, and to behold the eternal in ourselves under the guise of changelessness." I believed and still believe now that I have quite clearly discovered that most intimate ability within me—I have sensed this for quite some time ...' (GA 38, Letter I).[46] On this foundation he arrived in the following years to an experience of the second stream of time, namely to the understanding 'that there is a regressing evolution which interferes with the progressing one'.[47] In this way he was able to come to a full consciousness of his higher ego and thereby solve the problem which had most preoccupied him in his youth: the problem of time and specifically the second 'interfering' time-stream in which all beings of the spiritual world live and work. Already in the early period of his life he also posed the question of the third stream of time, which he was to resolve only much later. In his autobiography *The Course of My Life* Rudolf Steiner recalls this question, which had strongly stirred him around his twenty-first year, although at the time the young Rudolf Steiner posed this question not from the standpoint of cosmic existence but from that of a cognitive consciousness. He therefore formulated it in a reverse form. He writes: 'Behind the riddle of space [which had been solved for him by the new geometry] stood at that time in my life the riddle of time. Ought a conception to be possible there also which would contain within itself as an idea a return out of the past into the "infinitely distant" future?' (GA 28, ch. 3).

The further consequence of this question—in addition to much else which has already been described elsewhere[48]—led Rudolf Steiner at the turn of the century to 'stand spiritually before the Mystery of Golgotha'. The question specified was also finally answered for him out of this spiritual source.

On the basis of what has been said one can summarize Rudolf Steiner's spiritual development until his great Christ experience around the turn of the century as follows: becoming aware of the higher ego is like a foretaste of what the apostles experienced to a full extent through the event of Whitsun. Thus a first, albeit only preliminary sense of being touched by the Whitsun Spirit occurred in the life of Rudolf Steiner. For since the Turning Point of Time the Whitsun Spirit has participated in every inner awakening that leads to a taking hold of the higher ego.

Then around his thirty-third year Rudolf Steiner completed his main philosophical work *The Philosophy of Freedom*. Behind it stood the personal spiritual experience of its author, which—as was shown at the beginning of this chapter—was therefore only possible because the Ascension had taken place at the Turning Point of Time. Only through this could Rudolf Steiner find in his etheric body the forces which led to *The Philosophy of Freedom* coming into being.

This path reached its culmination in the spiritual experience of the Mystery of Golgotha, which also cast its light on the two previous stages representing the necessary preparation for this central event in Rudolf

Steiner's life. Anthroposophy could therefore now be founded on the Earth as modern spiritual science. However, the foundations for this event were laid by Rudolf Steiner in *The Philosophy of Freedom*. And by 'standing in spirit before the Mystery of Golgotha' he was able to gain access to the source of creating out of nothing, which he had previously described in his book as the aim of the free human being on the Earth. For as has already been described elsewhere, freely working in the world out of individual moral intuitions is none other than constantly creating out of nothing.[49] In this way, *The Philosophy of Freedom* has within it, albeit in an as yet germinal form, those spiritual forces which led to the founding of anthroposophy after the turn of the century. Behind the content of this book stands, as an individual Whitsun event, its author's experiencing of the higher ego. In the pure, etheric thinking out of which it was written there work the forces of the Ascension; and in the free deeds out of moral intuitions described in it the trend that led Rudolf Steiner to his Christ experience was already indicated. Hence *The Philosophy of Freedom* became an unshakeable foundation for the whole subsequent development of anthroposophy.

★

If one would now define with greater precision the stage of initiation attained by Rudolf Steiner through his Christ experience around the turn of the century, one can say that—while nevertheless on the path of modern initiation—it is comparable with that stage attained at the Turning Point of Time by the apostles as a result of the Whitsun event.

In the lectures on the Fifth Gospel it is related that the consciousness called forth in the circle of the apostles through the influence of the Spirit corresponded to the sixth stage of pre-Christian initiation, that of the 'Sun Hero'. 'What could be attained through initiation by a few single individuals in ancient times was attained as the result, so to speak, of a natural event during the days of Pentecost on the part of those who were the apostles of Christ. Whereas before then it was necessary for human souls to rise up to Christ, Christ had now come down to the apostles. And the apostles, in a certain respect, had developed to the point where they bore within themselves the substance and content that had belonged to the souls of the Sun Heroes of old' (GA 148, 3 October 1913).

On the Christian-mystical path the sixth stage is that of the 'Resurrection'. This confirms that the apostles were therefore the first people to enter into a direct relationship with Christ's Resurrection body. This became possible for them because 'the Christ had now come down to the apostles', bringing the forces of the Resurrection body which belong to the Vulcan stage of world evolution (and even beyond it). He brought these after Easter through the further stages of the Ascension (Venus aeon) and Whitsun (Jupiter aeon) into the second (Mercury) half of Earth evolution, so that mankind can fulfil its mission on the Earth. 'And lo, I am with you always, until the completion of the earthly age' (Matthew 28:20, after the Emil Bock translation).

What was attained at the Turning Point of Time through the Whitsun event only by the small circle of the immediate pupils of Christ is accessible today in the new mysteries to all people of good will. For the path of spiritual communion which stands at the centre of the new mysteries leads people today to an experience of everything that has been discussed up to this point. (See diagram on p. 87.)

★

The relationship of Christ's earthly life to world evolution as a whole that has been characterized can be further illumined by the Trinitarian aspect of this event. Thus the Baptism in the Jordan has mainly to do with the influence of the Holy Spirit. John the Baptist bore witness to this in the following words: 'I saw the Spirit descending as a dove from heaven and it remained on him' (John 1:32). At the Transfiguration, Christ then manifested His Sun nature. For His appearance as the Lord of the spiritual Sun ('And His face shone like the Sun', Matthew 17:2) at the same time signified the revelation of His Son forces.[50]

This was also the moment when the earthly Jesus principle completely withdrew and the divine nature of the Son began alone to shine. In this way the actual meaning of the words 'Not I, but Christ in me' (Galatians 2:20) was revealed to the three chosen disciples. But since they were not yet capable of rising to this stage of Christian initiation, they fell into deep sleep. Nevertheless, through their experience on Mount Tabor they acquired a presentiment of the new age now dawning in the evolution of mankind; and they became the first witnesses of how, without the old rites of initiation, one may now enter the spiritual world solely with the power of Christ in one's ego.[51]

Then followed Christ's 'farewell discourses', which John has preserved in his Gospel. These contain a reference to the mystery that behind death the Being of the divine Father is concealed and that the marriage of Christ with death is in reality none other than 'I and the Father are one' (John 10:30). This is also attested by the last words on the Cross: 'Father, into thy hands I commend my spirit' (Luke 23:46).

Because the death on the Cross is like a summation of the whole three years of Christ's earthly life ('for this purpose I have come to this hour', John 12:27), one can find on the Hill of Golgotha the revelation of the Holy Trinity, that is, also those spiritual forces which stood behind the Baptism and the Transfiguration. Hence Rudolf Steiner says: 'Anyone who beholds the Cross on Golgotha must at the same time behold the Trinity, for Christ indeed makes the Trinity manifest in His whole interrelationship with the earthly evolution of mankind' (GA 214, 30 July 1922). This manifestation of the Trinity on the Hill of Golgotha then appears in mirror form in the events after the Crucifixion. In the Resurrection the forces of the Father are manifested in a new, transformed way, in the Ascension the forces of the Son are active and at Whitsun the forces of the Holy Spirit are revealed.

Hence Peter and Paul said several times that it was the divine Father Himself who had awakened Christ from death.[52] Rudolf Steiner also sometimes used this formulation.[53] The reason for this is that in the Resurrection it was above all the forces of the Father that were at work, mediated by the First Hierarchy. Christ thereby accomplished what no initiate had ever been able to achieve in any initiation. It was possible for Him to take hold of His physical body even to the extent of the mineral substance of its bone system (in the form of a rib, ever the symbol of death) and wholly to transform it. Herein lay the decisive condition for the Resurrection which then ensued. 'He who was to vanquish death on the Earth had to have mastery over the skeleton' (GA 112, 3 July 1909).[54]

The influence of the forces of the Trinity in the totality of Christ's life on Earth therefore becomes clearly apparent: from the past, when the body of Jesus of Nazareth was prepared, through the Baptism and Transfiguration until the Mystery of Golgotha, when they came to manifestation together. Since then they have, by way of the stages of the Ascension and Whitsun, shed their light upon the future of mankind in order that they might increasingly take hold of and renew its whole existence on Earth.

In addition, there is also the 30-year life of Jesus of Nazareth as the true *Son of Man*, in whom the best forces of the heavenly (Nathan soul) and earthly (Zarathustra) development of mankind flowed together.[55] And after the event of Whitsun there followed the new life of Christ in the spiritual environment of the Earth as the *Representative of Humanity*, as Rudolf Steiner has portrayed Him in the Sculptural Group and in the middle motif of the painting in the small cupola of the First Goetheanum. (See illustration on p. 115.)

The whole picture can be clarified by the following diagram:

Easter, Ascension and Whitsun in the Light of Anthroposophy 87

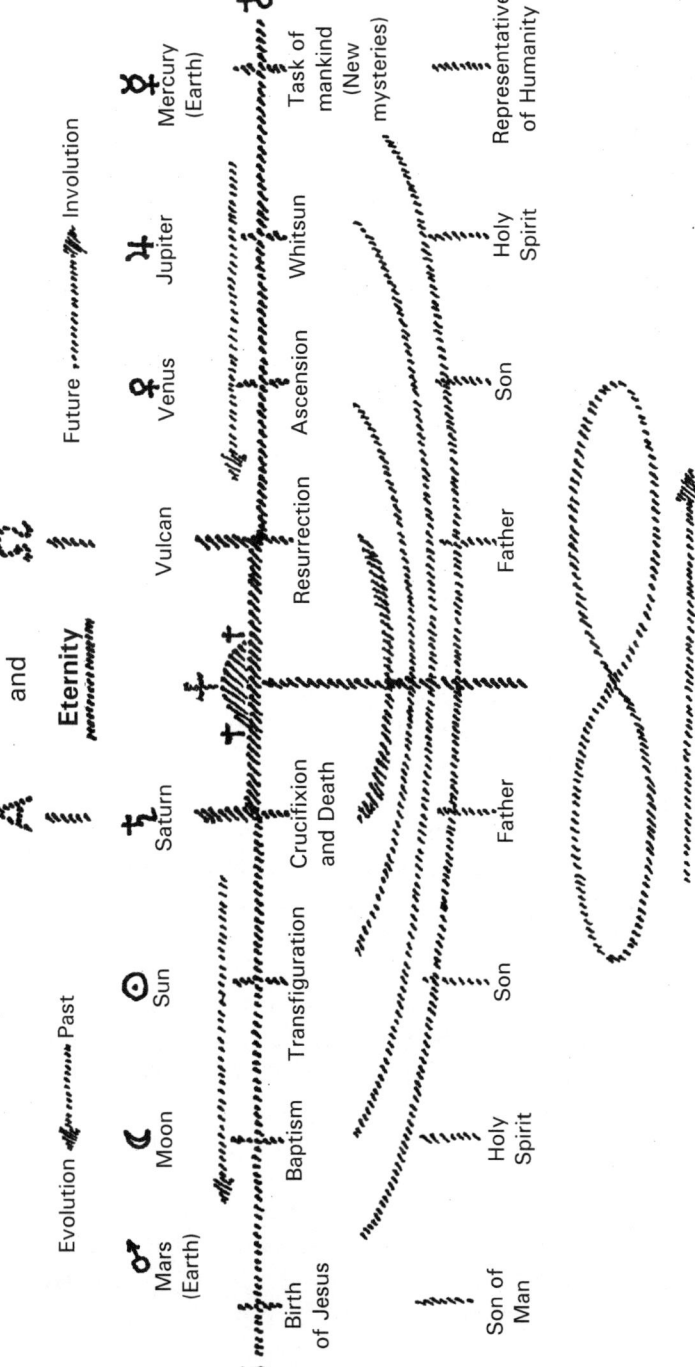

The Inner Relationship between Easter, Ascension and Whitsun

At this point, something further needs to be said concerning the inner relationship of the mystery of Easter to the further steps in the unfolding of the Christ impulse after the Mystery of Golgotha. As has already been described elsewhere,[56] in the Resurrection there occurred a mighty breakthrough into the earthly world of those forces which are otherwise experienced by man only in the Midnight Hour of cosmic existence, that is, at the highest point between two incarnations. Through the influence of the highest (First) Hierarchy, which carries the creative impulses of all the other hierarchies, a constant imprinting of world karma upon earthly matter is wrought from the heights of Cosmic Midnight. 'The rank of the Thrones, Cherubim and Seraphim in the spiritual cosmos is higher because they are mightier beings—mightier not merely in the realm of spiritual life but because they bring to effect in the physical world what they experience in the spiritual world' (GA 239, 9 June 1924). While, therefore, the karma-imprinting activity of the First Hierarchy works directly into the earthly world, its influence is enacted out of the forces of Cosmic Midnight, in contrast to the human sphere which lies on the midday side of cosmic existence. That is to say, the abyss between the two spheres of activity, the human realm and that of the First Hierarchy (or the midday and the midnight aspects of cosmic existence), within the earthly sphere is as great as the path of the soul from the physical world of the senses to the highest point of its journey between two incarnations. According to Rudolf Steiner, this highest point lies at the uppermost border of Higher Devachan (where it directly adjoins the Buddhi sphere) and, from a spiritual-cosmic standpoint, lies beyond the visible starry sky or zodiac.

In His Resurrection Christ bridged this abyss in a new and unique way: not in a vertical direction (as the soul accomplishes this each time after death in its ascent to the Cosmic Midnight Hour) but in a horizontal one, that is, directly on the Earth, without rising to the heights of the spiritual world. In other words, Christ connected the forces of the Cosmic Midnight Hour—which are at the same time the forces of all nine hierarchies[57]—directly with the spirit-form of the physical body (the phantom) of Jesus of Nazareth. The Resurrection body, which bears within itself the whole spirituality of the world (as was described at the beginning of the previous chapter in connection with the Foundation Stone Meditation, see pp. 7–8), was therefore not born beyond the stars but directly on the Earth.

Christ gave the apostles an indication of this mystery through His Ascension. For what is the meaning of the Ascension from the standpoint of the Fifth Gospel? In the Ascension, Christ—in contrast to man's life after death—did not leave the Earth in order to make His way to the realm beyond the stars but, in contrast, brought heavenly forces, the forces of Higher Devachan, down to the Earth. 'The further life of Christ in the earthly sphere since the Ascension or since the event of Whitsun [as we have seen, the latter can also be experienced by human beings] is to be compared with what the human soul lives through in the spirit-land, in what is known as Devachan' (GA 148, 3 October 1913). Instead of returning to the heights of the spiritual world Christ has, as we have seen, brought the highest forces of Devachan (those of the Midnight Hour itself), which He manifested to human beings in His Ascension, to the Earth. With this He also showed them the origin of those spiritual forces out of which He had accomplished His Resurrection in the physical body.

This is discernible above all from the following. Anthroposophy describes that the further stages of cosmic evolution, Jupiter, Venus and Vulcan, which represent the future for the Earth, are already part of a present reality—the Jupiter stage on the astral plane, the Venus stage on Lower Devachan and the Vulcan stage on Higher Devachan, so that the Midnight Hour represents the transition from Vulcan to a still higher cosmic state. Hence it becomes understandable what Rudolf Steiner meant when he said that in Christ a Being lived on the Earth such as man will in his way only be *at the end* of Vulcan.

This explains the manner in which, and why, the Ascension had to follow the Resurrection. What actually happened in the Resurrection— and out of which forces the Resurrection body was born—was made manifest by Christ to His most advanced pupils in the event of the Ascension. For in this event He revealed to them the great mystery that a new, 'horizontal' connection had been created between midday and midnight. Through His 'vertical' ascent Christ revealed to mankind in the Ascension that between the two shores of the cosmic abyss—which, as we have already seen, is as deep as the abyss between the Earth and the world of the fixed stars—an essential connection and a direct exchange of forces was established from out of the Earth after the Resurrection.[58]

The event of Whitsun developed as a third step out of the two previous events with the same logicality as the Ascension emerged after the Resurrection. What had previously taken place in the Resurrection as a 'mystical fact' that was as yet still external to human souls was to be connected with them. Human beings were now to understand with their individual ego-consciousness what had objectively happened in the cosmos itself at the two previous stages. This could come about only because something became accessible to them on the Earth which they were otherwise able to experience only in the Cosmic Midnight Hour between two incarnations.

At this point one needs to bear in mind what Rudolf Steiner described in the lecture of 13 April 1914. There he relates that at the Cosmic Midnight Hour not only is the karma-forming activity of all nine hierarchies manifested to the human soul but that at the upper border of Higher Devachan there comes about the direct revelation and inspiration of the Holy Spirit, sending its influences down from still higher spheres.

Thus at the highest point of its journey between two incarnations the human soul experiences a fructification by the Holy Spirit, enabling it to 'newly awaken in cosmic existence' (GA 153). In other words, at the Midnight Hour of existence the soul is thereby brought to its individual ego-consciousness through being filled with the Holy Spirit from above. 'We come to know the spirit of the spiritual world which now awakens us as a new light shines out from the Cosmic Midnight Hour and illumines our human past ... Our own true nature is reawakened out of the Cosmic Midnight Hour through this spirit. Thus we are awakened by the Holy Spirit at the Cosmic Midnight Hour. *Per spiritum sanctum reviviscimus*' (ibid.; italics Rudolf Steiner).

The soul thereby comes in contact with the cosmic sphere whence Christ derived the forces for His bodily Resurrection. And because in His Resurrection he united these forces of the heights of Cosmic Midnight directly with earthly evolution and thus created a bridge for all human beings over the cosmic abyss, or—in another picture—unlocked the cosmic gate between Cosmic Midnight and the midday of cosmic existence, the Holy Spirit who illuminates individual ego-consciousness was also able to appear in earthly evolution among human beings through this opened gate and to pour into them the true knowledge of the Mystery of Golgotha and of the Ascension. The message and meaning of Whitsun lie in this.

For this reason the outpouring of the Spirit is a direct consequence of the Resurrection and the Ascension. Since this time these events have remained inseparable from one another, as has become evident in the course of the year through the fact that they form the foundation of three *movable* festivals, which succeed one another in accordance with a strictly cosmic law. In this way the inner substance of this great threefold event of the Turning Point of Time is preserved in them for all people.

3. The Resurrection and the Interior of the Earth

The descriptions of the events of Good Friday and Easter Sunday that have been offered in the first two chapters of this book pose the justified question of the mystery of Easter Saturday, which in Christian tradition is brought into connection with Christ's 'journey into Hell'. From an anthroposophical standpoint what is meant by this is His path through the nine layers of the Earth's interior, characterized on several occasions by Rudolf Steiner above all in his early lectures. He also mentioned that this knowledge was from the outset imparted in true Rosicrucian schools. 'Only in true Rosicrucian schools can one speak about the interior of the Earth' (GA 94, 11 July 1906).

The decisive indication for a right understanding of the interior of the Earth is, however, to be found in a later lecture, in connection with insights on these lines which already lived in the ancient Egyptian mysteries. Thus Egyptian initiates already knew that what circles around the Earth in the form of the Moon is also to be found in a transmuted form within the Earth. 'What lies out there in the surroundings can be found reflected, though condensed, in an outer layer of the Earth itself' (GA 216, 29 September 1922). It is a similar situation with all other planets and even with the starry sky lying beyond them: 'If we now move to the next planet that encircles the Sun together with the Earth ... Venus[1] ... we must—if we draw the next layer of the Earth—draw this layer as a reflection of what lies outside' (ibid.). And then Rudolf Steiner widens his gaze to the entire cosmos: 'Thus the whole Earth becomes a reflection of the universe, though we would always find that what exists out there in a very delicate, rarefied form is pressed together and condensed if we dig down into the Earth. And if we were to come to the outermost periphery of the universe, this most outward periphery of the universe would be condensed in a single point at the centre of the Earth' (ibid.). Of particular significance here is the last sentence, for the 'outermost' boundary of the universe lies in the sphere of the fixed stars or, to be more precise, in the circle of the zodiac. The soul has a normal experience of its true nature only between two incarnations, when it has risen to the Cosmic Midnight Hour and is then able to behold the entire starry world from the other, spiritual side. Hence the outer boundary of the cosmos is at the same time indicative of the heights of the Cosmic Midnight Hour, when man's soul surveys all at once the whole spirituality of the cosmos.

It follows from the cited quotation that the interior of the Earth has within itself in a condensed form the forces of all seven planets from the Moon to Saturn and also those of the fixed stars, although these cosmic forces are as though in exile there and separated from their origin.

The transition from cosmic to spiritual communion already described in chapter 1 has the consequence that the common spirituality of the planets and fixed stars is deepened by the forces and influences of all the nine divine-spiritual hierarchies standing behind them. In the lecture cycle *The Spiritual Hierarchies and their Reflection in the Physical World* (GA 110) Rudolf Steiner describes the seven planetary spheres as the corresponding fields of activity of the hierarchic beings from the Angels upwards to the Thrones.[2] The two highest hierarchies, the Cherubim and Seraphim, alone reach beyond the planetary spheres in their activity and are active in the pure starry worlds.

Thus we see that in the interior of the Earth not only are the spiritual forces of the planets and fixed stars as though held fast but also in a deeper sense also the corresponding forces of the higher hierarchies, which are misused within the nine sub-earthly spheres for aims that are opposed to their own intentions. Thus one can say that in the first three layers of the Earth's interior the hierarchic forces are held back by luciferic spirits, in the next three by ahrimanic spirits and in the last three by asuric powers.

The relationship of these counter-forces to the layers of the Earth's interior becomes particularly clear from the following words of Rudolf Steiner: 'We have the physical world, the astral world, Lower Devachan and Higher Devachan. If a body is thrust down lower even than the physical world, one comes into the sub-physical world, the lower astral world, the lower or evil Lower Devachan and the lower or evil Higher Devachan. The evil astral world is the province of Lucifer, the evil Lower Devachan the province of Ahriman and the evil Higher Devachan the province of the Asuras' (GA 130, 1 October 1911, answers to questions at the end of the lecture). These sub-sensible reflections of the higher planes of the spiritual world are for their part connected with the corresponding layers of the Earth's interior. Thus one finds the forces of the astral plane trapped above all in the first three layers, in the next three the forces of Lower Devachan (see further in this chapter); while the seventh layer forms the transition to the forces of Higher Devachan that are held fast within the Earth's inner regions.

One can also say that these three categories of counter-forces are constantly drawing from these layers of the Earth's interior the forces which they use in their battle against the evolution of mankind as willed by the Gods. The Earth's core, however, which according to Rudolf

The Resurrection and the Interior of the Earth 93

Steiner forms the centre of evil on our planet, is connected with the Sun Demon (Sorath) himself.

★

Before we turn to the actual theme, something must briefly be said about the relationship between the temporal aspect of world evolution (as for the most part described in the first two chapters) and the spiritual-spatial aspect. The temporal aspect consists above all in world evolution, stretching from Old Saturn to the future Vulcan. The spiritual-spatial aspect is connected more with the knowledge of this evolution. Thus Rudolf Steiner writes in the last chapter of his book *An Outline of Occult Science* that, if an initiate wants to investigate the previous and future stages of the cosmic evolution of the Earth, he must rise correspondingly ever higher into the spiritual world. He mentions the following three stages: at the first stage the past condition of Old Moon and the future one of Jupiter are revealed to him *at the same time*; at the second stage he beholds the conditions of Old Sun and Venus; and at the third stage those of Old Sun and Vulcan.

It is not difficult to establish that at these three stages one has to do on the one hand with the cognitive faculties of Imagination, Inspiration and Intuition and, on the other, with the cosmic spheres in which this knowledge becomes possible. Thus one can say: on the astral plane one comes to know Old Moon and the future Jupiter in Imagination; on Lower Devachan, Old Sun and the future Venus through Inspiration; and on Higher Devachan, Old Saturn and the future Vulcan through Intuition. However, one can spiritually survey the whole of evolution only at the Cosmic Midnight Hour (as has already been shown at some length elsewhere).[3] The three cosmic stages mentioned here—astral plane, Lower and Higher Devachan—correspond cosmologically to the inner planets (astral plane), the outer planets (Lower Devachan) and the starry worlds, which extend in Higher Devachan to the Cosmic Midnight Hour where its outermost boundary lies. The Sun has a particular position here. In its planetary aspect it is the transition from the astral world to Devachan; in its starry aspect it encompasses all further cosmic stages as far as the sphere of the fixed stars.

These explanations regarding the temporal and spatial aspect of world evolution are of significance above all for an understanding of the Earth's interior. For the temporal aspect of evolution in all its metamorphoses connects our Earth with the whole cosmos. However, the spatial aspect mainly has to do with the interior of the Earth. Hence, the transition from the one to the other had first to be described in order to establish a basis for what is to follow. After this preparation a short description will be given of the nine layers of the Earth's interior, which—in accordance with what has already been said—contain as though under lock and key the forces of the planets and also of the corresponding hierarchies.

In order to gain a better understanding of the first three layers, which are associated both with the forces of the inner planets and with those of the Third Hierarchy, it is necessary to draw attention to a particular quality of this hierarchy. In the evening lecture of 16 April 1909, Rudolf Steiner describes how the Angels form their physical body in the watery element, the Archangels in the aeriform element and the Archai in the fiery element. In this way they also share in the material constituents of the Earth. However, this is denied to them in the first three layers of the Earth.

In the uppermost layer ('mineral Earth'), which forms the actual hard crust of the Earth,[4] the solid matter is condensed to such an extent by the Moon forces active within it that the Angels can no longer penetrate this layer.

The second layer ('fluid Earth') forms a substance imbued with illusory life to which the Archangels have no access. Everything solid becomes liquid. One can say, to put it in a pictorially real image: all silver here becomes quicksilver. But from the Mercury forces that have been banished here and then misused the illusory life of this layer acquires a negative character, which consists in that all life here is destroyed.

The third layer ('vapour Earth') is filled with a substance in which every kind of feeling is destroyed. Feelings in the cosmos are connected above all with the sphere of Venus. Here they are turned into their opposite. The forces of the Archai do not extend into this sphere, since they can form their physical body only in the fiery element and not in that of air. Thus these three layers are separated from the world of the Third Hierarchy and set in opposition to its influence in the cosmos.

Rudolf Steiner also mentions that these three layers of the Earth still retain a memory of the condition when the Moon was not yet separated from the Earth (see GA 94, 12 June 1906). Since the luciferic powers remained behind on Old Moon, they continue to have a strong influence over these three layers through their special relationship to the Moon.

With the fourth layer ('form or water Earth') one enters into a region where not only the forces of the astral plane but also those of Lower Devachan are trapped. Rudolf Steiner says in this regard: 'The fourth layer corresponds in a certain sense to the first region of Devachan' (GA 94, 11 July 1906). Thus we have arrived at a region beneath the surface of the Earth from which Sun forces, and hence those of the Sun Elohim or

Spirits of Form, are so to speak banished. Rudolf Steiner says of this layer that all forms here are turned into their negative opposites. A salt cube, which on Earth is filled substance, here becomes an empty cube whose substance has been squeezed out, thus endowing it with negative qualities. In this process, forces that are opposed to the good Spirits of Form are at work. All forms which the Exusiai have created on the Earth are here dissolved, so that they 'no longer have the substantial nature that can be encountered on the Earth'. Here everything visible is 'led back into an astral condition' (GA 96, 16 April 1906). All material substance is in a false

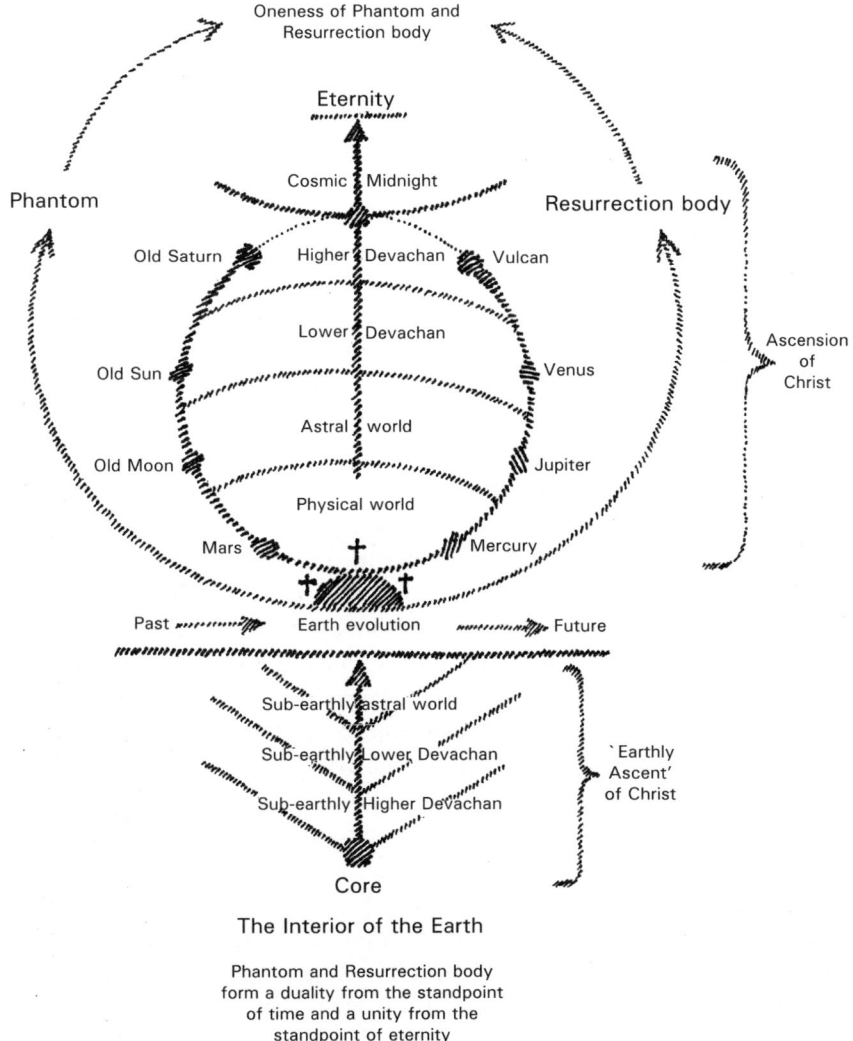

The Interior of the Earth

Phantom and Resurrection body
form a duality from the standpoint
of time and a unity from the
standpoint of eternity

way 'spiritualized' with misused Sun forces that have been imprisoned. Thus this layer is opposed to any influence of the Spirits of Form.

The fifth layer ('fruit Earth') manifests a wholly contrary quality. It produces 'continual forms on forms' that are then again destroyed (GA 97, 21 April 1906). This layer makes use of these forms to counteract the legitimate activity of the Spirits of Movement, who have nothing to do with the creating of forms but, rather, with the inner processes guiding evolution as a whole and generally bringing about the metamorphosis of forms. Thus in this layer resistance to the cosmos is generated out of an 'overwhelming energy of growth' (GA 95, 4 September 1906) with the help of misused Mars forces. Here, too, are found the forces of the primordial life of the Earth (life is always movement), which in this context, however, are opposed to the Spirits of Movement.

The next layer ('fire Earth') has the quality of developing the strongest passions out of every most insignificant sensation. These passions then work right into matter and are filled with a will that opposes every calming influence. In this layer it is mainly the wisdom and harmony of the Jupiter forces that is turned into its opposite and opposed to the Spirits of Wisdom. 'These forces are those into which the primal fires have been banished' (GA 107, 1 January 1909). By means of this primal fire this layer acts in opposition to the forces of the Kyriotetes. Rudolf Steiner relates that the three latter layers have within themselves a memory of the time when the Sun, Moon and Earth still together formed one body. (See GA 94, 12 June 1906.) Because the ahrimanic powers remained behind on Old Sun, they retain great power over these three layers. In another context Rudolf Steiner mentions that Ahriman is particularly concerned with this layer ('fire Earth'). 'In this layer the kingdom of Ahriman has its material focus of activity and its influence rays out from here,' for these 'inner fire forces of the Earth [are] at Ahriman's service. This is where he has the centre of his activity' (GA 107, 1 January 1909).

The seventh layer of the Earth ('Earth mirror' or 'Earth reflector') enables all conceivable qualities to appear in their polarity. Natural phenomena—including the forces of electricity and magnetism—here have a moral character, though turned into their opposite; they become decidedly evil. Everything that appears as good on the Earth is led here into a state of anti-morality. Just as Saturn at the boundary of our solar system preserves and reflects a memory of it, so from this layer is everything directed back (reflected away), though in a highly evil way. Rudolf Steiner says that Old Saturn represented something like a great mirror in the universe, which reflected back the primal activity of the Spirits of Will—whence world evolution had its origin—in 'a reflection into its opposite' (GA 95, 4 September 1906). Just as the warmth matter of Old Saturn was at the outset permeated by the good morality of the Thrones, so now is a caricature of it reflected back. Everything material is imbued with forces of immorality. One could also say that what existed at the beginning of world evolution as the sacrifice of the Thrones is thrust back by a mighty mirror. The cosmic power of sacrifice is confronted by its total repudiation.

In the eighth layer this process continues still further. Here earthly material is not only positively imbued with immorality but all morality existing in the world is actively fragmented and, hence, destroyed. For this reason Rudolf Steiner calls this layer the 'fragmenter'. He goes on to characterize this layer in the following way: 'All moral feelings, such as love and compassion, are turned there into their opposite, into hardness, brutality and so forth' (GA 94, 11 July 1906). 'All evil is to an essential degree prepared and organized here ... This layer has in an essential way brought evil into the world' (GA 95, 4 September 1906). Rudolf Steiner makes this sentence more explicit in another context: 'If a black magician succeeds in reaching it [this layer] ... the evil in him will be significantly intensified' (GA 97, 21 April 1906).

The evil characteristic of this layer is directed against everything that links human beings with one another, and that means the end of all brotherliness. Here evil works destructively right into the inner web of karma itself. Hence a black magician who draws his forces from this layer is also condemned for ever to remain alone, to the bitter end hating and fighting against the whole world; for he has himself destroyed all good karmic relationships with the world around him. 'This region is the seat of everything that is disharmonious, immoral and unpeaceful. Everything has a divergent tendency there' (ibid.). By means of this evil force that destroys all harmony, this layer opposes the influence of the Spirits of World harmony, the Cherubim. Moreover, everything that succeeds in reaching it is immediately broken into small pieces and multiplied to an infinite degree. In this dismembering and multiplying we have a distorted image of the starry sky. It is a collection of endless details without any relationship to one another. Thus in this layer the forces which were originally active in the starry world beyond the Saturn sphere are forcibly held fast.

The last layer belongs to the actual 'core of the Earth'. From here not only is immorality engendered by evil but it begins to exert a magical influence. 'This is essentially the source of the influence that gives rise to black magic in the world' (GA 95, 4 September 1906). Rudolf Steiner also indicates that two forces are connected in a deeply evil way here with one another: brain-bound thinking of a purely material kind and the forces of reproduction. (See GA 96, 16 April 1906.) In this layer resides the basest form of earthly sensuality with its automatic thinking processes. From this it becomes understandable why black magicians constantly strengthen their powers of thinking through meditation and then connect them with occult forces of sexuality. This union of thinking and sexuality works destructively on man's ego. The Asuras therefore derive their forces mainly from this last layer and the two previous ones. Rudolf Steiner says of them: 'The asuric spirits will ensure ... that the [human] ego is united with the sensuality of the Earth ... [and] be irretrievably lost' (GA 107, 22 March 1909).[5] If, however, the misuse of sexual forces passes from the stage of the wildest sensuality over into black magic within which spiritual forces have been brought to bear, one is no longer dealing only with the Asuras but with the Sun Demon himself. Rudolf Steiner speaks of him in his cycle on the Revelation of St John: 'The misuse of spiritual forces is connected with that seductive power of the beast with the two horns [these signify abstract brain-bound thinking and unbridled sensuality]. We call this abuse of spiritual power black magic ... Thus in the mystery of 666 or Sorath is hidden the secret of black magic' (GA 104, 29 June 1908). That the Earth's core is connected with the activity of Sorath follows in addition from the fact that its influence on man works simultaneously in the two directions referred to: on the one hand it works through the 'misguided understanding' or the 'misguided intelligence' (GA 104, 30 June 1908); on the other hand, through a boundless sensuality which even 'commits prostitution with matter'.[6]

By means of black magic a battle is being waged here against white magic, which can arise out of the forces of spiritualized love. The highest archetypes for this are the Seraphim, the Spirits of Universal Love, who create new worlds out of this love. Rudolf Steiner goes on to describe how the Heavenly Jerusalem will eventually arise out of white magic: 'We see the new Jerusalem arising out of white magic' (GA 104, 29 June 1908). From this it follows that it is above all from this evil core of our Earth that the battle against the transition of our planet to the Jupiter condition and thereafter to the further evolutionary forms of Venus and Vulcan is being conducted both now and—more especially—in the future. Thus behind this battle of the Asuras there stands the guiding and directive power of the Sun Demon himself, who, however, belongs not to the evolution of the Earth but to that of the Sun.[7]

In the cycle on the Book of Revelation Rudolf Steiner mentions that at the Turning Point of Time the attempt was made on the part of Sorath to prevent the development of the Christ impulse on the Earth. 'This being could only have got something from the Earth by being able to gain the rulership at a certain moment, namely when the Christ principle descended to the Earth. If the Christ principle had been stifled in its germinal stages, it would have been possible for the Earth in its entirety to succumb to this Sorath principle' (GA 104, 30 June 1908). However, these plans of Sorath were thwarted and destroyed at the mid-point of earthly evolution by Christ's Resurrection. An entirely new situation therefore arose on the Earth, which Rudolf Steiner describes as follows: 'This, however, did not take place, and so this being has to be content with the dregs of humanity who have no inclination towards the Christ principle, with those human beings who have remained embedded in matter' (ibid.). The danger which was thereby averted on a cosmic plane continues to exist on the human level, for those people who have remained embedded in matter 'will in the future form his cohorts' (ibid.). Such people who are inspired purely out of the evil core of the Earth will have a relentless inclination towards black magic.

★

The concentration of evil forces in the Earth's interior concerns only one aspect of our planet. From a cosmological point of view the forces of the Cosmic Midnight Hour, which as regards their origin belong to the extreme periphery of our universe and are, so to speak, in exile in the core of the Earth, are also to be found in the interior of the Earth. One can also say that the Earth's interior is like an antipode to Cosmic Midnight. Compressed to an infinite degree, these forces form the innermost core of the Earth and from the very outset they await—as do the cosmic-hierarchic forces of the other layers—an imminent redemption. How this can happen will be discussed in the following section.

In one particular context Rudolf Steiner brings a result of his spiritual research that initially appears to contradict everything that has been said. He says that it is from the centre of the Earth that the Thrones, Cherubim and Seraphim, as the First Hierarchy, unfold their forces. 'Thus we see how radiations from within out of the centre influence what goes on within our planet. So we can say: our planet is therefore so constituted that the Spirits of Will or Thrones, the Cherubim and Seraphim work from its centre ... When, therefore, we look towards the centre of our planet we can say: there are sublime beings there, Thrones, Cherubim and Seraphim' (GA 121, 11 June 1910). In order to understand how these sublime beings work out of the centre of the Earth, one must shift one's position to the sphere of the Cosmic Midnight Hour. There a human being experiences, when he is at the highest point between two incarnations, how a new heaven appears before his spiritual sight, though now not above but beneath him. 'But looking downwards towards the Earth, it does not appear to us in the physical form as we have it around us here; rather does there appear—to be precise, in the direction of the Earth—a mighty spiritual life ... woven out of the deeds of the Seraphim, Cherubim and Thrones' (GA 239, 25 May 1924). And these sublime spirits now imprint the consequences of human earthly karma into the material substance of the earthly world.

Thus one can say: at the centre of the Earth there is on the one hand the centre of black magic out of which the forces of the Sorath form of evil work upwards, while at the same time there unfolds from there also the activity of the highest hierarchy, led by the Spirits of Universal Love or of white magic. However, these two polar forces are active on two different shores of cosmic existence and are separated from one another by an abyss, which is as deep as the abyss between the centre of the Earth and the cosmic sphere of Cosmic Midnight, which lies behind the sphere of the fixed stars. In other words: in order to cross this abyss in the sense of the good powers, the human soul must ascend on its path between two incarnations to the Cosmic Midnight sphere, in order from there to work with the forces of the First Hierarchy on the forming of its karma right into the earthly world.[8]

To this original, *vertical* connection of the centre of the Earth to the Cosmic Midnight Hour, Christ has through His Resurrection added a new, *horizontal* connection. This came about at the centre of the Earth on Easter Saturday (see also in chapter 2). In order to understand how this deed of Christ was accomplished, one must take a further statement by Rudolf Steiner into account.

As already mentioned in chapter 1, the phantom of the physical body had been completely restored in its original form by the time of the Crucifixion. Rudolf Steiner even indicates that at this time it was already wholly separate from the substance of the body, so that the body was no longer held together by the phantom but continued to exist solely 'in accordance with the law of inertia' (GA 131, 12 October 1911).[9] And when the phantom-less body was subsequently treated before the burial with certain spices, it disintegrated into the finest dust soon after being laid in the grave and was then received into the Earth through the fissure that arose in it. (See GA 130, 9 January 1912.)

What then happened to this restored phantom? First, the paths of the phantom and the Christ Spirit separated. The latter followed the same path that the phantom of every human body takes after death. It goes into the interior of the Earth as far as the seventh sphere, where it remains for a while. Rudolf Steiner describes this process as follows: 'What one generally calls the human body is destroyed after death in a physical-material sense. It disintegrates in the uppermost layers of the Earth, but the sum total of forces that maintain the form of the physical body [the phantom] does not. This you can find in the seventh layer, the so-called Earth mirror ... Actually, this [the seventh layer] is a kind of reservoir for the forms which remain in existence. The material substance disintegrates, but the form [the phantom] is preserved' (GA 96, 16 April 1906). The preserving of the form in this layer results from the fact that it has to do with the Saturn forces, or with the imprisoned forces of the Thrones. They were the actual creators of the phantom on Old Saturn, which is why there is a natural force of attraction between the phantom and the seventh layer.

Rudolf Steiner describes the ensuing destiny of the phantom thus: 'If you pursue a human form that has been preserved in this way, you see that it remains for a time in this seventh layer. Then in the eighth layer, the fragmenter or number generator,[10] it is indeed split into fragments' (ibid.).

This has primarily to do not with dividing the phantom into pieces but with its multiplying, as is clearly apparent from Rudolf Steiner's following remark: 'What happens is *exactly the same* as I told you earlier when speaking of a flower' (ibid.). What is being referred to here is the previous section in the same lecture, where Rudolf Steiner describes in connection with his characterization of the eighth layer how the initiate, if he spiritually imagines a flower—or it could be an animal or a person's work of art—and then, as though gazing through it, concentrates on this place in the Earth's interior, is able to experience that this flower (or whatever it may be) appears to his spiritual sight to have been '*multiplied* ... many times over' (ibid.).

The phantom forms of the physical body which have been multiplied in this way can therefore turn into the phantoms of other human beings when they are born on the Earth. Then 'the person concerned has with respect to their form other people within himself, deeply ensconced in his body' (ibid.).[11] Such a fragmentation or multiplying of the phantom in the eighth layer of the Earth is possible only through its having received into itself the forces of death and disintegration with the Fall. These enable the phantom to exist in a manner other than its original one.

In contrast, the destiny of the phantom of Christ Jesus was altogether different. It first descended as through a natural force of attraction into the seventh layer. After a certain time it passed, as do all other phantoms, from there into the eighth layer, where on account of its restored original forces it was not shattered. In exoteric Christianity this process is brought to expression in the picture that the mouth of Hell was not able to swallow the Risen One.

In this eighth layer the unfragmented phantom was newly taken hold of and permeated by the Christ Spirit, who had meanwhile passed through the seven previous layers (see below). Thus Christ, clothed with the phantom, stood at the threshold of the very depths of Hell and now accomplished the last step *together with the phantom*: entry into the core of the Earth, in order from thence to establish the *horizontal* connection that has already been mentioned with the other shore of cosmic existence. Like a mighty, barely conceivable breakthrough what happened here was a completely new union with the sphere of the Cosmic Midnight Hour or with the influence of the First Hierarchy, and then also with the two other hierarchies. And so the spiritual 'Christ Sun' shone forth at the centre of the Earth, betokening the beginning of the event of Easter. Or, in the words of Emil Bock: 'While on Earth the dark Sabbath of the grave prevails, in the realm of the dead the Sun rises. This is the meaning of Christ's descent into Hell ... While it was still Easter Saturday on Earth, it was already Easter in the kingdom of the dead.'[12]

The description given in chapter 2 of the coming into being of the Resurrection body (as distinct from the phantom) refers to what was accomplished in the core of the Earth on Easter Saturday. Now the phantom, which had hitherto still belonged to the earthly shore of cosmic existence, was fully imbued by Christ out of the forces of the Holy Trinity with the cosmic spirituality that lay on yonder side (the Cosmic Midnight Hour): the limb system of the phantom with the forces of the First Hierarchy, the rhythmic system with those of the Second Hierarchy and the head system with those of the Third Hierarchy. (See chapter 1.) In this way the phantom was transformed into the Resurrection body. And just as the restored phantom could not be shattered by the eighth layer, so was the Resurrection body not subject to any black magic from Hell. Filled with the Christ Spirit, it now undertook a kind of 'ascension' or, to be precise, an 'earthly ascent' out of the earth's core through all nine layers to the surface of the Earth, in order to appear before the disciples on Easter Sunday as the Risen One.

In the lecture of 16 April 1906 Rudolf Steiner mentions that spiritual streams flowed through the centre of the Earth taking the form of a cross. 'Two lines of force clearly perpendicular to one another pass exactly through the centre of the Earth. They are not strands but directions in which forces move' (GA 96).

Thus two crosses are connected with the physical Cross of Golgotha: the cross described above in the depths of the Earth, and the great cosmic cross shining in the heights of the spiritual world, as described in the Foundation Stone Meditation.[13] There one finds how through the First Hierarchy the forces of the divine Father work from above downwards, the forces of the Son through the Second Hierarchy radiate from East to West and the forces of the Holy Spirit through the Third Hierarchy rise upwards from below.

On the basis of what has been said, it is possible to discover a further aspect of Christ's descent into Hell and the beginning of the Resurrection process at the centre of the Earth. For one can say that, through His Resurrection, Christ brought the great cosmic cross of hierarchic forces into the centre of the Earth and connected them there with the inner cross of the Earth. By this means the final victory of the Golgotha Cross over evil was achieved at the centre of the Earth and the possibility established for the future incorporation of the Earth in the hierarchic cosmos. Since then the Earth has borne the Golgotha Cross within itself. It has become the cosmic body of Christ. Herein lies the significance of the occult sign with which Rudolf Steiner concluded the cultic act of the laying of the Foundation Stone at the Christmas Conference.[14]

In order to gain a better understanding of the 'earthly ascent' described above, one must include a further aspect of the spiritual-scientific research into the Earth's interior. In several lectures Rudolf Steiner mentions that a knowledge of the nine layers of the Earth as already described can be attained pre-eminently on the path of Christian-mystical initiation. Thus its seven stages are in a direct relationship to the first seven layers.

Washing of the Feet	— mineral Earth
Scourging	— fluid Earth
Crowning with Thorns	— air (vapour) Earth
Bearing the Cross	— form (water) Earth
Mystical Death	— fruit Earth
Entombment	— fire Earth
Resurrection	— Earth mirror

(See GA 96, 16 April 1906)

It is striking that Rudolf Steiner here, as in some other lectures also, consistently concludes the sequence with the Resurrection as the seventh stage. This becomes understandable if one recalls that the seventh stage has to do with the forces of Saturn or the exiled forces of the Spirits of Will and, hence, with the being of the phantom, whose restoration forms the basis and pre-condition for the Resurrection.

At this point there arises the question of researching into the last three layers of the Earth. The answer to this question can be found in another lecture, where Rudolf Steiner indicates that 'the eighth layer ... can *likewise* be perceived at the seventh stage of initiation' (GA 94, 11 July 1906). So the correspondence can be extended as follows:

 Resurrection   — Earth mirror
 Resurrection   — Fragmenter

It is clear from what was said previously why the seventh stage of initiation extends to two layers. The reason is that the seventh and eighth layers have a particular relationship to the human phantom (as was described above). As for the last stage, on the Christian-mystical path it is called 'the Ascension' and, in accordance with what has been said, is connected with the ninth layer, the Earth's core itself:

 Ascension   — Core of the Earth

In this way a reference is made to the mystery of the 'earthly ascent' of the Christ Spirit, that is, to His ascent—clothed in the Resurrection body—through the core of the Earth and all its further eight layers to its surface and beyond.

★

The descent of Christ through all the layers of the Earth's interior also forms a key for the deeper understanding of the subsequent 'multiplying' of His phantom in the spiritual surroundings of the Earth, so that in the perspective of Earth evolution every human being can receive a spiritual reflection of it. Rudolf Steiner speaks of this in the lecture cycle *From Jesus to Christ*. 'Now imagine that, through what one may call a mystical Christological process, man acquires a body quite other than the one he has gradually acquired in the descending line of evolution. Then think of each of these bodies that human beings have acquired as having a connection with what rose from the grave, somewhat as the human cells of the physical body are connected with the original cell. That is, we must think of that which rose from the grave as multiplying itself as does the cell which gives rise to the physical body' (GA 131, 11 October 1911).[15]

 In this description it is striking that Rudolf Steiner in this connection again and again refers to the apostle Paul, who was the first to have knowledge of the mystery of the multiplying of the phantom in the spiritual sphere of the Earth and had proclaimed it in his esoteric teaching. In the cycle referred to, Rudolf Steiner indicates 'that He [Christ] appeared in the spiritual body, the body of which Paul says that it increases as a grain of seed and passes over into all people' (GA 131, 12 October 1911).

This process of the spiritual multiplying of the phantom forms the opposite pole to its multiplication in the eighth layer of the Earth's interior. What continually happens there in a negative sense as the consequence of the Fall has since the Resurrection taken place in the spiritual surroundings of the Earth in a positive way that has decisive significance for the future of mankind. However, both processes are closely connected with one another. For through the fact that the restored phantom of Christ was not—like all normal human bodies—shattered or multiplied in the eighth layer, the particular quality of this multiplying process was wrenched away from the dark powers of the Earth's interior and employed altogether differently. Thereafter this multiplied phantom served *intrinsically* to connect human beings with the forces of the Resurrection (that is, through the implanting of copies of the phantom).

In this way there took place in the evolution of mankind what Rudolf Steiner refers to as 'the rescuing of the human ego'. This will have the consequence that 'in so far as man ... clothes himself with this incorruptible body, he will become more and more aware of his ego-consciousness, and of that part of his nature which journeys on from one incarnation to another' (GA 131, 11 October 1911). In other words, through a conscious connection with a copy of the multiplied phantom of Christ the human individual will come to an experience of the immortality of his individual ego and, hence, rise to consciously taking hold of his *higher ego* in the spiritual world.[16]

The next step for the individual human being will be the taking hold of his *true ego*.[17] This will likewise take place in the spiritual world, though now through a conscious connection with the other aspect of the Resurrection, with the Resurrection body itself. Through this it will be possible for the person concerned to unite his earthly ego, whose development constitutes the essential nature and significance of earthly existence, with the higher ego (that which 'journeys on from one incarnation to another') initially through the forces of the phantom and subsequently with the true ego through the forces of the Resurrection body, without losing the earthly ego. In other words, in order to embark upon the transforming of the phantom, one has to reach the stage of the higher ego; but in order to get to know the nature and origin of the Resurrection body the forces of the true ego are also necessary. For only with these forces can the initiate really gain insight into the mystery of the Earth's core and, hence, the mystery of evil.

In order now to establish more precisely when the multiplication of the phantom happened in the life of Christ after the Resurrection, the following also needs to be taken into consideration. In the lecture of 16 April

1906, which has already been quoted, Rudolf Steiner describes in the greatest detail the possibility of investigating the interior of the Earth on the path of Christian-mystical initiation. In this respect there would seem to be a discrepancy between this lecture and the one he gave on 11 July 1906. For in the latter lecture he said that the seventh and eighth layers become accessible to the person undergoing initiation at the stage of the 'Resurrection'. (A consequence of this is that the mysteries of the ninth layer only become discernible at the stage of the 'Ascension'.)

In the lecture of 16 April, on the other hand, Rudolf Steiner states with regard to the cognitive potential of the eighth sphere ('fragmenter') that one has to do here with that level of initiation which the spirit-pupil 'attains in Christian initiation only *after* the Resurrection'. It follows from this that, in order to research into the mysteries of the eighth sphere, one must have reached the stage of the 'Ascension' on the Christian-mystical path.

However, these two statements of Rudolf Steiner's are not in contradiction with one another if one bears in mind that it is a question here of researching into *various* mysteries in the *same* layer of the Earth's interior, for which first one and then the other stage of initiation is necessary. Thus one must have reached the stage of the 'Resurrection' in order to be able to investigate the mysteries of the shattering or multiplying of the phantom in the eighth sphere of the Earth's interior. On the other hand, one needs the still higher stage of the 'Ascension' in order to come to a knowledge in the same sphere of the connection between the negative multiplying and its positive archetype in the spiritual surroundings of the Earth.

It must still be taken into account here that this multiplying relates from the outset *only* to the phantom and not the Resurrection body. For, as we have already seen, the restoring of the phantom and its preparation for every individual human being (multiplication) at the same time bring about a compensation for the so-called Fall, which the Gods allowed to happen in world evolution without man's agreement. Hence it was the concern of the Gods to establish a counterbalance to the Fall of Man. (See GA 143, 17 December 1912.) In this sense the creating of the Resurrection body is alone connected with the future of earthly evolution and is therefore the only guarantee that mankind can at all reach its final goal on Vulcan. Hence this Resurrection body can only gradually and out of full freedom be achieved and individualized by human beings through their own inner work. For what this really amounts to is not the balancing out of a past event but the beginning of the new humanity as far as Vulcan (and even beyond it). It is from this *common* source that human beings will derive the strength that is necessary for consciously taking hold of the true ego with which alone a further evolutionary process can be accomplished.

As the stage of Ascension on the Christian-mystical path of initiation also has a real relationship to the Ascension at the Turning Point of Time (in the sense of the microcosm in which the macrocosm is reflected), it can therefore be established that the multiplying of the phantom of Christ was encapsulated and, hence, made a reality by Him in the process of His Ascension. For, as has been said, Christ Himself drew the possibility for this forth from out of the depths of the Earth's interior into the spiritual surroundings of the Earth.

At this point the question now arises as to which stage of initiation is necessary in order to be able to research also the core of the Earth. In accordance with the lecture of 16 April such a stage of initiation must lie beyond that of the 'Ascension'. This is also confirmed by a portion of the lecture itself, where Rudolf Steiner indicates that the ninth layer does not correspond exactly to the core of the Earth but surrounds it like a final sheath. ('Then comes the ninth layer, which directly surrounds the centre of the Earth.') Which stage leads beyond that of the 'Ascension'? In the sequence of the stations of Christ Jesus's life in the sense of the path of Christian-mystical initiation, the stages of Resurrection and Ascension are followed by that of 'Whitsun'. In this case, however, this cannot be related to the stage of the historical Whitsun event but to something even higher.[18]

Rudolf Steiner actually mentions this higher stage in one place. It does indeed have an intrinsic connection with the Whitsun event at the Turning Point of Time (for this is where the spiritual source of its endeavours lies[19]), but in comparison to this event it represents a further stage. It is obvious that only a few *leading initiates of the Earth* are able to reach such a stage of initiation. In the following words Rudolf Steiner describes this stage using the example of Mani, the founder of Manicheism in the fourth century: 'However, Mani described himself as the "Paraclete", the Holy Spirit promised to mankind by Christ. We should understand by this that he saw himself as *one* incarnation of the Holy Spirit; he did not mean that he was the *only* one. He explained that the Holy Spirit appears in reincarnations, and that he was only *one* such reincarnation of the Holy Spirit' (GA 93, 11 November 1904; italics Rudolf Steiner).[20]

This has to do with a connection with the Holy Spirit which is even more intrinsic than that in which the apostles were engaged at the Turning Point of Time as a result of the event of Whitsun. Nevertheless, this higher stage is inseparably connected with it as its direct continuation.[21]

There is no doubt that Rudolf Steiner, too, was deeply connected with this stage of initiation. For how otherwise would he have been able to give so much information *out of his own spiritual research* about the Earth's interior and about the nature of evil (of the counter-forces), a deed which has no comparison in the whole evolution of humanity to this day? Above all he was enabled out of this source to enter so deeply into the essential nature of the Mystery of Golgotha that he was the first to speak not only of the phantom of Christ but, in addition, also of His Resurrection body. And in the Foundation Stone Meditation he revealed to all people of good will the modern path to the experiencing of the full reality of the Resurrection. Herein lies the real mystery of Rudolf Steiner's initiation.

★

At this point something further needs to be said about the nature and origin of the *three* earthquakes; for they can only rightly be understood on the basis of what has already been considered. The first of these earthquakes took place on Good Friday, the second on Easter Saturday and the third in the early morning of Easter Sunday. From a spiritual-scientific point of view, earthquakes are always associated with influences from the fifth and sixth layers of the Earth's interior (fruit Earth and fire Earth: see GA 96, 16 April 1906), which naturally does not exclude the possibility that other factors are also involved.[22]

The first earthquake occurred after the death of Christ Jesus on the Cross. Only St Matthew's Gospel gives an account of it: 'And behold, the curtain of the temple was torn in two, from top to bottom; and the earth shook, and the rocks were split' (27:51).[23] The tearing of the curtain in the temple is here a true symbol for the beginning of the union of the Christ Spirit with the spiritual atmosphere of the Earth; for the temple is also an image of the human body. The process of leaving the body had already begun before the death on the Cross. It is in this sense that Rudolf Steiner reports from his research in the domain of the Fifth Gospel: 'With this darkening process [that started during the Crucifixion] one is beholding the connection of the cosmic Christ impulse with the Earth's aura *before His death*' (GA 148, 16 November 1913). And he then supplements this testimony with a personal remark: 'Thus to behold the Cross on Golgotha in the spirit, and to see the Christ pour Himself out over earthly life through the darkened Earth, is an impression of the most overwhelming magnitude' (ibid.).

It is in this sense important that one finds this result of Rudolf Steiner's research indicated only in St Luke's Gospel. Thus the evangelist reports that the curtain of the temple was torn *before* the death on the Cross (23:45).[24] Whereas the two other evangelists, Matthew and Mark, shift the tearing of the curtain to the moment immediately *following* the death on the Cross (27:51 and 15:38). This difference stems from the fact that Luke focuses mainly on the beginning of the process of the Christ's Being's union with the Earth's aura, while Matthew and Mark look more towards its end.

From a spiritual-scientific standpoint one can say that Christ's union with the aura of the Earth began at the moment when the phantom of the physical body of Jesus had been fully restored, which—as Rudolf Steiner indicates—was achieved already before the death on the Cross. (See chapter 1.)[25] The earthquake reported by St Matthew's Gospel at this point, on the other hand, refers to the descent of the fully restored phantom into the interior of the Earth, or its passage through the fifth and sixth layers on its way to the place that was described earlier in this chapter. This was a completely new occurrence for the whole of earthly evolution.

The second earthquake is associated by Rudolf Steiner with the receiving of the body into the fissure in the earth: 'The Earth opened, the dust of the corpse fell into the chasm and united with the whole substance of the Earth' (GA 130, 9 January 1912). At this point it is necessary to recall that the body of the Crucified One—once the phantom had separated from it—first crumbled in the grave to the finest, almost non-material dust and was only then received by the Earth like a kind of homoeopathic medicine. In the lectures on the Fifth Gospel Rudolf Steiner describes this process in further detail: 'That earthquake shook the grave in which the body of Jesus had been laid and the stone covering it was wrenched away; a fissure was rent in the Earth and the corpse was received into it. Another tremor caused the fissure to close again over the corpse. And when the people came in the morning the grave was empty, for the earth had received the dead body of Jesus. Only the stone still lay there, flung from where it had been' (GA 148, 2 October 1913).

This second earthquake was a sign that the Christ Spirit, having first formed a connection with the Earth's aura, had now embarked upon His 'Descent into Hell', that is, His path into the interior of the Earth in order to take hold of His phantom in a renewed way. The earthquake was the consequence of His *first* passage through the fifth and sixth layers of the Earth.

Only St Matthew gives an account of the third earthquake early on Easter morning (28:2). It occurred at the moment when the Christ Spirit, clothed in the Resurrection body, *for the second time* passed through the layers mentioned above. The consequence of this last earthquake was the closing of the fissure which had previously received the dust of the body. At one point in the lectures on the Fifth Gospel Rudolf Steiner indicates in this connection that the moving of the stone was associated not with the opening up of the fissure but with its closing, that is, it occurred because of this. Thus in summarizing these events he describes the following sequence of happenings: 'Once again let us follow the sequence of pictures! Jesus dies on the Cross of Golgotha. Darkness breaks in upon the earth. The corpse of Jesus is laid into the grave. A tremor shakes the land and the corpse of Jesus is received into the Earth. The fissure caused by the tremor closes; the stone is flung aside. These are all actual happenings' (GA 148, 2 October 1913).

Here lies the possibility of bringing the fruits of Rudolf Steiner's research into harmony with the account in St Matthew's Gospel. For in the above quotation there is the sentence 'And when they came in the morning the grave was empty, for the earth had received the dead body of Jesus. Only the stone still lay there, flung from where it had been', from which it is quite clear that this earthquake had taken place *before* their arrival at the grave.[26]

The reason why Rudolf Steiner's account differs from what is stated in St Matthew's Gospel is, in my view, that Rudolf Steiner starts more from the spiritual source of the second and third earthquakes, both of which are associated with Christ's passage through the fifth and sixth layers of the Earth, which is why he considers these two events together without mentioning the temporal interval between them. Herein lies the difference between these and the first earthquake; for this latter is associated with the *path of the phantom* into the Earth's interior, whereas the two subsequent ones have to do with the *path of Christ Himself*. Matthew, on the other hand, concentrates in his reading in the Akashic Record upon the first and third earthquakes and connects the latter directly with the event of the Resurrection (the conclusion of Christ's 'earthly ascent') and, hence, temporally with Easter morning and the arrival of the women.

Thus one can have the following overall view of the three earthquakes:

First earthquake	after the death on the Cross on Good Friday (Matthew 27:51)	brought about by the *phantom's* passage through the fifth and sixth layers of the Earth
Second earthquake	some time after the Entombment on Easter Saturday	brought about by the *first* passage (the Descent into Hell) of the *Christ Spirit* through the fifth and sixth layers of the Earth (opening of the fissure)

| Third earthquake | on Easter morning at the rising of the Sun (Mark 16:2)[27] | brought about by the *second* passage (the 'earthly ascent') of the *Christ Spirit* in the *Resurrection body* through the fifth and sixth layers of the Earth (closing of the fissure, moving of the stone). |

As we have seen, St Matthew's Gospel speaks only of the first and third earthquakes, whereas Rudolf Steiner describes a second and a third.[28]

One important result of what has been described is that the last two earthquakes, through which the fissure in the Earth was opened and closed up again, were brought about by the Christ Spirit Himself.

Furthermore, we also see from the fruits of Rudolf Steiner's research that have been cited that the Christ Spirit had begun to leave Jesus shortly before death and to merge into the aura of the Earth, thus causing Jesus to say: 'My God, my God, why hast thou forsaken me?' (Matthew 27:46). In the present context these words must be regarded as an expression of a specific supersensible fact. However, one should not imagine this separation to be of an absolute nature but only to the degree that Jesus was able to experience this sense of abandonment consciously. In the deeper levels of His being the Christ Spirit did of course remain inseparably connected with Jesus until the moment of death, in order then finally to merge into the Earth's aura *together with him*. For this reason Rudolf Steiner could in many other contexts indicate with full justice that Christ too (and not only Jesus) passed through the death on Golgotha.[29] Thus, for example, he could say in one of the lectures on the Fifth Gospel: 'Through the death of Christ Jesus, the Earth received the Christ impulse' (GA 148, 18 December 1913).

However, the loosening, or distancing, of the Christ from Jesus was absolutely necessary in order that Jesus could actually die. For this would not have been possible if Christ had been fully present in him.[30]

Jesus was, however, received by the Christ Spirit in the aura of the Earth immediately after death; and they remained united here until the beginning of the Christ Spirit's 'Descent into Hell' on Easter Saturday. Thus He first merged into the aura of the Earth, in order from thence to descend into the depths of the Earth as far as its centre. In this way the foundation was laid, and the process initiated, for the Earth increasingly to become the planetary body of Christ. (The total permeation of the Earth's aura did not, however, happen until later and is, as already described in chapter 3, associated with the mystery of the Ascension.)

This union of the Christ Spirit with the earthly sphere is portrayed in the central motif of the paintings in the small cupola of the First Goetheanum. That this motif is primarily concerned with this mystery is apparent if one carefully studies the pastel sketch which Rudolf Steiner personally made for this motif in 1914. (See the illustration on p. 115.) Somewhat to the right of the middle of this sketch is the Hill of Golgotha with the three crosses, where one can discern the outlines of the three bodies hanging on them. The three crosses are clearly surrounded by darkness, which wholly corresponds to what is said in the Gospels: 'Now from the sixth hour there was darkness over all the land until the ninth hour' (Matthew 27:45), when Jesus passed away (27:46 and 50). That is, what is being portrayed here is the time from immediately before until directly after Jesus' death, though before the body had been taken down from the Cross.

Then we have adjacent to the three crosses the mighty form of the Christ in radiant gold, surrounded by an oval-shaped etheric aura in peach-blossom. This figure is at the mid-point of the semicircular form of the Earth's aura in rainbow colours, while the Sun—likewise surrounded by peach-blossom—shines powerfully into the aura of Christ as a sign of the future transformation of the Earth into a new Sun. In contrast, the waning Moon testifies to the end of the old world. The ascending Lucifer[31] and the image of Ahriman enchained beneath the Earth are an indication of the arising of a middle sphere which later becomes the Resurrection sphere of Christ and in which Jesus' etheric review (*Rückschau*) begins after his death, under the protection and guardianship of Christ. In this way Christ laid the foundation for the 'new etheric body' (GA 130, 9 January 1912) which after the Resurrection becomes His outermost sheath. And at the same time the spiritual space was prepared in the spiritual surroundings of the Earth out of which He could subsequently work as the Risen One.

The Christ Himself still awaits the beginning of His 'Descent into Hell', when He will unite with the restored phantom in the depths of the Earth. One can also say that He is waiting until the phantom has reached the seventh layer of the Earth's interior, in order thereafter to begin the process of Resurrection.

★

If one contemplates the path of the Christ Spirit from the Hill of Golgotha through all seven layers of the Earth to the point of His union with His phantom in the eighth layer, one can understand this path as follows. Christ journeyed through these dark spheres like a lightning-flash of the Spirit—and none of them could halt His Spirit in its path. By this means, however, the adversarial powers reigning there were limited in their influence—the luciferic powers being confined to the first three layers, the ahrimanic powers to the next three and the asuric powers to the last three. In the Resurrection the influence of the Sun Demon was likewise similarly kept within bounds in the Earth's interior.

As we have already seen, the Resurrection consisted in the transformation of the phantom into the Resurrection body out of the forces of Cosmic Midnight, when Christ entered into a connection with all nine hierarchies on a horizontal plane out of the forces of the Holy Trinity and imbued the three systems of the phantom body with their forces.[32] He was therefore able to pass again through all nine spheres, sowing the seeds of hierarchic forces from His Resurrection body of which they had been deprived. This happened in the sequence:

Core of the Earth	— Forces of the Seraphim
Fragmenter	— Forces of the Cherubim
Earth mirror	— Forces of the Thrones
Fire Earth	— Forces of the Kyriotetes
Fruit Earth	— Forces of the Dynamis
Form Earth	— Forces of the Exusiai
Air Earth	— Forces of the Archai
Fluid Earth	— Forces of the Archangeloi
Mineral Earth	— Forces of the Angels

Through this deed the seeds for its future spiritualization were sown in all nine layers of the Earth, a process which will lead eventually to its union with the Sun. Moreover, the possibility thereby arose for human beings to be able to work from this time onward out of their own freedom on the transforming of the interior of the Earth—and not only from above downwards but also in the direction of Christ's 'earthly ascent', upwards beginning from the lowest layers. Hence Rudolf Steiner could say: 'Its aim [that of the anthroposophical movement[33]] shall therefore be: to redeem [improve] the fragmenter, the eighth sphere; its endeavour shall be to rescue what can be salvaged from the centre of the Earth' (GA 94, 11 July 1906).[34] For with His 'earthly ascent' Christ laid the foundations for the future victory of human beings over the sub-earthly powers in all layers of the Earth's interior.

Rudolf Steiner sums up the whole evolutionary journey in the following words: 'Thus a connection exists between man's inner nature and the interior of the Earth ... What man does on Earth gradually transforms the whole earthly planet. And if white magic really makes good progress, the core of the Earth will also become different. Only the black magicians will be excluded on a kind of Moon when our planet eventually passes away' (GA 94, 11 July 1906).

From the standpoint of the Christmas Conference the transformation of the core of the Earth is associated with the Foundation Stone, which has a connection with the New Jerusalem.[35] Rudolf Steiner created it out of white magic. Hence its nurturing in the human heart can transform the core of the Earth. The Foundation Stone was then handed on to the members in order that they might build a community upon it. The new brotherliness working within this community right into the forming of karma can transform the 'fragmenter'.[36] For the transforming of the 'Earth mirror', the Society must become a reflection of relations in the heavens. This will be achieved when the members work together with the Third Hierarchy.[37]

Working upon the other layers can come about as follows: on the first layer the training of logical thinking has an influence, as belongs to the first stage of the path of schooling. It must, however, be conducted with a respect for the thinking of all other people. For the transforming of the 'fluid Earth' it is necessary to reach the stage of living thinking, associated with a deep respect for everything living in nature. And the 'air Earth' can be transformed if thinking becomes an organ of perception for imaginations. This must involve a respect for the soul-life of other human beings (and that of animals).

The transition to the 'form Earth' has to do with the achieving of an empty consciousness. Imaginations that have been dissolved out of free will create an inner space of freedom in the soul into which inspirations of the good can stream out of the spiritual world. The good then becomes a substance of real potency, and it has a redemptive effect upon the fourth layer. The transforming of the 'fruit Earth' occurs when man becomes creative out of the wellspring of the good in his soul. And the 'fire Earth' is transformed when he develops such an enthusiasm for the moral ideals of the world that it becomes an inner fire in the heart, which can overcome the destructive powers of the seventh layer.

One can best arrive at an understanding of the process of the Resurrection itself—as it took its course in the core of the Earth—through meditatively working with the Foundation Stone Meditation, specifically in the sequence of its parts as given by Rudolf Steiner at the laying of the Foundation Stone on 25 December 1923. On that day he first read the three microcosmic sections of the first three parts, then the fourth part

The Resurrection and the Interior of the Earth

with the radiating of the 'Christ Sun' in the middle and, in conclusion, again the three microcosmic parts, though now associated with their macrocosmic counterparts. In the sense of what has already been presented here one can recognize in the following six lines of the microcosmic sections the path to a meditative union with the forms of the restored phantom:

> 'And thou wilt truly *live*
> In the World-Being of Man'

> 'And thou wilt truly *feel*
> In the soul-weaving of Man'

> 'And thou wilt truly *think*
> In the Spirit-Foundation of Man'.

This is the inner path whereby man can today succeed in thinking, feeling and living (willing) in the bodily nature of the restored phantom.

On Easter Saturday the spiritual 'Christ-Sun' then dawned at the centre of the Earth, whereupon the breakthrough described above occurred: the uniting of the three systems of the phantom with the forces of all nine hierarchies up to the Trinity. Thus the restored phantom became the Resurrection body.

The consequence of this is that, if the three microcosmic sections are meditated together with the three macrocosmic sections, one is on the way towards uniting the full reality of the Resurrection body (and the phantom that is connected with it) with one's own being. This will be possible only if one has previously forged a direct inner connection to the *present* Christ impulse through the content of the fourth part. For all true knowledge of Christ, including knowledge that seeks to comprehend the essential nature of the Mystery of Golgotha, must always have as its starting point and spiritual source a direct connection to His *eternal present*.

★

Just as the Christ Spirit was able to form a connection with His phantom in a new way in the depths of the Earth, so after the conclusion of His 'earthly ascent' there took place a renewed association with His etheric body. For in contrast to the destiny of an ordinary etheric body after death (its dissolution in the etheric cosmos after three days), the etheric body of Christ Jesus remained completely intact in the etheric surroundings of the Earth. The individuality of Jesus of Nazareth also continued to be connected with it. For, in common with every other person, this individuality likewise beheld the great panorama of its former 33-year earthly life during the three days after death. Nevertheless, as has been said, this special etheric body did not dissolve at the end of this time.[38]

Thus the Resurrection encompasses all the events, from the great breakthrough to the highest spiritual forces in the centre of the Earth—which forces brought about the transformation of the phantom into the Resurrection body—to the latter's union with the transformed etheric body at the end of the 'earthly ascent', through which the Risen One became visible first to the women and then to all the disciples. The individual events should not, however, be understood in a temporal succession but as belonging to the sphere of duration. Hence one can with complete justice speak of the Resurrection as a single event.

As was shown in the second chapter, through His subsequent Ascension Christ united Himself with the destiny of the etheric bodies of all individual human beings after death. Now, however, He concluded His 'earthly ascent' by uniting with His own transformed etheric body. In this way the foundation was laid for the future overcoming of the 'second death',[39] just as through the Resurrection at the centre of the Earth the foundation was laid for overcoming the death of the body for the whole of mankind. Emil Bock writes in this regard: 'The death struggle will not be able to dissolve the etheric body of Christ on the third day. Through the power that the Christ retains over His own being, this etheric sheath will not withdraw from the Earth; rather will it become more substantial so that Christ can form a proper connection with the Earth as a whole only through it' (Emil Bock, the chapter entitled 'Good Friday'). In other words, at the moment when after three days Jesus's etheric body was to be dissolved in the cosmic ether and would have succumbed to the 'second death', the Christ, having resurrected in the transformed phantom, united with it (this etheric body) on Easter morning so as to appear to the disciples as the Risen One in a new etheric sheath which surrounded and guarded the Resurrection body.[40]

In one single instance Rudolf Steiner indicates that with this etheric body, too, a transformation took place which, on the basis of what has been said previously, can be described as a metamorphosis which corresponds to that from the phantom to the Resurrection body. In the lecture of 9 January 1912 we read of the 'particularly contracted etheric body,[41] from which the constituents of the *new etheric body* were drawn with which the Christ Being clothed Himself [after the Resurrection]' (GA 130). One could also say that this 'contracted etheric body' stands with regard to the 'new etheric body' referred to as does the phantom to the Resurrection body: they are like two essences which at the same time form an inseparable unity.

Consequently the Christ Spirit appeared first to the women and then also to the disciples in the form that His Resurrection body was outwardly as though 'clothed' by this 'new etheric body'. Herein lies the twofold mystery of the Resurrection already mentioned in the first chapter, which was characterized in the description of spiritual communion as a connection with the spiritual body *and* blood of the Risen One.

★

There is in Rudolf Steiner's work a description which can be regarded as a key whereby the essential nature of this process can be investigated more precisely. It is not without significance that the place in question is only to be found among the research that he shared from the Fifth Gospel. Thus Rudolf Steiner indicates in the lecture of 10 February 1914 that both the forces of the etherized blood and also those of the body of the Risen One are perceived by every human being who has found a conscious relationship to Christ on Earth during the first three days after death when the etheric body is dissolved. What Rudolf Steiner describes here in general terms for the whole of humanity was in just this way experienced for the first time in spiritual history—and, hence, in an archetypal form—by Jesus of Nazareth after his death on Golgotha during the three following days in the etheric surroundings of the Earth. And because he was the first human being on Earth who entered into a relationship with Christ—and *his* relationship to Him during the three years was deeper and more intrinsic than any person on Earth has ever or will ever achieve—it is wholly justified to relate the following results of Rudolf Steiner's spiritual research also to the experiences of Jesus of Nazareth after death.

In the lecture referred to Rudolf Steiner speaks of the forces in man's etheric body which have been active within it since the Mystery of Golgotha.[42] They are present within it because it received the etherized blood of Christ or, to be more precise, that part of the blood which flowed from the Cross directly down to the Earth and was etherized there.[43] 'This part of the blood was etherized, it was indeed received by the Earth's etheric forces, so that the blood which flowed at that time from the wounds became an etheric substance. This etheric substance sparkles, shimmers and lights up in the etheric body' (GA 148). And if a person perceives it after death in his etheric body, he knows directly that Christ will lead the whole of earthly evolution in the future Jupiter. The next incarnation of our Earth is thereby spiritually assured: 'This is a freshly germinating life [in the human etheric body] which leads man viably towards the future' (ibid.). In this way it becomes possible that by the end of the Earth aeon man will not only reach his original position in the cosmos but is able to develop further. Man '... would arrive on Jupiter and not suit the life there if what had been attained on the Earth were not to have been passed on to Jupiter' (ibid.). The manifestation of Christ's etherized blood in the etheric body of every human being after death is a clear testimony that He will ensure that all fruits of Earth evolution are not lost in the cosmos but will be preserved for the future Jupiter.

Thus one can say that in what he experienced after death Jesus of Nazareth was the first human being to receive this etherized substance of the holy blood into his etheric body, thus giving him the confidence that the Earth will indeed reach the Jupiter condition. In order that this will eventually become possible, something else was absolutely necessary. For the blood alone was not sufficient to secure the future; the holy body had to be included as well. Just as man's etheric body is permeated by the etheric substance of Christ's blood every time after death, so is the whole cosmically extended tableau of this etheric body *enlivened* by the forces of the Resurrection body when it is spread out after death, with the result that the etherized substance of Christ's blood becomes *visible* to man in his etheric body.

In many places in the lectures on the Fifth Gospel Rudolf Steiner describes how the 'blood-drained' body of Jesus was received by the Earth into a fissure caused by an earthquake, in order then to pass through the metamorphosis already described in this chapter. But then, as has already been described, after the conclusion of Christ's 'earthly ascent' there occurred on Easter morning the connection of the Resurrection body with the etheric body of Jesus which had continued to remain in the spiritual surroundings of the Earth, with the result that the blood and the body came together for the first time in this new form. 'Thus something else has entered into the etheric body: what has been received by the fissure in the Earth has permeated that which we have called the blood that shimmers and glistens in etheric substance, with the result that the shimmering and glistening blood becomes visible. One therefore has the feeling, as I said just now, that the etheric body expands after death and one perceives it as a kind of firmament from which everything else stands out; and then, like a fundamental substance, the body, the blood-drained body of Christ Jesus, which has been received by the fissure in the Earth and has therefore passed into the Earth and appears as an enlivening element in the extended tableau of the etheric body, stretches out in this extended etheric body' (ibid.).

Only the perception of the etherized blood with the blood-drained body of Christ Jesus gives the dead person in his etheric panorama after death 'the confidence that mankind will not be destroyed but will live on as the spiritual content of the Earth when the physical matter of the Earth falls away, as an individual human corpse falls away from a person's spiritual being' (ibid.).

In this way there appears before every person after his death one of the most important consequences of the events at the Turning Point of Time. Since the etheric body of Jesus was as has been described connected with the Resurrection body on Easter morning, every human individual can perceive this process in his existence after death as a pledge for the future Jupiter. Only through this beholding of the future of the Earth can man attain to true bliss after death. For only that 'which the Christ impulse has made out of the spiritual part of the Earth [gives] bliss to the soul ... in the life between death and a new birth' (ibid.). However, the possibility of thus gaining insight into the 'spiritual part of the Earth' results from spiritual communion with the blood and the body of the Risen One, as is accessible to man after his death through experiencing the Christ impulse in his etheric body.

As a result of the Mystery of Golgotha this union of the blood and body of Christ Jesus has an influence not only at this first, etheric level, for it is only the starting point for further development. Thus on the next highest, astral level this connection is revealed as a promise for the future transition of Jupiter to the ensuing Venus condition; and on the Devachan plane it signifies the foundation for the future Vulcan. From this there results the threefold communion of man, which takes place on three cosmic levels and, hence, ensures mankind's future on Jupiter, Venus and Vulcan. The condition, however, remains the same: man must already here on Earth consciously establish a relationship to Christ and to His deed on Golgotha out of his own freedom.

It is clear from what has been said how Rudolf Steiner's words about 'the *new etheric body* with which the Christ Being clothed Himself [after the Resurrection]' (see above) can be better understood. For the 'new' consists in that the etheric body of Jesus was imbued on Easter Saturday with the etherized and, hence, 'shimmering and glistening blood'. As the bearer of this etherized blood substance the etheric body of the Risen One became quite different to what it had been on Good Friday.

Moreover, the consequence of the appearance of this substance in the etheric body of Jesus of Nazareth is that it can be found from that time until now within man not only after death but also during earthly life. Hence Rudolf Steiner speaks of how in every human being, in addition to the stream of human etherized blood ascending from the heart to the head, a second stream—that of the etherized blood of Christ Jesus—has since the Mystery of Golgotha been flowing in the same direction. And if both of these streams are united within a human being through his work with anthroposophy, he can succeed in beholding the Etheric Christ. Herein lies the most important task of anthroposophy today. 'A union of these two streams can, however, come about only if a person is able to unfold a *true understanding* of what is contained in the Christ impulse. Otherwise there can be no union; the two streams mutually repel each other' (GA 130, 1 October 1911). And an understanding of the events taking place at the Turning Point of Time *out of anthroposophy* forms a substantial part of such a 'true understanding'.

These three aspects are also contained in the fourth part of the Foundation Stone Meditation. The path from the heart to the head is mentioned there three times. In the first section this occurs in relation to the shepherds and kings. This is also a reference to the human stream of etherized blood which flowed already in pre-Christian times in all human beings from the heart to the head. In the second section there is a reference to the shining of the 'Christ Sun' in Earth evolution as a consequence of the Mystery of Golgotha and, hence, to the source of the other stream, that of the blood of Christ. And the last section has to do with the deeds of human beings who have brought about within themselves the union of the two streams and seek to accomplish the good in the world out of these conjoined streams.

★

The twofold nature of the Resurrection, consisting in the duality of blood and body, or condensed etheric body and Resurrection body, is referred to in the Book of Revelation at the point where the revelation of the Christ Sun between two 'pillars of fire', one of which is on the sea and the other on the land (Rev. 10:1–2; see also the fourth apocalyptic seal in GA 104). Of these two pillars, the one connected with the land, refers to the Resurrection body, and the one connected with the water refers to the new etheric body of the Risen One. (Water always stands for the revelation of the etheric in the realm of the senses.)

Later on in the Book of Revelation the two beasts approach this twofold mystery of the Resurrection. Thus the beast with seven heads and ten horns first appears out of the water (Rev. 13:1). This beast tries on behalf of Sorath to prevent human souls from having any connection with the Resurrection body.[44]

After this emissary of Sorath, this being himself appears out of the Earth's core in the form of the second beast. 'Then I saw another beast which rose out of the earth; it had two horns like a lamb and it spoke like a dragon' (Rev. 13:11). He will make every possible effort to prevent human beings from having any connection with the Resurrection body. For anyone who does not consciously and freely establish this connection will not find the path to the Heavenly Jerusalem or to the next cosmic condition of the Earth.

In the 21st chapter of the Book of Revelation, which is devoted to the future Jupiter aeon as the Heavenly Jerusalem, mention is made of the overcoming of the first and the second death (verses 4 and 8). As we have already seen, man will achieve victory over the first death by receiving the forces of the Resurrection body, while victory over the second[45] happens through the receiving of the forces of the new etheric body of the Risen One. In this first great step in the spiritualizing of the Earth (the dissolving of its physical substances), the forces of the Resurrection body will make a decisive contribution towards the Earth's uniting with the Sun, which will bring the Earth aeon to an end. Then, however, the new etheric body of the Risen One will play a decisive part in the second step of its spiritualization (the dissolving of its etheric constituents, which must likewise be achieved with the union with the Sun; see GA 104, 30 June 1908).

However, this process of the spiritualization of the Earth must be preceded by the total transformation of the Earth's interior out of the moral power of human beings, who will endeavour to develop in themselves the qualities of white magic or the pure magic of love. 'If white magic achieves the mastery, there will no longer be any evil in the world. Thus human evolution signifies a transforming of the Earth's interior ... Ultimately the whole Earth will be a spiritualized Earth, transformed through the power of mankind' (GA 95, 4 September 1906). However, this lofty goal, representing the consequence of Christ's 'Descent into Hell' and 'earthly ascent', can be attained only in connection with the forces of His Resurrection body.

If Christ appears in the Resurrection as the Alpha and Omega of the whole of world evolution, stretching as it does from Old Saturn to the future Vulcan, so is the Resurrection at the same time the source of the spiritual forces with whose help the interior of the Earth will be transformed, in order thereby to open up the path to the future aeon of Jupiter.

Regarding the Relationship of the Earth Spirit to the Interior of the Earth

The period that Christ spent at the centre of the Earth is connected with the being whom Rudolf Steiner calls the spirit of the Earth. In describing the interior of the Earth Rudolf Steiner mentions this being only in a few words. It does indeed belong to the centre of the Earth, though not to the evil forces that are active there. Rudolf Steiner has this to say about this spirit: 'The ninth and last layer is, so to speak, the abode of the planetary spirit. This being manifests two distinctive characteristics. One could compare it with a human being, for it possesses an organ resembling a brain. Another organ is similar to a heart' (GA 97, 21 April 1906).

It can be assumed that through Christ's appearances in the dwelling-place of the planetary spirit this being experienced a great metamorphosis, which also signified the beginning of a wholly new development for it. For in future Christ would Himself increasingly take over its function as lord of the Earth planet. 'Christ becomes more and more the Earth Spirit, and the true Christian understands the words "He who eats my bread treads me underfoot" [John 13:18], for he considers the body of the Earth to be the body of Christ; *of course at present this is only at its beginning*. Christ has still to become the Earth Spirit; He will unite Himself fully with the Earth. And when the Earth later unites with the Sun, the great Earth Spirit, Christ, will be the Sun Spirit' (GA 104, 30 June 1908).

What does it mean that Christ, as is indicated in the above words, increasingly becomes the new Spirit of the Earth and therefore transforms it to its very core into His cosmic body? The Foundation Stone Meditation can also give us significant help in answering this question. As has already been described, the Resurrection or the transforming of the phantom into the Resurrection body took place through its connection forged by Christ with the forces of the Trinity at the centre of the Earth. With the ensuing 'earthly ascent' Christ was able out of these forces to establish a new relationship between the nine hierarchies and the nine layers of the earth. In this way the foundation was laid for the future transformation of the Earth into a planetary reflection of His Resurrection body, a process which must be completed by the end of the Earth age. This means, quite literally, that the Earth will one day become the body of Christ. For the only true body of Christ is His Resurrection body. Hence in order to be His planetary body, the Earth must itself become similar in nature to the Resurrection body.

This could be imagined as follows. At the end of earthly times—in order to achieve the union with the Sun and the transition to the Jupiter condition—the three times three layers of the Earth's interior are transformed as follows: the three lowest layers are permeated by the forces of the First Hierarchy, the three middle layers by the Second Hierarchy and the three upper layers by the Third Hierarchy (see p. 113). In the sense of the Foundation Stone Meditation the three lowest layers thereby become the limb system of the Earth as the body of Christ and, in this respect, the new wellspring of the good. The good that is engendered in this way must work formatively into the karma of mankind and, hence, of the entire earthly planet. The three middle layers are transformed into the rhythmic system of His planetary body. What is today the source of so many disastrous earthquakes and volcanic eruptions will take on a harmonious, rhythmic character and only follow the laws of the starry world. And the three upper layers will be metamorphosed into a kind of head system, which will impart to human beings the inspirations of the Third Hierarchy.

Today all life dies away behind the solid bone surface of the human skull. This has to be so in order that man can take hold of the impulse of freedom in the dead thinking of the brain. In our time the forces of death have already progressed so far in modern intellectualism that even the merest feeling that is permeated by them fades away. But just as man can inwardly enliven his thinking on the path of schooling in order to achieve the stage of living thinking, so will it also be possible for him gradually to transform the three upper layers of the Earth through working spiritually on himself.[46]

The world of the elemental spirits, which pervades the whole of nature on the Earth's surface, will likewise be increasingly included in this process. This is why in the Foundation Stone Meditation there is the threefold allusion to the 'elemental spirits', who today longingly await this transformation of the Earth as a consequence of the Mystery of Golgotha (the Rosicrucian dicta). The apostle Paul expresses this in the familiar words: 'For the creation waits with eager longing for the revealing of the Sons of God; for the creation was subjected to futility, not of its own will but by the will of him who subjected it in hope; because the creation itself will be set free from its bondage to decay and obtain the glorious liberty of the children of God. We know that the whole creation has been groaning in travail together until now' (Romans 8:19–22).

However, this aim of the Earth will only be achieved if mankind rises to its full worth as 'children of God'. This can happen only if individual human beings fully receive the forces of the Resurrection body and learn 'truly [to] think' in their heads, 'truly [to] feel' in their hearts and 'truly

[to] live' in their limbs (that is, to bring the good into the world through their free deeds). In other words, only out of his conscious connection with the Resurrection body will man be capable of bringing what was instituted within the Earth through Christ's Resurrection to a true fulfilment. If he learns to think out of the power of the Resurrection body, he will bring about the transformation of the three upper layers of the Earth's interior. If he learns to feel out of the Resurrection body, he can transform the three middle layers. And through his deeds out of the Resurrection body, if, that is, it fills the whole of man's being with true life, the three lowest layers extending to the very centre of the Earth will be made free for the forces of the Christ Sun.

If one adds the transforming of nature out of the forces of the Resurrection body, which will be possible in the future through man's collaborative work with the elemental spirits, we have in the macrocosmic sections of the Foundation Stone Meditation also the key for understanding Christ's 'earthly ascent': His connection with the forces of the Trinity in the centre of the Earth; the subsequent allocation of the forces of the nine hierarchies to its nine layers; and the transformation of the world of the elemental spirits on its surface, who would seek already today to impart to human beings the mystery of the new Spirit of the Earth: 'May human beings hear it!' Thus these two processes—man's connection with the three systems of the Resurrection body and the transformation of the Earth into the threefold body of Christ—should not be separated from one another. This planetary body then becomes the cosmic reflection of His Resurrection body, which alone enables the eventual union of the Earth with the Sun to take place and the circumstances to be created for the future Jupiter.

What has been said here is also associated with the gradual transformation of the Earth spirit, a task with which human beings must likewise collaborate out of the Christ impulse. To this end the fourth part of the Foundation Stone Meditation was given to them, highlighting the transforming of human hearts and then of human heads out of the power of the 'Christ Sun'. This twofold transformation of man's being leads to changes in the brain and heart systems of the Earth spirit, who will be increasingly connected with Christ, the new Spirit of the Earth, as His sheath. Rudolf Steiner says in this regard: 'The planetary spirit is also subject to changes that are intimately related to the evolution of human beings' (GA 97, 21 April 1906). The cosmic communion described in the first chapter and its twofold mantric encapsulation lead to this same goal. Thus from both these different directions human beings will prepare the future union of the Earth with the Sun.

On the basis of Rudolf Steiner's indications there arises at this point a further question which is not easy to resolve, namely, regarding the actual composition of the Earth's core, with which both the Earth spirit and also the origin of evil are connected. In order that the attempt be made to answer this question even only to some extent, something must first be extracted from what has been said about the nature of the Earth spirit. Rudolf Steiner speaks about this being in the greatest detail in the cycle *The Spiritual Beings in the Heavenly Bodies and in the Kingdoms of Nature* (GA 136). There he describes how each of the three groups of divine-spiritual hierarchies bequeathes a kind of offspring in the realm of the Earth. From the Third Hierarchy (Angeloi, Archangeloi and Archai) there derive the nature-spirits, from the Second Hierarchy (Exusiai, Dynamis and Kyriotetes) the group-souls of plants and animals, and from the First Hierarchy (Thrones, Cherubim and Seraphim) the spirits of the rotation of time.

Rudolf Steiner speaks in the same vein about the spirit of the Earth and also about the spirits of the other planets, which, however, are at a higher level than the spirits of the rotation of time. The following correspondences result from a comparison with the structure of man's being:

Physical body — sense-world
Etheric body — world of the nature-spirits
Astral body — spirits of the rotation of time
Ego — planetary spirit

(See ibid., 4 April 1912.)

In the realm of perceptible nature the nature-spirits function as nature-forces; the spirits of the rotation of time reveal themselves in it as the laws of nature and the planetary spirit constitutes the meaning of the whole of nature (ibid.).

From this description there arises the next question: to which group of offspring does the spirit of the Earth belong, if the spirits of the rotation of time derive from the First Hierarchy, which is the highest in the hierarchic cosmos? One can find at least an indication of this spirit's origin in the cycle referred to. After Rudolf Steiner has described the influence wrought by the nine hierarchies, he mentions completely different kinds of hierarchic beings who have a far greater creative potential than even the spirits of the First Hierarchy. These are essences composed of several beings and, hence, are of a higher standing than the individual hierarchic orders viewed individually.

In the lecture of 7 April 1912 Rudolf Steiner cites an example of such

The Resurrection and the Interior of the Earth

composite beings. In the beings in question the Spirits of Form correspond to the physical body, the Spirits of Movement to the etheric body and the Spirits of Wisdom to the astral body. In addition, they have the Thrones as a kind of sentient soul, the Cherubim as intellectual soul and the Seraphim as consciousness soul: 'And just as we [human beings] look up to what we will only gradually acquire in future earthly ages, so do these beings look up to what towers above the being of the hierarchies. As we speak of our ... Spirit Self, Life Spirit and Spirit Man, so does this being look up to an archetypal spirituality from its seraphic member as we would from our vantage-point of the consciousness soul' (GA 136).

It is apparent from the context of the cycle that the only kind of beings who include both the spirit of the Earth and also similar spirits of other planets among their offspring are these composite beings. This supposition is confirmed when Rudolf Steiner finally indicates that behind each planet of our solar system there stands an ascending sequence of hierarchies beginning with the Spirits of Form and reaching up to the Seraphim. All these six-membered beings have their abode on the Sun, from where they guide the respective planets. (See ibid., 10 April 1912.)

The spirit of the Earth, who endows the whole of nature with its spiritual significance, has its origin in one of these composite beings. Rudolf Steiner describes this being's task in the following way: 'So just as the human ego perceives the physical earthly environment, the planetary spirit likewise perceives everything that is in the environment and in the world of space surrounding the planet, and orders the deeds of the planet and also the feeling of the planet ... in accordance with these perceptions out of the spatial world' (ibid., 4 April 1912). Thus the body of the Earth is enlivened and guided by the spirit of the Earth, who has its origin in one of these special beings inhabiting the Sun.

In accordance with these preparatory observations one can now make the attempt to investigate the original question as to the relationship of Christ to the spirit of the Earth. The analogy to man, as employed on numerous occasions by Rudolf Steiner, must again be taken as a point of departure. Man consists of three systems, those of the head, the heart and lungs, and the limbs. With regard to the spirit of the Earth, however, only the first two systems are mentioned. What is its relationship to the third? Rudolf Steiner describes how every person bears something in his body which he calls the 'focus of destruction in man'. This is necessary in order constantly to destroy matter in the human body. It lies behind the memory-mirror and was originally necessary for the forming and strengthening of man's ego. 'By what means does this ego arise? It is formed by man's capacity to plunge into the chaos of destruction. This ego must be forged and hardened in that world lying within man as a focus of destruction' (GA 207, 23 September 1921). This focus of destruction which is so necessary for the evolution of man can, however, at any time become a mighty source of evil within him, in so far as its forces find a way out and extend their influence: 'If what is within [man] were to spread out over the whole world, what would then live in the world through man? Evil! Evil is nothing other than the outward extension of the chaos that is necessary in man's inner being' (ibid.).

It is true that Rudolf Steiner mentions in the same lecture that the focus of destruction actually 'extends throughout the human organism', even though in another context he says that it is mainly concentrated in the limbs.[47] Hence it is understandable why Rudolf Steiner, in the words quoted above, only speaks of the head and the heart of the Earth spirit, though not of its limb system. For in the organism of the planetary Earth the focus of destruction functions in this system in the form of the layers of the Earth's interior together with their centre, as these have already been described in the present chapter. And just as in man the ego—if it does not succumb to evil—experiences a strengthening effect from the focus of destruction, the same is also true of the spirit of the Earth. As it remains uninfluenced by the evil in the interior of the Earth and, moreover, does not allow it to go beyond the bounds of the earthly body, it similarly receives a strengthening effect in its ego which it needs for its tasks in the cosmos.[48]

An altogether different situation presents itself for those human beings who have not been able to keep the forces of the destructive focus within permissible bounds and, hence, acquire a relentless tendency towards evil. 'The evil person carries it into the outer world; the good person keeps it inside him' (GA 207, 24 September 1921). Such an 'evil person' then becomes susceptible to the influences of the interior of the Earth and its various layers, as a result of which evil can be immeasurably intensified within him.

From this derives the special relationship that exists between man's inner being and the interior of the Earth. The understanding of this relationship can be further deepened if one bears the following in mind. In his characterization of the focus of destruction Rudolf Steiner also mentions that it lies behind the memory-mirror which protects man's soul from its influences. 'Thus the world that manifests itself as such a destructive focus lies within [man], beyond the memory-mirror' (ibid., 23 September 1921). We find something similar in the interior of the Earth. Here the seventh layer is referred to as an 'Earth mirror' (GA 97, 21 April 1906). It likewise to a certain extent protects the upper layers from the black-magical influences of evil coming from the core of the Earth. That this mirror acts as such an impermeable seal is evident from the fact that the vertical shafts or canals which connect the inner regions of the Earth with its surface extend only to the fifth layer (fruit Earth). As has already been described, the tectonic forces thrusting themselves up from the sixth layer (fire Earth) ascend upwards from this region, where they then cause earthquakes and volcanic eruptions. The seventh layer is accordingly the first that cannot exert a direct influence upon the surface of the Earth. Thus this layer forms an outer sheath for the two lowest layers, which already belong to the Earth's core. Hence Rudolf Steiner says that the transformation of the seventh layer is of particular importance: 'When our human race will have progressed so far that it will have produced the highest morality, everything anti-moral in this Earth mirror will have been overcome and transformed into something moral' (GA 96, 16 April 1906). Thus the path to the eventual transformation of the Earth's core has been opened up for human beings in our time.

However, this stage will be reached only if, in the course of earthly evolution, not only the ahrimanic but also the asuric powers have to a sufficient degree been overcome. For the forces of Ahriman extend only to the sixth layer: 'There he has the centre of his activity' (GA 107, 1 January 1909). Beneath this layer begin the regions whence the Asuras pre-eminently derive their forces of evil.[49] Here ordinary evil makes the transition to black magic, which 'consists above all in the misuse of the physical body' (ibid.). Hence Rudolf Steiner says: 'It is a fact that in certain schools of black magic such practices are taught very extensively. One of the most terrible perversions to which man may be subjected occurs when the forces of the physical body are taken as the starting point for occult training' (ibid.). For by this means man hands himself over not only to ahrimanic but to asuric powers, which have a direct connection with the Earth's core. Hence 'in the future, to be immoral will be possible only for individuals who are goaded in this direction, who are possessed by evil demons, by ahrimanic, asuric powers, and moreover aspire to be so' (GA 130, 1 October 1911).

And so, just as in the Earth's interior the fragmenter and the Earth's core itself—the centre of earthly evil—are behind the Earth mirror, so does the focus of destruction within man lie behind the memory-mirror, while at an even deeper level within man's being there resides the *potential tendency* towards every kind of evil which all human beings in our time carry in themselves as a microcosmic reflection of the core of the Earth. Rudolf Steiner says in this regard: 'Anyone who crosses the threshold has the experience that there is no crime of whatever kind to which every person, in so far as he belongs to the fifth post-Atlantean period, is not subconsciously prone. Whether in any particular case the inclination towards evil leads outwardly to an evil action depends upon entirely different circumstances and not upon the inclination itself' (GA 185, 26 October 1918). Hence above all the ahrimanic and asuric powers try to take possession of man and entice him into implementing the inner inclinations referred to. For it is not in the inclinations themselves but in the urge to deploy them outwardly that the forces of the Earth's interior are active in the human soul.[50]

However, a relationship to the interior of the Earth extending to its core is necessary, since from our time onwards man must begin to work consciously on its transformation. This work can be accomplished only if it is founded upon a new relationship to the Christ impulse, in order that—strengthened by Him—moral forces might ray out into all layers of the interior of the Earth. For man bears all these layers, reaching right to the Earth's core, within himself in the form of a reflection. If this were not so, he would never be able to transform the Earth. Only through the total purification of his soul will he be capable of enabling the forces of the highest good to stream into the focus of destruction residing within him, in order then to liberate and redeem the Earth even to its very centre out of the Christ impulse within his ego.[51]

A decisive task for earthly man with respect to the 'focus of destruction', and, hence, also the Earth's interior, results from this state of affairs: 'In this focus of destruction ... matter is truly annihilated. Matter is thrown back into its nothingness. Then if instead of giving rein to our instincts and impulses, which are bound to cultivate the development of egotism, we imbue the focus of destruction with moral, ethical ideals out of a moral attitude of soul, we can enable the good to arise within this nothingness. *Something new can then come into being.* In this very focus of destruction the seeds of future worlds spring forth' (GA 207, 24 September 1921).[52] In other words: if man works inwardly on the transforming of the focus of destruction and constantly changes its influences for the good, he is at the same time exerting an influence upon the interior of the Earth and its transformation. And as for the 'new' element which thereby merges within the Earth, Rudolf Steiner in the same lecture calls it the future Jupiter existence. 'In this Jupiter existence there will only be the new creation that is already being formed today in human beings out of moral ideals within this focus of destruction ...' And then he adds, as a word of warning: 'To be sure, [there will also be present what] works out of his anti-moral impulses, out of what works as evil from his egoity' (ibid.). For man as a free being is in our time, both in himself and in the world, indeed placed between good and evil.

It follows from this that not only man's own destiny but also that of the whole earthly planet depends upon his decision in this regard. For by working on himself he also transforms the entire Earth from within outwards through its nine layers. In this way man imbues all natural laws with his moral power. 'Within our inner being matter, and with it all the laws of nature, is annihilated. Material life, together with all the laws of nature, is thrown back into chaos, and out of the chaos a new nature is able to arise, saturated with the moral impulses that we impart to it from within ourselves' (ibid.). In this way the whole of the Earth's interior is gradually transformed and the Earth itself prepared for the Jupiter condition.

This transforming of the Earth out of the inner work of man upon himself is possible only if he freely and consciously takes the Christ impulse into himself. 'In the inner being of man are the seeds of future worlds. And if into these seeds human beings receive the Christ, heaven and Earth may pass away; but the Logos, the Christ, cannot pass away' (ibid.).

In anthroposophy, the modern 'knowledge of the Grail'—that is, 'the new initiation-knowledge centred around the Christ mystery' (GA 13)—was given so that man may be able consciously to take the Christ impulse into himself in our time. Through this means man can also gradually reach the goal of Earth evolution, which Rudolf Steiner describes thus: 'We see then that the "knowledge of the Grail" culminates in the highest imaginable ideal of human evolution: that of *spiritualization*, which man attains through his own efforts' (ibid.). Out of this spiritualization of man the spiritualization of the entire Earth will in the future be achieved through man's connection with the Christ.

Through Christ's 'Descent into Hell' and the union with the Earth that was associated with it, what He did in this respect for all human beings was accomplished also for the spirit of the Earth. He linked this spirit in a wholly new way with the divine being whence it originated on the Sun and thereby gave it a completely new possibility for evolution, which it needs for the future union of the Earth with the Sun. Until the Turning Point of Time the spirit of the Earth was merely the bearer of the meaning of nature. Now it has received the new Sun-meaning of the Earth planet. Rudolf Steiner brings this to expression in the following words: 'Before the Mystery of Golgotha the meaning of the Earth was on the Sun. Since the Mystery of Golgotha the meaning of the Earth has been united with the Earth itself. This is what anthroposophy would seek to bring to mankind as a perpetual Whitsun mystery' (GA 226, 17 May 1923).

What was instituted for human beings through the Whitsun event took place for the spirit of the Earth as a cosmic reality through Christ's descent into the interior of the Earth. The Earth thereby received the Sun impulse into itself, in order that it might again become united with the Sun at the end of the Earth aeon under the guidance of Christ.

This cosmic process can be clothed in the following picture, which wholly corresponds to the actual reality. Just as man in the course of his own evolution will, through the Grail initiation, gradually become a Christ bearer (in the same way that in the Grail mysteries the Moon chalice bears within itself the forces of the spiritual Sun), so will the spirit of the Earth likewise achieve its new goal with the help of those human beings who follow this inner path. In the same way it will, once the Moon is reunited with the Earth, then receive the spiritual Sun into this cosmic Moon chalice and hence bring about the union with the Sun, so that the Earth itself becomes the cosmic Grail in the universe.

Appendix: The Forces of the Phantom and Stigmatization

> 'People refuse to look into these more subtle aspects of the spiritual world. They very often want to perceive the spiritual not only through inner experiences but in what they behold outwardly. They want to perceive the spiritual in outwardly visible, sense-perceptible phenomena.'
>
> Rudolf Steiner, lecture of 20 August 1924

It follows from what was presented in the first chapter that the phenomenon of what is known as stigmatization[1]—as frequently encountered in the history of the Roman Catholic Church—has in itself no relationship to the phantom. For the bleeding wounds on the physical body form part of what happened *before* the Resurrection. After the Resurrection the phantom was no longer imbued with any material substance. It did indeed continue to bear the five bodily marks, but these have a completely different significance. They are the expression of the victory of the Ego over the physical body—and, hence, over death—and, as the spiritual sources of the power of Christ's Ego, are only supersensibly perceptible. They are signs of victory and no longer of suffering. Likewise, the points of densification on the etheric body of the Risen One (etheric 'scars') are of a supersensible, etheric nature and as such are unable to engender any material effect.

The appearance of the stigmata on the Christian-mystical path of initiation, which Rudolf Steiner describes in many of his lectures, has an altogether different significance. They merely indicate that the person undergoing initiation has through his inner exertions caused his soul to have a direct influence on his physical body. Such an influence is indeed striven for at the beginning of this path. Hence a pupil, in so far as he had rightly completed the first stage, had already arrived at the experience 'as though his feet were being dipped in water' (GA 97, 22 February 1907). It is important for Rudolf Steiner at this initial stage to refer to the *transitory* character of these *bodily* sensations: 'No one need fear this sensation, for it soon passes' (ibid.). Something similar happens at the second stage: the pupil 'sees himself in the vision of the scourging, and a similar sensation appears on the entire body'. And then Rudolf Steiner adds that 'this likewise passes'. At the third stage 'a new vision appears: the pupil sees himself as crowned with thorns. As an outward symptom, he experiences a kind of headache ...' But this symptom also soon fades. It should be pointed out that, at these and the further stages, the person being initiated experiences not Christ but himself as the one suffering in the situation described.

Now comes the fourth station, where the pupil acquires a completely objective relationship to his physical body. The pupil's body has to become 'like a piece of wood' which he carries like a heavy cross. Only once this stage has been reached and inwardly and comprehensively completed does a further experience arise. Then 'after weeks and months' of meditative exercises a new vision presents itself as a purely 'astral experience: he sees himself being crucified'. That the pupil has indeed risen to this stage is borne out by the following experience: 'As external signs, wounds—the stigmata—appear *for a short time* during meditation' (ibid.). And in another lecture Rudolf Steiner explains this process more precisely: 'These symptoms [the stigmata] appeared more frequently in periods of meditation' (GA 97, 3 February 1907). That is, when this stage is rightly accomplished—in accordance with the strength of the meditation—the stigmata appear and then also disappear again.

In a further lecture Rudolf Steiner describes the symptoms more exactly: 'The pupil is capable in meditation of *voluntarily* bringing forth the wounds on his body' (GA 100, 27 June 1907). That the pupil has his inner experiences constantly in hand and can consciously control them is what is decisive on this path. He also has the features that become visible on his body fully under control. For only in this way can he maintain his inner freedom and not for even a moment be at the mercy of forces which he does not fully comprehend.[2] Moreover, the stigmata themselves do not have a bloody aspect, as is familiar from Catholic contexts, but look quite tender and intimate, manifesting themselves simply as outward signs that the inner stage of the pupil's development that is in question here has indeed been reached. 'Red spots appear, which are reminiscent of the wounds of the Crucified One' (ibid.). In another context Rudolf Steiner expresses himself even more specifically: 'Red markings on the skin appear in certain places in such a way that the pupil can evoke the manifestation of the wounds of Christ, on the hands, the feet and on the right side of the chest' (GA 99, 6 June 1907).[3] An 'inner experience' is likewise associated with this: 'One sees *oneself* hanging on the Cross in astral vision' (GA 100, 27 June 1907). Rudolf Steiner calls this experience the 'trial by blood' (ibid.). If this trial is rightly undergone, the external features of the stigmata cease to be visible, for they do not belong to the further, higher stages of this initiation, where—as we shall see—there is an association no longer with the Crucifixion but with the Resurrection and also the Ascension.

Let us now summarize these descriptions of the 'trial by blood' (the fourth stage of the Christian-mystical path). If it takes its rightful course, the bodily symptoms do not resemble open, bleeding wounds but, rather, red spots, which only appear for a short time during meditation and then disappear again. They are voluntarily called forth by the meditant through his constant exercises and merely represent a temporary 'trial' on the further path to the higher stages of initiation.[4] It is also possible that they do not appear as a bodily phenomenon at all. At any rate, this could be deduced from the following words: 'The pupil then receives ... proper stigmata, which *can* temporarily manifest themselves'; 'can manifest themselves', or also not (GA 94, 11 July 1906). In the latter case they are only present inwardly and do not appear outwardly in visible form at all.[5]

What is of decisive significance here is that at this stage the red markings on the body are called forth by the inner strength of the spirit-pupil, who is therefore constantly in control of the whole situation. Rudolf Steiner indicates in this regard: 'He is able to bring about the reddening of his skin through the inner strength of his spirituality precisely in those places of his body which are associated with the wounds' (GA 284/285, 19 May 1907). This experience therefore has nothing to do with the permanent stigmata familiar from the Roman Catholic Church.

Rudolf Steiner also characterizes the spiritual experiences accompanying those bodily phenomena as 'astral visions' (GA 100, 27 June 1907). In them the pupil sees above all *himself* scourged, crowned with thorns and crucified. For where a rightful crossing of the threshold is concerned, one experiences the inner processes of one's own soul as objective facts, which are the first thing that one encounters in the spiritual world. Rudolf Steiner goes on to say: 'This is not merely an outwardly historical but a spiritual picture which every person can have [on this path]' (GA 284/285, 19 May 1907).

With regard to the bodily experiences described Rudolf Steiner emphasizes: 'It is not the [outward] symptoms that matter, for they arise *as a result of the exercises*' (GA 103, 30 May 1908–II). This makes it clear that on this path it is not the stigmata (and other bodily experiences) that are of importance but solely the objective of the whole path, which is only fully attained at the last two stages.[6] Rudolf Steiner describes this as follows: 'I have explained to you how Christian initiation was undergone. The pupil developed something called the "Christ-eye"'—a new supersensible organ with which Christ can be beheld in a purely spiritual way (not dependent on the senses). 'If you had no eyes, everything around you would be dark; and just as you would not be able to see the Sun without any eyes, you would not be able to perceive the Christ without the Christ-organ ... Human beings can develop the capacity of beholding Christ through the exercises which are being spoken of' (GA 100, 27 June 1907).

Furthermore, as a direct consequence of the whole path of initiation a state of being is arrived at which Rudolf Steiner summarizes as follows: 'When a person has lived through this seventh stage, Christianity will have become an inner experience of his soul. He is then wholly united with Christ Jesus; Christ Jesus is within him' (GA 95, 3 September 1906). Since in this description the last, seventh stage is called that of the 'Resurrection', it is obvious that the words 'Christ Jesus is within him' must also be understood in the sense of receiving the forces of the Resurrection body.

However, the path as a whole is not so much concerned with visions of events at the Turning Point of Time as with the acquiring of a purely spiritual (non-visionary) relationship to the living, *present* Christ, who as the spiritual Sun thenceforth irradiates the whole inner life of the pupil. In this way, the words from the Gospel 'And lo, I am with you always, to the close of the age' (Matthew 28:20) become for him a reality that he has experienced for himself.

The words about the Christ-eye were spoken shortly after Rudolf Steiner described the three further, still higher stages of this path of initiation: mystical death, the Resurrection (together with the Entombment that preceded it) and, lastly, the Ascension. These further stages no longer have anything to do with the outward signs of a stigmatization, for these, as already mentioned, appear 'only temporarily' at the fourth stage. Already at the fifth stage quite other inner processes are involved. In mystical death the pupil experiences how everything appears to his inner sight as 'plunged into the darkest darkness'. 'The whole sense-world is as though extinguished and sunk into oblivion' (GA 100, 27 June 1907). And the whole evil aspect of Earth evolution appears before his inner eye. All at once it is as though an inner curtain is rent before him, and for the first time he looks fully conscious 'up into the spiritual world' (ibid.).

All that he has already experienced is, however, far outweighed in its significance by the two concluding stages. At the sixth stage the pupil is united with the entire Earth. He experiences how 'the whole Earth still belongs to him' (ibid.). The sheer splendour of this experience is difficult to clothe in earthly words. The pupil experiences here that, since His death on the Cross, Christ 'has indeed become' the new 'Spirit of the Earth' (ibid.). From this point onwards the person being initiated bears co-responsibility for the entire future of the Earth. And as for the last stage Rudolf Steiner says: 'The seventh stage cannot be described further, for no human soul whose thinking is still brain-bound can comprehend the greatness and the sublimity of its significance' (GA 94, 11 July 1906). For 'it surpasses everything that man is capable of imagining' (GA 103, 30 May 1908–II) and signifies a 'complete absorption into the spiritual world' (ibid.).[7]

In his descriptions of the Christian-mystical path of initiation Rudolf Steiner also refers repeatedly to dangers which can, however, be avoided above all through the personal help and the constant assistance of an experienced spiritual teacher, who is therefore indispensable in this kind of initiation. Rudolf Steiner also emphasizes that with this initiation there is really only one hierophant, and that is Christ Jesus Himself. Nevertheless, the fact that Rudolf Steiner presents virtually all his descriptions of this path in the form of a teacher's instructions to his pupils makes it quite clear that earthly guidance is also needed.[8] And in the lecture of 3 June 1906 he expresses this quite clearly: 'The Christian schooling can take place with the advice of a teacher who knows what is to be done and who can always at every step put straight what has gone wrong' (GA 95).

The dangers of this path are especially great at the fourth stage, the 'trial by blood' (stigmatization). Rudolf Steiner reports: 'Then something occurs which is called the "trial by blood". *What in many cases might be a condition of sickness* is in this case [if the path of initiation is rightly followed] a consequence of meditation, because all sickness must be eliminated' (GA 103, 30 May 1908–II). Only as a result of pure and selfless meditation on the content of St John's Gospel is it permissible at this stage—and even so only for a short time—for red markings to appear on the five places of the body, for otherwise the pupil is in danger of 'a condition of sickness' which 'in many cases' can come over him. Hence Rudolf Steiner emphasizes in the same lecture: 'Care is also taken [probably by the accompanying teacher] that there is no question of suggestion and autosuggestion'. It follows from this observation that 'suggestion and autosuggestion' present a great danger especially at this stage, because one is working here with *bodily* symptoms and sensations.

At this point a short interpolation needs to be made. It has to do with the one single instance of stigmatization which, so far as is known, featured in the Anthroposophical Society during Rudolf Steiner's lifetime. The person in question was Richard Pollak (1867–1943), who came from a prosperous business family of Jewish origin in Prague and worked for several years with his wife Hilde on the ceiling paintings of the First Goetheanum. From his early youth onwards he had a strongly Christian orientation, and already during his art studies in Munich he ardently followed the Christian-mystical path of schooling. Shortly afterwards his body came to manifest the wounds, as Rudolf Steiner describes for this path. They were clearly to be seen in all places, though without any issue of blood. At the beginning of the century Richard Pollak came to Vienna, where he became acquainted with a friend of Rudolf Steiner's youth, Friedrich Eckstein, who introduced him to Rudolf Steiner's writings. Two years later Pollak for the first time heard a lecture by Rudolf Steiner, at whose request he moved with his wife to Dornach in 1914 for five years. As Richard Pollak was the only stigmatic who was closely connected with Rudolf Steiner, it is obvious that he must have discussed the phenomenon with him. It is possible that Richard Pollak gathered from such a conversation that in a previous life he had been a Franciscan. In any event, after they had returned from Dornach to Prague in the 1920s, his wife painted him in Franciscan clothes. When asked about this by a friend, Hilde Pollak replied: 'Richard had in this incarnation indeed taken on a Jewish bodily organism, but several decades ago the wounds of Christ appeared on his body, thus showing where he belonged as regards his inner nature. Nevertheless, he kept these phenomena hidden as far as possible. For he wants to be recognized not out of the reverberation of a former incarnation but from what he has achieved in the present one. You can experience for yourself how little he cares about himself.'[9] There is much to be said for the idea that this objectively distant attitude of Richard Pollak to his own stigmatization could have had its origin in the conversation with Rudolf Steiner or would have been supported by him. There is in this connection an oral record that Rudolf Steiner even gave Richard Pollak a special meditation which was to lead to the disappearance of the stigmata, whose appearance outside a rightly followed Christian-mystical path of initiation is not only inappropriate for the times but must be regarded as abnormal.[10]

However, what is most deeply stirring about Richard Pollak's destiny are not his stigmata but the moral greatness and true Christlike quality which this man showed in later years. After the Nazi invasion of Prague and the beginning of the persecution of the Jews, anthroposophical friends of the Pollaks gave them the prospect of escape. Richard Pollak's answer was along these lines: in this incarnation I have been born into the Jewish race; and in these difficult times I would not wish to separate myself from my destiny. When asked whether this made him sad—for Richard Pollak well knew what his decision signified—he replied: 'I am not sad. If one has had the good fortune to meet Rudolf Steiner in one's life, one can never again be sad.'

Shortly afterwards they were both arrested and initially taken to Theresienstadt. There and in another camp to which he was moved later, Richard Pollak gave more than one hundred lectures on anthroposophy to his fellow prisoners until he suffered a martyr's death. His wife was likewise put in an extermination camp after she refused to sew uniforms for German soldiers.

One experiences in this extraordinary human and anthroposophical destiny how the Christ impulse works in a very real way in a human being. The deeply Christian nature of Richard Pollak manifested itself not in stigmatization but in moral strength, in courage and faithfulness.

★

In the cycle *From Jesus to Christ* Rudolf Steiner brings the Christian-mystical path of initiation into connection with the being of the phantom. Having briefly characterized the seven stages of Christian-mystical initiation (significantly, the 'Resurrection' appeared as the seventh stage in this description), he said: 'When we do this ["drive our feelings into the physical body"] we are doing nothing less than *making ourselves ready* in our physical body gradually to receive the phantom that derives from the grave on Golgotha' (GA 131, 14 October 1911). In other words: at this fourth stage, one has 'made oneself ready ... gradually to receive the phantom'. What is being referred to here is simply the *preparation* of what will attain its full reality only at the further stages. Rudolf Steiner continues in this same sense: 'Hence we work into our physical body [on the path of innermost meditation] in order to make it so living that it *feels* an affinity, a force of attraction, towards the phantom' (ibid.). Here too it is merely a question of the *feeling* of a 'force of attraction' which is experienced in the physical body, representing only a preparatory stage.

Finally Rudolf Steiner expresses this even more clearly by describing it as follows: '... how an individual, through the corresponding feeling experiences of Christian initiation, *makes himself mature enough* to receive the phantom which rose from the grave on Golgotha'. Hence this 'state of maturity' is in point of fact extended to the *whole* sevenfold path of Christian-mystical initiation, at the end of which is the stage of the 'Resurrection', when the connection of the person undergoing initiation with the phantom is brought about. Whereas at the fourth stage, the *Bearing of the Cross*, one cannot as yet speak of an actual connection with the phantom, not least because—and this must again be reiterated—this stage of initiation reflects that stage of the Way of the Passion which lies *before* the Resurrection.

In this connection the following indication by Rudolf Steiner concerning the spiritual leadership of his first Esoteric School is of significance: 'The Master Jesus and the Master Christian Rosenkreutz have prepared two paths of initiation for us: the Christian-esoteric path and the Christian-Rosicrucian one. These two paths have existed ever since the Middle Ages' (GA 264, 1 June 1907). It follows from this that the greatest master of the Christian-mystical path is to this day Master Jesus. He himself travelled this path above all in the time before the inauguration of Rosicrucian initiation. 'Until that time Christian-mystical initiation was given to the Occident in the form in which it passed through its founder, the "Unknown One from the Highland", to St Victor, Meister Eckhart, Tauler, etc.' (GA 262, 'The Barr Manuscript', II.) The 'Unknown One' or 'Friend of God from the Highland' was the incarnation of Master Jesus in the fourteenth century, who was at that time following the Christian-mystical path together with his pupils. After his incarnation at the Turning Point of Time, when he was the most important witness of the Mystery of Golgotha, Christian Rosenkreutz likewise followed this Christian-mystical path in his further incarnations until the founding of Rosicrucianism in the thirteenth century. There is, however, no record that either of these two masters had ever received the stigmata.

It follows from what has been said that the only stigmata of which it is justified to speak are those that only appear temporarily on the fourth stage of the Christian-mystical path. They are, as already stated, always voluntarily called forth and become visible on the physical plane as a pure consequence of meditation. The situation is completely different with stigmata which are permanent and, moreover, manifest themselves as open, bleeding wounds.

The first historically proven case of this kind is, as is well known, that of Francis of Assisi (1181/82–1226). In this connection it is significant that wherever Rudolf Steiner ventured to speak about the occult antecedents of this individuality he never mentioned his stigmatization. This is, for example, even the case in the lecture of 28 May 1912, where he considers the biography of Francis of Assisi in the greatest detail. There he merely refers to how in this soul 'moral impulses had developed in such a manner that they were strengthened in a particular way in his meditations and appeared to him as the Cross with the Crucified One upon it. In these circumstances he felt an inner, personal relationship to the Cross and to the Christ, and from this there came to him the forces through which he could so immeasurably intensify the moral impulses which now flowed through him' (GA 155). Not a word about stigmatization! Nor was there any mention of it in other lectures, the listener's attention being focused exclusively on the universal, outstanding and well-nigh unique moral impulses that lived in Francis of Assisi's soul and were so mighty that he was able to heal even lepers who could not otherwise be cured out of his infinite forces of compassion and love.

Rudolf Steiner referred from a more esoteric standpoint to above all two occult aspects of Francis of Assisi's life. One of these was his pupilship with Gautama Buddha, who taught in a supersensible way at an esoteric school on the Black Sea in the seventh–eighth centuries AD. The future Francis of Assisi was at that time one of his most advanced pupils. 'The characteristic quality of Francis of Assisi and of the life of his monks—which has so much similarity with that of the disciples of the Buddha—is due to the circumstance that Francis of Assisi was a pupil of Buddha [in this esoteric school]' (GA 130, 18 December 1912).

The second, even more decisive aspect of Francis of Assisi's life was that it was granted him to receive a copy of the astral body of Christ Jesus in his own astral body. This—and not the stigmata—was for Rudolf Steiner what was most characteristic about St Francis. In several lectures he mentions this quality of St Francis's astral body as the real esoteric wellspring of this deeply Christian life and of its immense capacity for love. It was not the appearance of the bodily wounds but the high moral strength which he possessed through bearing a likeness of Jesus' astral body that was of central significance for Rudolf Steiner. With regard to Francis of Assisi's stigmata, it is known that they appeared only two years before his death and that he concealed them so carefully that they were only discovered on his dead body after he passed away.[11] It is, moreover, of significance that, after his life as Francis of Assisi, this individuality in his next incarnation died while still a little child and thereafter did not appear again on the Earth but followed his master, Gautama Buddha, to Mars in order to work further with him there. (See GA 130, 18 December 1912.)

Francis of Assisi was not the only person of his time who received this astral likeness. Elisabeth of Thuringia (1207–31)—and in a somewhat different way Thomas of Aquinas (1225/7–74) and surely some others—were the bearers of such an astral likeness in this epoch. Of his contemporaries, St Clare (1194–1253) also belonged to this category. According to tradition, when the two of them met for a conversation about spiritual matters the whole region was as though illumined by a heavenly light. This was called forth by the moral atmosphere which indeed surrounded them. Hence Francis of Assisi is so highly venerated in the cultural history of the West especially because of his morality.

The moral elevation that this individuality had attained in his incarnation as Francis of Assisi was in itself no guarantee that what he had in his head by way of intellectual content was on the same level as this morality. Rudolf Steiner says in this regard: 'What must sometimes strike us as being so strange especially in these personalities [the bearers of copies of the astral body of Christ Jesus] is that their ego development was often not on a par with what was living in their astral body ... There often seemed to be something grotesque about the way they behaved in their ego, whereas the world of their moods and feelings, together with their fervour, was magnificent and sublime' (GA 109/111, 15 February 1909). In another context Rudolf Steiner also mentions 'all his mistakes' (ibid., 6 April 1909), because the cognitive powers associated with his ego were not commensurate with the grandeur of his astral body. It follows from this that also the stigmata can never furnish a proof of what an individual can himself attain solely through the free development of higher cognitive powers.

This contrast between an imperfect ego and a perfect astral body—as was the case with Francis of Assisi—resulted from the fact that in his earthly life in the thirteenth century he had not undergone a proper Christian initiation but, rather, derived his extraordinary soul capacities above all from the astral copy that he bore within himself. Likewise during his schooling with Gautama Buddha in his previous incarnation it was more a question of the training of moral qualities than of true knowledge.[12]

Thus the discrepancy that manifested itself in the being of Francis of Assisi is a confirmation that by his time a true Christian-mystical initiation was no longer fully a possibility. Its heyday was in earlier centuries.[13] Hence the decision was made by the spiritual leadership of mankind[14] to found a new esoteric stream within Christendom in the middle of the thirteenth century, the aim of which was to correspond to present-day human beings and to their completely different inner faculties. This is the Rosicrucian stream, whence also the sevenfold path of initiation of anthroposophy is derived. This initiation is in our time the only one appropriate to people of the West who seek the Christ. For it is scarcely possible any longer to follow the Christian-mystical path of initiation, mainly for three reasons:

1. It demands the total isolation of the pupil from the outside world, which is not appropriate for people today.

2. It requires an intensity of the feeling life, which for a contemporary humanity increasingly orientated towards knowledge is no longer achievable.

3. It works directly with the forces of the physical body, which presents great dangers and therefore renders necessary the personal guidance of an experienced teacher, which is no longer appropriate for our time.

In order to avoid especially the great dangers that are associated with a *direct* influence upon the physical body, the opposite path was established by true Rosicrucians, one that strictly excludes from the outset any *direct* influence upon the physical body. (In Christian-mystical initiation, in contrast, there was a direct influence out of the realm of feeling upon the physical body, in order to evoke the bodily experiences described—which are no longer appropriate.) Of course, the transforming and spiritualizing of the physical body was also the ultimate aim of the Rosicrucian path. But in Rosicrucian initiation this happened by dint of purified cognitive forces *through the mediation of the spirit*, while fully maintaining individual freedom.[15]

The anthroposophical path of schooling (as a modern form, and continuation, of the Rosicrucian path) leads to the same goal as Christian-mystical initiation. However, it corresponds to all the characteristics and life-circumstances of people today: no physical teacher is needed any longer, individual freedom is unreservedly respected, and there is no direct influence upon the physical body (not even through the feelings).[16] For the foundation and the point of departure of modern initiation is the development and application of a pure, sense-free thinking, which leads man consciously out of the body with its sense-perceptions[17] in order on this wholly new path to lead to the same great goal: union with the Resurrection body of Christ.

Rudolf Steiner describes in the following words how the Rosicrucian—and, hence, by other means also the anthroposophical—path leads to this same goal: 'Through what has been characterized as Rosicrucian initiation, and through what an individual can experience by way of initiation today, the same thing is also attained in a certain sense, only by somewhat different means: a bond of attraction is formed between the individual—in so far as he is incarnated in a physical body—and that which arose as the true archetype of the physical body from the grave of Golgotha' (GA 131, 14 October 1911). Even in the formulation the difference as compared to the Christian-mystical path is apparent. What happens with this latter path is that the pupil 'feels a power of attraction' to the phantom; whereas on the Rosicrucian path a real 'bond of attraction [to it] is *formed*'.[18]

The difference in this respect between the Christian-mystical path and the modern continuation of the Rosicrucian path in anthroposophy is even greater. In this sense the appearance of vestiges of blood, especially if they are not of the kind that belong to a rightly followed Christian-mystical path, has to be judged differently and considered to be no longer appropriate. Above all, their appearance today has nothing to do with the Rosicrucian—and hence also the anthroposophical—path of initiation.

★

Everything that has been said so far can be investigated through the actual example of perhaps the most famous of Catholic stigmatics. This was Anna Katharina Emmerich (1774–1824), who lived at the turn of the century in Germany and whose visions have been made known through the reports of Clemens Brentano (1778–1842). The only remark that Rudolf Steiner made about her which has been handed down is of decisive significance. It is striking that in his vast legacy he never spoke once out of himself about Anna Katharina Emmerich. The only observation that he did make was prompted by a question about her that was directly put to him by a member of the audience after the cycle in Leipzig on *Egyptian Myths and Mysteries* (GA 106) on 14 September 1908. To this he gave a remarkable answer, which was formulated as follows: ' "Katharina Emmerich" by Clemens v. Brentano? The sightings recorded here are of an exceptionally good somnambulist. Especially the parts which relate to mirror-vision have without any doubt something extraordinarily right about them.'[19]

Anna Katharina Emmerich reports that on several occasions she was on a 'time-journey'—as one might call it—to the events of the Turning Point of Time, in order that she might participate in them by means of *sensory perceptions*, that is, with all five bodily senses: seeing, hearing, smelling and so on. She then shared these 'sense' experiences from the past with Clemens Brentano, who committed them to paper and later published them. However, such 'time-journeys' are, from a spiritual-scientific point of view, none other than a particular form of somnambulism.

In a lecture where Rudolf Steiner explains the origin and nature of somnambulism from the spiritual-scientific point of view, he mentions how in certain forms of this state of being the following occurs. 'The ego [of a somnambulist] has the opportunity to become more involved with its environment. It is not embedded in the system of ganglia and is therefore free to make use of channels to the outside world which enable it to perceive from a distance all kinds of processes in space and *in time* which, when it is embedded in the system of ganglia, are processes which

Appendix: The Forces of the Phantom and Stigmatization 145

it cannot normally perceive' (GA 174, 14 January 1917). As 'an exceptionally good somnambulist' Anna Katharina Emmerich was also in this way able to carry out her 'time-journeys' to the Turning Point of Time and beyond, even to the creation of man in paradise. Thus when Rudolf Steiner is characterizing the nature of Anna Katharina Emmerich's spiritual experiences, he uses not the word 'visions' (*Visionen*) but 'sightings' (*Gesichte*).[*] For the former can also relate to the purely spiritual world, whereas the latter are mainly associated with perceptions from the sense world, hence their strong relationship to the physical body.

In this respect Rudolf Steiner characterizes the nature of somnambulism in another lecture as follows: 'Whereas an individual in normal life is in contact with his environment only through his senses, in the case of the somnambulist ... the whole person is connected with his environment through the mechanism of his will. This makes it possible for influences from a distance to have an effect, a thought can extend its influence into the distance, and *distant* spatial and *temporal vistas* can open up.'[20] Thus with certain somnambulists there is an inner tendency for 'the whole man to be as it were transformed into sense-organs, with the result that *automatic and temporal sightings from a distance* arise. Their foundation is always a sick or enfeebled life of soul. They have nothing to do with the world to which man belongs with the immortal part of his being; they have to do with the spiritual aspect of the physical environment of the senses, and specifically with what the human will enacts there' (ibid.).

In both quotations Rudolf Steiner speaks either of the 'mechanism of the will' or of 'automatically' appearing vistas. For as is evident above all in the case of Anna Katharina Emmerich, though also in that of Therese Neumann from Konnersreuth (1898–1962), who was stigmatized in the twentieth century, such people can never become masters of their 'sightings', which engulf them mainly during Passiontide, though sometimes every week with the intensity of natural phenomena, totally claiming all their physical, soul and spiritual forces. In such circumstances there can be no question whatever of human freedom, which must be the highest requirement of every modern initiation from the outset and at all its further stages.

As a person of today one can of course have one's own opinion about the 'sightings' of Anna Katharina Emmerich or Therese Neumann; one

---

[*] The German word used here has no exact English equivalent in the present context. In the present translator's view, 'sightings' seems to convey the meaning better than any other word. However, it is not always used here to render the German word in question, or its compounds. In another context, 'visions' could be an appropriate translation, but this is specifically ruled out here.—Translator

can find them fascinating and even worthy of admiration, and consider them true and authentic, because the stigmata have been adduced as proof of their genuineness. However, one can also sense that their descriptions are—at least to some extent—thoroughly odd, above all through the fact that the spiritual dimension of the Christ event, which for Rudolf Steiner was always its most important aspect, comes to the fore in only a very limited way. It is clearly apparent that the sufferings of the human being Jesus have more weight for Anna Katharina Emmerich than the actual mystery of the Christ.[21] As one becomes familiar with the experiences that she reports, it is difficult to avoid the impression that the actual step from Jesus to Christ was not really fully taken in her inner experience.[22]

Rudolf Steiner on the other hand, above all in the lectures on the Fifth Gospel, makes every possible effort to point out that the Mystery of Golgotha is not only an affair of human beings on the Earth but also, and quite especially, one of the Gods themselves—an affair of the spiritual world. 'We must imbue ourselves ever more deeply with the notion that in the Mystery of Golgotha we are beholding an affair of the Gods' (GA 148, 18 December 1913). Rudolf Steiner speaks in this regard of the 'anxiety and fear' of the Gods (ibid.) at the time of the Mystery of Golgotha that because of the increasing influence of the adversarial powers the whole evolution of mankind could be led onto a false track. And in the 'sweat of anguish upon the brow' of Christ Jesus on the Mount of Olives (GA 148, 3 October 1913) we must also see a reflection of this anxiety of the Gods over the future of mankind as a whole. This decisive cosmic dimension of the events of the Turning Point of Time is almost completely absent in the accounts of Anna Katharina Emmerich and Therese Neumann.

For this and also many other reasons, one has to ask from an anthroposophical standpoint the thoroughly important question: why are these 'sightings' in a multitude of instances different in content, and even often contradictory, to Rudolf Steiner's spiritual research, as regards not only the point mentioned above but also many of its other areas? Out of the many examples which show that Anna Katharina Emmerich's experiences are at variance with the results of Rudolf Steiner's research, four will be mentioned here:

- She states that the form of the Cross on which Jesus was crucified did not have the form of a cross but that of the letter 'Y'. This corresponds neither to Christian tradition nor to the fruits of Rudolf Steiner's research. In all his pictures and sketches Rudolf Steiner constantly used only the true form of the Cross: †. (See his water-

Appendix: The Forces of the Phantom and Stigmatization   147

colour painting 'Three Crosses (Easter)', his pastel sketch for the Christ motif in the small cupola and the sketches for the rose and violet window in the north.) Rudolf Steiner also confirms the corresponding artistic tradition through the spiritual-scientifically deduced fact that the painters who established it bore within themselves copies of the etheric body of Jesus and were therefore able to behold the true imaginations of the events of the Turning Point of Time. (See GA 109/111, 7 March 1909.) However, the tradition of the cross is still older and goes back to Plato's mystery-imagination of the world cross with the world soul crucified upon it. (See GA 105, 12 August 1908.) In this connection it is important that, at the founding of the Rosicrucian Order in the fourteenth century, Christian Rosenkreutz gave his pupils this familiar form of the Cross, though surrounded by seven roses. In his book *An Outline of Occult Science* Rudolf Steiner forms a link with this through the Rose-Cross Meditation. If one now bears in mind that Christian Rosenkreutz was personally 'present at the Mystery of Golgotha' (GA 130, 27 January 1912), that is, he saw the Cross with his own eyes and communicated its true form to his pupils, how is it then possible that Anna Katharina Emmerich speaks of a completely different form of the Cross? It is fairly obvious that, although she beheld her sightings with her physical eyes, she must nonetheless have seen incorrectly.

- Anna Katharina Emmerich also describes the Grail chalice used by Christ Jesus during the Last Supper, in contrast to esoteric Grail tradition, as having a very complicated structure. According to her, it was made from an unknown metallic material, coated with gold, had a pearlike shape and contained a smaller chalice. At the base of the larger chalice there was a place for a small spoon and a little table which could be pulled out. The big chalice was, in addition, surrounded by six small bowls. However, Rudolf Steiner clearly states, in accordance with all Grail traditions: 'The sacred jasper cup of the Holy Grail which Christ made use of when He broke the bread ...' (GA 26). Thus there was a simple chalice, as has always been indicated from earliest Christian times. (See also GA 112, 24 June 1909.)

- Jesus' Baptism, which all four Gospels, Rudolf Steiner's spiritual research and innumerable works of art indicate as having taken place in the River Jordan, happened according to Anna Katharina Emmerich on an island which miraculously came into being for this purpose, with a natural pool in the middle in which the Baptism was enacted. Moreover, what is most essential about the Baptism, namely the union of the cosmic Christ with the bodily sheaths of Jesus of Nazareth, is lost to Anna Katharina Emmerich's view behind a multitude of often fancifully suggested details. In her sightings Christ came to Earth not with the Baptism but with Jesus' birth. In other words, she does not know the difference between Christ and Jesus.

- Anna Katharina Emmerich beholds the scene in Gethsemane in such a way that Christ will take upon Himself all the subjective sins of human individuals in the past, present and future. From this it becomes clear that she cannot distinguish the decisive difference between subjective karma, for which every human being must himself make compensation, and objective karma, which Christ takes upon Himself. (See in this regard GA 155, 15 July 1914.)[23]

On a fundamental level, every anthroposophist who is well familiar with Rudolf Steiner's Christological research—and especially his reports from the Fifth Gospel (GA 148)—will immediately recognize in them a *completely different spirit* from what was beheld and described by Anna Katharina Emmerich. It is also striking to what extent the pure spirit which reigns in Rudolf Steiner's research along these lines is utterly similar to that of the four other Gospels, which is why the name 'Fifth' Gospel is absolutely justified; whereas the descriptions of Anna Katharina Emmerich and Therese Neumann are of a different kind and are imbued with a spirit that is alien to the five Gospels.[24]

Nor can the argument be adduced with regard to Anna Katharina Emmerich's sightings that she may perhaps herself have been incarnated at the Turning Point of Time and that she bore memories of this time in her etheric body.[25] For in what she communicates she often gives an account of scenes and conversations which no one else around Christ Jesus could have experienced or shared in some way. Similarly, she describes in detail the youth of Mary and Jesus, episodes from the life of the Patriarchs, even Adam's experiences before the Fall—and all this in the same sense-perceptible manner as her sightings of the events at the Turning Point of Time. Only in this sensory way is Anna Katharina Emmerich able to perceive both physical and spiritual events (for example, what happened in paradise). It follows from this that what she describes has nothing to do with memories deriving from her own etheric body but, rather, with a certain form of somnambulistic experience.

Thus with respect to such sense-perceptible sightings several questions need to be resolved. However, for an anthroposophist one thing is absolutely clear: *all this has nothing to do with anthroposophy and its spiritual-scientific research!* And if such somnambulistic 'methods of research' enter into anthroposophy and become widespread within it, this would mean the abandonment of the spiritual-scientific method of research and, hence, the end of anthroposophy as spiritual science.

With regard to such phenomena, Rudolf Steiner himself clearly refers to two dangers which arise here. Firstly, that of sensationalism. For 'what the spirit-researcher has to do in order to penetrate into the world of the spirit is not so entertaining, interesting or demanding of attention as the experiences of a somnambulist' (GA 72, 28 November 1917). Hence it can easily happen that someone may find descriptions of the nature of an Anna Katharina Emmerich—not least because they work directly on the feelings—far more impressive that the content of the Fifth Gospel.

Secondly, there is the far greater danger that such a somnambulistic seeress would in certain places give voice to utterly correct facts. But as these can never be verified by her and she does not know their source, what she imparts is for the most part mixed up with numerous mistakes and errors. For even in the *process of the origination* of such sightings, it is never possible for alien influences and interferences to be completely excluded. 'Somnambulistic consciousness in a certain sense produces similar teachings [to 'theosophical' ones[26]], and what a somnambulistic individual can see by eliminating the lucidity of waking consciousness is often the same as a [rightly schooled] clairvoyant sees with his lucid waking consciousness. But the somnambulist is never able to verify what she sees ... She cannot even verify whether what she perceives is indeed the truth in the way that she perceives it.'[27] Nevertheless—and this belongs to the psychic qualities of somnambulism—somnambulists are for the most part convinced of the 'truth' of everything that is revealed to them in this way from sources that they do not understand. This was, moreover, precisely the state in which Anna Katharina Emmerich was with regard to what she perceived. The times in which she had inwardly completely segregated her sightings from her earthly surroundings were those that she experienced as moments of the highest grace in which it was neither possible nor permissible to doubt.

Moreover, she could not for a moment question what she saw (not least because she perceived her sightings directly with 'physical eyes' and other sense-organs), just as any ordinary person never doubts his sense-perceptions[28] but considers them to be the full reality. However, what somnambulists do not notice is that 'whereas people are in this way led into a state where something is revealed to them which would otherwise remain concealed, they are themselves obliged to forfeit a stage that they have attained [in their waking consciousness]' (ibid.).

For this reason Rudolf Steiner frequently emphasizes that, especially in our time, it is not only of importance whether perceptions of the spiritual world are true or false but, above all, in what way they were arrived at. Hence any mingling of what was received on somnambulistic paths with the fruits of anthroposophical spiritual-scientific research can only work to the latter's detriment.

In the case of Anna Katharina Emmerich, whose sightings were unmistakably Roman Catholic in spirit, there arises the additional danger—to which Rudolf Steiner likewise referred—of the 'Catholicisation' of anthroposophy itself, which needs to be prevented in every way possible.[29]

*

It is revealing in this connection that Anna Katharina Emmerich, with her sensory perceptions of the Turning Point of Time, was almost exactly the same age as Novalis. Moreover, Clemens Brentano, who subsequently recorded her sightings in written form, in his youth belonged to the circle of early Jena romantics, where he quite possibly met Novalis—who was a little older than he was—personally.

After his sudden initiation at the grave of his dead bride Sophie von Kühn, Novalis experienced a richness of imaginations, inspirations and even intuitions with respect to the events of the Turning Point of Time. However, his spiritual experiences were no 'time-journeys' but the justified consequences of his particular Christian initiation. Novalis could supersensibly behold the mysteries of Christ's life, the life of Mary and the Mystery of Golgotha—mysteries which he brought to expression in wonderful poems and prose works—not with his physical senses but with his 'Christ-eye' bestowed upon him as though by grace. Thus Rudolf Steiner devoted dozens of lectures to Novalis and his initiation experiences, culminating in the final legacy of his 'Last Address', where he describes him as 'a radiant forerunner ... of [the] Michael stream' and, hence, of the whole of anthroposophy (GA 238, 28 September 1924). For the spiritual experiences of Novalis lie absolutely in the mainstream of the anthroposophical path of schooling, whereas those of Anna Katharina Emmerich are essentially alien to this path. The reason is that Novalis did not for a single moment in his life fall victim to a somnambulistic state in order to behold the events of the Turning Point of Time as sensory sightings. On the contrary, he always experienced them through the higher cognitive forces that had awoken in him, of which he himself spoke and wrote.[30] Moreover, his spiritual experiences never involved the slightest dulling of his ego consciousness, which illumined everything around him in the spiritual world like a bright star.

Appendix: The Forces of the Phantom and Stigmatization

From what has been said it becomes understandable why Rudolf Steiner never mentioned Anna Katharina Emmerich in any of his writings or lectures. Quite apart from the true or erroneous nature of her sightings, it is above all the *way* in which she arrived at her perceptions that is not merely fundamentally different from but completely opposed to the research methods of anthroposophy.[31] For in the case of Anna Katharina Emmerich (and later also of Therese Neumannn) everything that was beheld passed through the physical senses and was therefore body-bound, as is characteristic of this kind of somnambulism. Thus for the moments of such time-journeys their ordinary waking consciousness was 'thrust down' to a deeper level, as Rudolf Steiner puts it.

However, the anthroposophical path of schooling goes in the opposite direction. As we have seen, the pupil arrives on the path of pure thinking to a purely spiritual, sense-free perception of the spiritual world, and from thence—through reading in the Akashic Record—also to sharing in the experience of earthly events.

One can find an exact example of this in the way that the central figure of Rudolf Steiner's sculptural Group came into being. In a conversation with Friedrich Rittelmeyer (1872–1938) in the spring of 1915, Rudolf Steiner confirmed the latter's experience that, through pure meditation, one can come to the inner experience of what Christ actually looked like in Palestine. When Rittelmeyer asked further, Rudolf Steiner began to describe Christ's appearance.[32] Thus, for instance, he said about His mouth: '*When I saw it for the first time*, I had the impression: this mouth has never eaten food, but has been proclaiming divine truths from all eternity.'[33] And in response to a further query from Rittelmeyer as to whether such an image already existed and could be seen, Rudolf Steiner explained: 'That is why I have told an artist in Dornach to make a model of Christ *in accordance with my indications*' (ibid.). This refers to the sculptress Edith Maryon (1872–1924), who, as Rudolf Steiner's selfless and executive hand, had dedicated herself to this task. But where it concerned the figure of Christ Himself, Rudolf Steiner always worked alone, without any help. Thus he fashioned all three sculptures of Christ's head *with his own hands*: the first small one in autumn 1914, the life-size one—also in plasticine—around Easter 1915 and finally, in accordance with this model, the wooden one which formed the central figure of the Sculptural Group. This is attested by the two photographs showing him at work.[34]

Rudolf Steiner could directly behold this figure of Christ in the spiritual world through the 'Christ-eye' (mentioned earlier in connection with the Christian-mystical path), which Rudolf Steiner had himself acquired on the modern Rosicrucian path. It was from this mode of perception that above all the life-size bust of Christ arose, which was then translated into the wood of the Group. Friedrich Rittelmeyer reports: 'At that time [summer 1915] there was only a bust of Christ in plasticine modelled by Rudolf Steiner himself,' (ibid.). Thus he engraved Christ's countenance upon earthly substance directly from his supersensible perception. He would therefore repeatedly say to those visiting his studio, referring to this bust and subsequently to the central figure of the sculptural Group: 'This is how I see Him.'[35]

Similarly in the public lecture of 29 June 1921, 'Goethe and the Goetheanum', he expressed himself unambiguously with regard to the same motif in the painting that he did in the eastern part of the small cupola: 'One can imagine this figure (the painted image of the Representative of Humanity) as the Christ. I have formed it as a Christ figure wholly out of my own perception ... It is the Christ, as He presented Himself to me in spiritual contemplation.'[36]

In other words, it is always a question here of a *present* experience of Christ, out of which the great Christian initiate of our time beholds His countenance and seeks to impart it to all human beings in this artistically liberating form.[37] Rudolf Steiner also describes how the whole sculptural Group with all its figures was fashioned by him out of a spiritual experiencing of the course of the year as a mighty Easter imagination. In this sense both the Christ motifs of the First Goetheanum, the painted and the sculptural forms, represent 'the figure of Christ freeing Himself from matter' and overcoming the forces of Lucifer and Ahriman in the natural world both today and on into the future. It is 'the image of Christ ... that is born out of cosmic happenings in the course of the year' (GA 229, 7 October 1923).

What is expressed here is not at variance with the fact that Rudolf Steiner also said of the same figure of the sculptural Group: 'This is how Christ walked the Earth in the human being Jesus of Nazareth in Palestine at the beginning of our era ... Here the endeavour has been to create a true likeness of Christ' (GA 194, 13 December 1919). This apparent contradiction is resolved through words spoken by Rudolf Steiner and passed on by Heinz Müller as he was describing his visit to the studio: 'Then Rudolf Steiner also spoke about the similarity between his [plasticine] study and the countenance of Christ. If one encounters Him in the spiritual world, the first impression is that He changes to a most surprising degree with every thought, feeling and will impulse ... Now as His Being dwells freely in the etheric heights independent from the body of Jesus of Nazareth, this constant changing of His countenance, and indeed of His whole figure, increases still further.'[38] Through this description all further 'contradictions' which may result from Rudolf Steiner's various testimonies about his sculptural Group also resolve themselves. Thus, for example, that in its central figure the Christ is depicted immediately after the Baptism in the Jordan, at the time of the Temptation in the wilderness, during the three years of His earthly life and finally after the Resurrection. For in the etheric body of the Risen One the whole life of Christ Jesus on Earth lives as a memory. And this memory appears in all its phases, spiritually reflected by the phantom, in the 'constant changing of His countenance'. 'But nevertheless,' Heinz Müller continues, 'Rudolf Steiner gave the assurance that both the sculpture and also the coloured portrayals of the Representative of Humanity [what is meant here is the Christ figure in the paintings on the ceiling] were fashioned in such a way that, if one were to meet Him, one would inevitably recognize Him at once. Thus here too [as with the depiction of the counter-forces] one may speak absolutely of a kind of likeness in the portrait' (ibid.).

'If one were to meet Him'—with these words Rudolf Steiner refers again to his direct, and for our time quite unique, relationship to the living Christ in the spiritual world, that is, to the Risen Christ in His *eternal presence* in the sense of the words that Rudolf Steiner so often quoted: 'And lo, I am with you always, to the close of the age' (Matthew 28:20). Thus through the constant changeability of His countenance this presence of Christ encompasses also all stages of His earthly life at the Turning Point of Time.

This does not exclude in any way Rudolf Steiner's research in the Akashic Record as regards the appearance of Christ Jesus at the time of His life in Palestine, which he did indeed carry out. However, what was most important about this was that he always did this research out of an inner connection with the present Christ. On one occasion he expressed himself very clearly about this: 'In the moment that I imbue myself with Christ, when I research the Akashic Record with Him, I discover the fact [that I am seeking] ... For only being imbued with the Christ impulse makes the soul capable of seeing things [in the Akashic Record] as they really are' (GA 155, 15 July 1914). Thus out of the constant presence of Christ in his soul he was able to portray the entire past and future of human evolution, often extending even to the smallest physical details. Many people, especially those who were able to hear his discourses about the Fifth Gospel (but also his other Christological lectures) therefore felt what Friedrich Rittelmeyer brought to expression in the following way: 'Then it was that I experienced how one speaks of Christ in the presence of Christ.'[39]

We are dealing here with the decisive principle pertaining in our time to the path leading to a true knowledge of the Christ Being. The Christ must first always be found in His eternal *present*. Only if He is experienced in *this* form as the highest God of the human ego can an understanding in accordance with the spirit of the Mystery of Golgotha, and the whole future evolution arising from it, be reached. For a true insight into the past and future of world evolution and the history of mankind is revealed only in the presence of the *living Christ*. Otherwise, the spirit-researcher is never sure whether Lucifer or Ahriman creep in unnoticed and obscure or even distort his gaze.

From this it follows that Rudolf Steiner always beheld Christ *in the present* in connection with His Resurrection body. That he was able to do this is to be explained by the conclusive experience of his Christian-Rosicrucian initiation, through which at the turn of the century he experienced Christ in Intuition. But because this highest form of knowledge leads to an experience of the physical (though from the spiritual aspect), he was in a position to understand the entire significance of the Mystery of Golgotha from his own experience. 'Having thus come through Intuition to a knowledge of Christ in the spiritual world, the pupil will find that he is able also to understand what took place historically on Earth in the fourth post-Atlantean period.' This is how he described this experience himself in a wholly objective form in the book *An Outline of Occult Science* (GA 13, p. 296). Rudolf Steiner then gives a personal testimony of how concretely this happened in his own initiation: 'My soul development rested upon the fact that I had stood in spirit before the Mystery of Golgotha in the most inward, most earnest celebration of knowledge' (GA 28, ch. 26).[40]

From an esoteric standpoint one can stand before the Mystery of Golgotha *in the spirit* only if one has in full consciousness taken the forces of the Resurrection body into one's own being and transformed them into new forces of cognition. This is why Rudolf Steiner speaks in this connection of a 'celebration of knowledge'. Here we have the principal source of all the anthroposophical spiritual research of Rudolf Steiner.[41] He could consciously and independently research all regions of the spiritual world and also describe faithfully and accurately the earthly events taking place at the Turning Point of Time out of his intuitive knowledge not, like the 'exceptionally good somnambulist' Anna Katharina Emmerich, with physical senses but with the spiritual organs of perception of the Resurrection body. The lectures on the Fifth Gospel form a supreme example of this. Moreover, by creating the supersensible Foundation Stone of Love at the Christmas Conference and the Foundation Stone Meditation that is inseparably connected with it, Rudolf

Steiner made the modern meditative path to spiritual communion accessible to all human beings, enabling them inwardly to gain knowledge of and participate in the whole reality of the Resurrection from their own experience.

At this point it must once again be emphasized that man's true relationship to the Resurrection body of Christ does indeed bring about the exact opposite to what can be observed in the example of Anna Katharina Emmerich. By uniting with the Resurrection body one perceives the events of the Turning Point of Time not with physical eyes and other bodily senses but *in a purely spiritual way*, with the exalted supersensible forces which Christ Himself brought to the Earth out of the realm of the Cosmic Midnight Hour (see chapters 1 and 2). Rudolf Steiner's spiritual research taken as a whole stands as a testimony of what this actually means—and this applies pre-eminently to what he imparted about the earthly life of Christ Jesus out of the Fifth Gospel.

Anna Katharina Emmerich's sightings can be understood from an anthroposophical standpoint as follows. According to Rudolf Steiner the *true* Akashic Record manifests itself only from the fourth realm of the spirit-land onwards.[42] However, its origin lies in yet higher spheres. This surest aspect is accessible to the spirit-researcher if he reaches the stage of modern initiation where it becomes possible for him to read the Akashic Record not from the earthly but from the cosmic aspect, that is, from a standpoint lying beyond the fixed stars. Rudolf Steiner speaks of this as follows: 'One reads the Akashic Record no longer from the earthly side but from the heavenly aspect; it becomes the occult script of the stars. One gains insight into the inner regions of the starry sphere, and acquires a feeling for the wellspring of the universe, the Logos' (GA 94, 8 June 1906). This is the plane of the Akashic Record, where it is itself permeated with the forces of the cosmic Word and where Rudolf Steiner mainly undertook his research, because this plane offers the greater security for the spirit-researcher. 'The Akashic Record can indeed be found in Devachan, but it extends down into the astral world, with the result that in this lower world pictures from the Akashic Record may often be like a mirage' (GA 99, 28 May 1907). It is obviously the case that distinguishing between truth and falsehood in this astral reflection of the Akashic Record is extraordinarily difficult.

However, this 'mirage' of the Akashic Record can descend to a still deeper level. Thus it can be reflected back as though from below through the Moon sphere. For what is characteristic about this Moon sphere is 'that the Moon actually reflects back *everything* that is in the cosmos, not merely the light of the Sun but actually everything' (GA 225, 23 September 1923). And because this Moon sphere itself belongs to the lowest regions of the astral world, it mirrors back among other things also the lower (astral) Akashic Record. So when Rudolf Steiner characterizes the sightings of Anna Katharina Emmerich he speaks of a 'mirror-vision', because she sees in the Moon sphere only the astral mirror images of the true Akashic Record (and even only individual 'parts' of it).

Because the Moon sphere borders upon the physical world of the senses, it has in itself a further quality: everything that is reflected back is similar to earthly sense-perceptions. Everything reflected by it appears to be material, as though one could actually perceive these mirror images with physical eyes and other bodily senses. And because somnambulists have—through their whole constitution of body and soul—an involvement with Moon forces, they are gripped and subconsciously imbued by them with particular ease.

In a case where a somnambulist has a constitutional weakness between the etheric and astral bodies, that is, when her ego is attracted by Moon forces and only takes her astral body with her and not the etheric body, the person concerned falls into a kind of waking dream and can do all manner of things in the earthly world with her physical and etheric bodies without being aware of it.

If, however, there is an organic weakness between the physical and etheric bodies,[43] such a somnambulistic individual no longer carries out dreamy outward movements but begins to perceive various facts from the mirroring of the Moon sphere, that is, to perceive in the reflected Akashic Record the distant vistas opening up in spatial and temporal sightings from the past. Then what has been beheld in the lunar mirror penetrates into the physical body, though now not as sense-impressions from without but comes before the senses from within, so that what was beheld in the Akashic Record—which one cannot otherwise perceive physically—appears before the soul in the form of sensory phenomena.[44]

What in the true Akashic Record has long become spiritual in the upper regions of Devachan and can be experienced only in a spiritual way becomes perceptible with, as it were, physical senses in the process described. Consequently, the spiritual element appears as though marked by physical qualities, as is the case in permanent stigmatization. And somnambulists who perceive such sensory sightings enter into the situation whereby, instead of reaching the spiritual world, they are influenced still more strongly by the physical body and are connected all the more closely with it. During the time of the sightings their experiences are translated to a stage lower than normal waking consciousness. Hence Rudolf Steiner emphasizes: 'What principally comes to expression on this

Appendix: The Forces of the Phantom and Stigmatization 157

path [where 'temporal distant vistas' appear] derives from the physical surroundings', even when these surroundings—through the lunar reflection of the Akashic Record which has been described—manifest themselves as the events of the Turning Point of Time. Irrespective of whether it is the present or the past that is becoming perceptible, one does not, therefore, escape from the physical domain.[45] Thus anyone who perceives these sightings remains unfree in them. 'The result is that, because of the exclusion of consciousness, the person concerned becomes like an automaton [for the time that the sightings are being experienced], and that actually only what belongs outwardly to cultural or moral life comes to expression in this person who is becoming like an automaton' (GA 67, 21 March 1918).[46]

The inner lack of freedom which befalls a person here brings a deeply unchristian element into such an approach to the events of the Turning Point of Time. For the living, present Christ wholly respects human freedom and does not do anything today that stands in contradiction to it. Thus one of Rudolf Steiner's profoundest Christological insights is here clothed in these words: 'That we can be free beings we owe to a divine deed of love. As human beings we may feel ourselves to be free, but we should never forget that we owe this freedom ... to the Christ!' (GA 131, 14 October 1911). Can one imagine that He who brought freedom to us human beings through His immeasurable sacrifice would take it away again in one way or another? But it is just this which happens with Anna Katharina Emmerich and Therese Neumann in the moments of their 'time-journeys'. For in these moments they are completely taken up by their sightings and wholly overpowered by them.[47] The sensory sightings come before their souls as though with an iron necessity, whether the somnambulist wants to see them or not. It follows from this that in such sightings are active not the pure Christ forces, to which the Sun nature inherently belongs, but the Moon forces which reflect them in the cosmos.[48]

Nevertheless, such sensory sightings exert such a fascination upon people today because they have been allowed to remain out and out materialists, who are used to perceive their surroundings with their five senses and judge them only from this *bodily* standpoint. Such people are then gladly prepared to accept also the events of the Turning Point of Time from this purely physical standpoint and even to be enthusiastic about this. However, this merely encourages the further spread of materialism amongst mankind and does not, therefore, harmonize with the impulse of the present living Christ.

Modern spiritual science, on the other hand, aspires to bring man to a body-free perception of the spiritual world in a manner appropriate to the present Michaelic Time Spirit, namely through pure thinking. That is to say, it seeks to a quite definite degree to overcome what is associated with the activity of the five senses in order to arrive at a sense-free experience of the spirit. That this is at all possible today can be attributed by human beings to Christ's Ascension (see chapter 1). The consequence, moreover, of all this is the encounter with the Etheric Christ. It follows from what has been said that one cannot in any way compare the sightings of Anna Katharina Emmerich or similar stigmatics with the spiritual experiences to which Theodora prophetically refers in Rudolf Steiner's mystery plays (GA 14). For in the former case there is a residual element of atavistic forces from the past. Theodora, on the other hand, tells of altogether new clairvoyant forces which will develop amongst mankind during the next three thousand years and lead to a *present* experience of Christ. Hence they must, in addition, be understood and nurtured in the Anthroposophical Society. Their foundation is not a stronger bond with the physical bodily nature but a liberation from it, just as in a somewhat different way the modern path of initiation aspires to achieve. Thus the new experiences that Theodora proclaims correspond to the fundamental character of the spiritual experiences of the future, which will be associated not with the bodily senses but with the inner experience of the body-free spirit: 'God is spirit, and those who worship Him must worship in spirit and truth' (John 4:24). For in spiritual research truth can only be reached through the spirit and never through perceptions resembling those deriving from the senses.

This is why modern initiation requires a complete separation from all sense-perceptions as its basic condition if the stage of Imagination is to be reached.[49] Anyone who does not know this has not yet grasped what it means to approach the spiritual world in the modern Michaelic sense. For Michael has no wish to come in contact with anything in man that derives from mere sense-impressions or from what is similar to them. This would signify for him 'a pollution of his being'.[50] This was also known by the old Rosicrucians, because already in their time they sought a Michaelic path to Christ.[51]

In contrast, what a somnambulist undertakes as a kind of 'time-journey', where everything is perceived only in a sensory way, is precisely what must be fully overcome on the modern path of schooling. On this path sense-free thinking becomes a spiritual organ of perception, with which man can initially behold true imaginations of the spiritual world. Thereafter he rises to further stages of initiation: to Inspiration, which can alone give him certainty of knowledge in the spiritual world; and finally

Appendix: The Forces of the Phantom and Stigmatization 159

he reaches the stage of Intuition, with which he is able to research the whole of world evolution, from Saturn to Vulcan.[52] Now he has reached 'cosmic consciousness' (GA 105, 12 August 1908). Only now are the spiritual foundations of the whole physical world of the senses also revealed to him, a world which came into being on Saturn and will on Vulcan finally pass over into a purely spiritual form of existence. Now the initiate so to speak returns to the physical world of the senses with his spiritual consciousness, though from the other, spiritual direction. At this stage he is also able precisely to research the individual facts of earthly history in the Akashic Record. In the following words Rudolf Steiner describes what this means, using as an example his researching of the actual events in the life of Jesus of Nazareth from the realm of the Fifth Gospel: 'The soul offers itself as food to the Archai,' it is spiritually 'digested' by them, for only thereby can one 'be transported into the consciousness of the Archai' (GA 148, 18 December 1913). Only then is one in a position truly to research the earthly life of Christ Jesus, as perceived in the Akashic Record.

And so present and future are united in such research. From the present of Archai consciousness one penetrates in a wholly spiritual way to the facts of the past history of humanity that one is seeking. This is only possible with the power of Christ in one's soul. It was in this way, that is, out of the Christ consciousness, that Rudolf Steiner researched the content of the Fifth Gospel.

Only at the higher stage of initiation that has been described, where the fully developed Intuition of the Christian initiate begins to research events of the physical life of the senses also from the moral-spiritual aspect, can

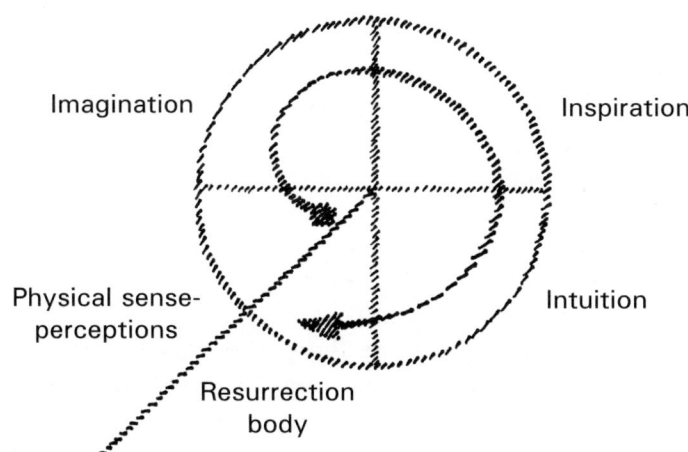

one come to know the essential nature of the Resurrection body. For the Resurrection body encompasses in its cosmic dimension the whole of world evolution from Old Saturn to Vulcan. (See chapters 1 and 2.) Hence for someone who is truly imbued with these forces, the world looks in such a way that everything material becomes as though transparent to him, and he is able to perceive and describe everything pertaining to the senses, down to the smallest everyday occurrences, *out of the pure spirit*. What happens as a result is not a refining of sense-perceptions but their total spiritualization. For at this stage of initiation a person can precisely describe earthly images out of the world of archetypes (Higher Devachan) and, hence, subject the whole process of spiritual research constantly to the strictest examination and surveillance, because description and error do not lie in the world of archetypes but only on the level of images.

On the other hand, it is hardly necessary to remark that, in all sensory perceptions of reflections in the Moon sphere, the human individual is constantly at the mercy of countless possibilities for mistakes and errors. And he cannot himself in any way monitor, still less examine, what he perceives on his 'time-journeys'. Moreover, he is constantly caught up in a dangerous illusion which he can see through only with difficulty. For his sightings appear before him with the power of conviction of sensory reality, without, however, actually being such a reality. The situation is made still more difficult through all that is being described remaining connected exclusively with the Moon sphere, which in this respect represents a particular difficulty, since the influence of the adversarial powers is very strong there.

It was for this reason so important for Rudolf Steiner to emphasize ever and again that the evangelists wrote their accounts not from physical documents, accounts of other people or their own recollections as physical witnesses, but from a faultless reading of the Akashic Record, 'where one actually experiences everything that happened at that time [at the Turning Point of Time]' (GA 95, 3 September 1906). Hence their accounts have nothing in common with the sensory sightings of 'time-journeys'. For they followed and described the events of the Turning Point of Time not from sensory, but from spiritual perceptions. That their sources were the same as those of the modern spirit-researcher is evident from the following words of Rudolf Steiner: 'Initiates can still perceive today what happened on Golgotha; those who carry through the principle of initiation are still able in our time to view the Akashic Record. The writers of the Gospels wrote what they did solely out of the Akashic Record. An event is described, but it did not occur to the original writers of the Gospels to draw upon perceptions of the physical plane. People were at that time so strongly aware that one was concerned here with something that had a connection with the supersensible worlds, and that it was of the greatest importance to achieve a relationship to the supersensible worlds. *A right relation to these events cannot be achieved from the world of the senses*' (GA 143, 17 April 1912). The force of this latter statement applies especially where these events manifest themselves in sightings which appear as sensory perceptions. For in such a case too the relationship to the spiritual world is disturbed, and without this relationship the essential nature of the Mystery of Golgotha can never be rightly grasped.

Thus every anthroposophist who unites himself meditatively with the content of the Fifth Gospel can immediately appreciate its deep relationship to the other four Gospels. For *all five* have the same source in the spiritual world in the true Akashic Record, whence they were brought to the Earth; whereas the sightings of Anna Katharina Emmerich and Therese Neumann—even though they may contain some accurate facts—belong to a completely different sphere.

In summary, one can characterize the mode of perception that arises out of man's connection with the Resurrection body as follows. First, through the restoration of the phantom, the physical body is led back into its original form as belonging to it on Old Saturn. At this stage of evolution the phantom was living—still completely transparent—in what we may think of as paradise, and was as such not yet perceptible with earthly senses. Moreover, man could himself perceive nothing of a sensory nature there. Only after the Fall were his earthly eyes opened ('then your eyes shall be opened', Genesis 3:5), and he could see (hear, smell, etc.) physical objects. In the cycle *From Jesus to Christ* Rudolf Steiner also calls the phantom the 'spirit-body', with which one can of course perceive only the spiritual world, and the physical world of the senses only from the spiritual aspect. Moreover, in the same cycle the phantom is also referred to as 'a real thought in the external world' (10 October 1911). This formulation also completely excludes the possibility that one can form a sensory impression of it. This is a familiar fact to every pupil of the spirit who rises through pure thinking to the world of imaginations, so that thinking itself becomes for him an organ of perception with which he can behold the supersensible world. Still less is it possible to have sense-perceptions with the Resurrection body. For this corresponds to the condition of Vulcan, where the highest spiritualization will be achieved, the nature of which cannot be grasped in any way with earthly concepts.[54]

In other words: forming a connection with the forces of the Resurrection body has nothing to do with stigmata or other outward signs but with a completely new union on the part of man with Christ and the spiritual world. What the physical body perceives by way of the senses on Earth is beheld purely spiritually by the Resurrection body,[55] as Rudolf Steiner was able to do in his spiritual research. For, as we have already seen, this capacity has its origin in his direct and conscious connection with the Resurrection body.

★

On the basis of what has already been said in the first chapter of this book, one can best understand Rudolf Steiner's unique capacity of freely researching in all regions of the spiritual world while maintaining full ego-consciousness from the nature of the Foundation Stone Meditation. Thus in the three microcosmic sections there is portrayed the path of modern initiation, which through the threefold exercise gives man's free ego the possibility of transforming his thinking, feeling and will (life) or spirit, soul and body (the latter initially in their supersensible parts) and make them ready to receive the forces of the Resurrection body. Consequently, the three macrocosmic sections describe what becomes accessible to man's cognitive forces in the spiritual world from this connection with the Resurrection body.

There first appear the highest forces, those of the Trinity, out of which Rudolf Steiner created the threefold Foundation Stone of Love at the Christmas Conference.[56] Then the whole cosmos of the nine divine-spiritual hierarchies comes towards us in their manifold, creative activity, which Rudolf Steiner has spiritually researched in all their different aspects—past, present and future—in his anthroposophical legacy. This world of the hierarchies at the same time forms the cosmic stages at which Christ as the divine Sun and the cosmic Word descended to the Earth out of the realm of the Trinity.[57] For Christ is from the outset 'the leader and guide also of *all* beings of the higher hierarchies' (GA 129, 21 August 1911).

Then come the three Rosicrucian dicta, which describe the quintessence of the whole inner task of all true Rosicrucians with regard to the purpose of their initiation—the acquiring of the forces of the phantom. Thus at the Baptism in the Jordan Christ is born on Earth out of divine forces, He dies a martyr's death at the end of three years in the body of Jesus of Nazareth and rises again on Easter morning out of the forces of the Spirit which master the bodily nature and overcome death.

All this was researched by Rudolf Steiner with the cognitive forces of

Appendix: The Forces of the Phantom and Stigmatization 163

the Resurrection body and presented down to the very details of earthly events in his Christological cycles, above all in the lectures on the Fifth Gospel. Rudolf Steiner brought us a new understanding of Christ and the Mystery of Golgotha not out of sightings perceived by the senses or visions that can be apprehended only spiritually but from pure, sense-free perceptions of the Spirit, which permeates everything on Earth and therefore makes the historical and physical events of the Turning Point of Time transparent and comprehensible.

At the end of the macrocosmic sections of the Foundation Stone Meditation there follows the call to the elemental spirits, who after the Resurrection of Christ became the guardians of the great mystery that Christ has, since then, become the new Spirit of the Earth and thenceforth remains connected with its evolution until Vulcan.

This gives one an idea of the extent of the knowledge available to the Christian initiate who can research the spiritual world out of the power of the Resurrection body. The path associated with sense-bound 'time-journeys' stands in sharp contrast to this path of modern initiation. For the latter leads, as has been described, to sense-free knowledge of the spiritual world and from there to a sure and fully verified description of the physical world from the Akashic Record. The former, in contrast, enters still more deeply into the bodily nature than is the case with normal people, in order to behold the past—which does not any longer exist as a *sensory* phenomenon—as though with bodily senses.

With regard to the appearance of permanent stigmata (their temporary manifestation at the fourth stage of the Christian-mystical path of initiation has, as we have seen, a completely different significance), it should also be noted that neither the apostles nor the other disciples of Christ ever had them, also not the great, leading initiates of Earth evolution such as Manes, Master Jesus, Christian Rosenkreutz and Scythianos, all of whom in the deepest sense worked out of the forces of the Resurrection body and continue to do so today, and are therefore to be regarded as those who most deeply recognize and understand the Mystery of Golgotha. Rudolf Steiner says of these initiates: 'Those who know that the progress of mankind depends upon an understanding of the mighty event of Golgotha are they who, as the Masters of Wisdom and of the Harmony of Feelings, are united in the great, guiding Lodge of mankind. And just as the tongues of fire [of the Whitsun event] glided down as a living cosmic symbol upon the community [of the apostles], so does the Holy Spirit whom Christ Himself has sent reign as the light over the Lodge of the Twelve ... The Holy Spirit is the great teacher of those whom we call the Masters of Wisdom and of the Harmony of Feelings' (GA 107, 22 March 1909).

The Lodge of the Holy Spirit, which guards the mystery of the Resurrection, includes among its members also Rudolf Steiner, who had the task in the twentieth century of bringing to mankind in the early stages of the Michael epoch—not through bodily features but *in full freedom*, because out of pure (body-free) knowledge[58]—the inner path on which a person today can receive into himself the substance of the Resurrection body out of the strength of his ego, in order out of his own experience to attain to the full reality of the Resurrection.

Thus it would be almost absurd to seek in the sightings of Anna Katharina Emmerich or Therese Neumann traits of the future Christ consciousness, which can and should gradually be achieved by more and more people on the anthroposophical path of schooling. If one is looking for a model of this spiritual consciousness, Rudolf Steiner stands before us as a prime example. For the Christ consciousness that he exemplified is possible only through the connection with the Resurrection body.[59] However, there are also other initiates, whose names are mentioned above and are among the great inspirers of anthroposophy, who can serve as models for this.

Furthermore, one should not forget that we are living today at a time which stands under the great sign of the appearance of Christ in the etheric body. This is why Rudolf Steiner never grew weary of emphasizing that one of the most important tasks of anthroposophy is the proclaiming of this fact, together with preparing humanity rightly to apprehend it. This event, which was inaugurated in the 1930s and will embrace a time-span of three thousand years (see GA 130, 4 November 1911) is linked to a second happening which is a kind of continuation of it and whose beginning came about at the end of the twentieth century. 'In the course of the twentieth century *and towards the end of it*, a significant event will take place, not in the physical world but in the higher worlds. This event will have as fundamental a significance for the evolution of humanity as the event of Palestine had at the beginning of our era' (GA 131, 7 October 1911). By this is meant that from this time 'Christ becomes the Lord of Karma for human evolution' (ibid.).

This is a fact to which anthroposophists need to refer today in full clarity. An inseparable component of this fact is that people must learn to direct their attention no longer to the suffering Jesus aspect of the Mystery of Golgotha but to the Christ aspect, which overcomes matter and triumphs over death. According to Rudolf Steiner, herein lies the central task of anthroposophy in the present.

Rudolf Steiner has the following to say as he brings these two most important events of our time together: 'In this connection we have pointed out what is so essential and of such consequence for our age: the new appearance of Christ in an etheric body, *for His reappearance in a physical body is ruled out* by the whole character of our times. Thus we have shown that the Christ, in contrast as it were to the suffering Christ of Golgotha, is appearing on Earth in His office as Judge, as Christ triumphant and Lord of Karma. This has been foreshadowed by those who have painted Him as the Christ of the Last Judgment' (GA 130, 2 December 1911). This is the mighty picture of the future, which alone corresponds to our apocalyptic age and can endow mankind with the strength to withstand the imminent encounter with evil.

Rudolf Steiner then continues: 'In truth, this begins in the twentieth century and will hold good until the end of the Earth. This judgment, this ordering of karma, begins from our twentieth century onwards' (ibid.). And the great karma revelations that he gave after the Christmas Conference in a series of 82 lectures, which he wanted to continue further, can be rightly understood only in the light of this observation.

This experience of the apocalyptic Christ in the full power of His heavenly glory will in the future—which is already beginning in our time—be made manifest above all to those people who are gripped and inspired by the power of Christ's Ego. They will behold not the suffering Jesus but the apocalyptic Christ. 'The Christians of the future who are inspired and imbued by the Ego of Christ will understand something else as well. They will not only understand the Christ who has passed through death; they will also understand the triumphant Christ of the Book of Revelation, resurrected in spiritual fire, He whose coming has been prophesied' (GA 109/111, 11 April 1909).

Thus the ecstatic sightings of Anna Katharina Emmerich and Therese Neumann, which are oriented mainly towards Jesus' way of sorrows, need to be countered by the spiritual-scientific research of Rudolf Steiner. For this derives from the new Michaelic initiation-knowledge and is disseminated amongst mankind today on behalf of the *present* Christ.

The Etheric Christ and His etheric revelation to mankind stand today at the centre of earthly evolution and at the heart of anthroposophy.[60] Only through this revelation and not through somnambulistic experiences of whatever kind can an appropriate access to the events of the Turning Point of Time be found. All other paths that do not begin from this central event of our time, that is, from the present activity of the Etheric Christ—even if they appeal to Christ and call upon His influence—actually lead not to Him but away from Him. At this point we are touching upon the most important task of the anthroposophical spiritual stream, which Rudolf Steiner formulates in the following words: 'The mission of the spiritual-scientific movement is to create the conditions which make an understanding of Christ possible on the physical plane, so that the [Etheric] Christ may be beheld' (GA 130, 21 September 1911). Herein also lies the particular responsibility of anthroposophy towards contemporary humanity. 'We thus comprehend spiritual science in a completely different sense. We learn that it imposes a tremendous responsibility upon us, for it is a preparation for the actual event of the reappearance of Christ' (GA 118, 25 January 1910). This 'preparation' consists—among other things—in that one expressly approaches it in a pure, that is to say, sense-free way and not through the forces and impressions of the physical body.

Moreover, the somnambulistic sightings that have been mentioned cannot be regarded as deriving from a normal Christian-mystical path. For this path has the task of guiding the human individual pre-eminently to a true knowledge of the spiritual world and not to beholding past events with bodily senses.[61] Hence at the end of this Appendix some words of Carl Unger should be quoted from his article from 1927, 'Was hat Anthroposophie zu Konnersreuth zu sagen?' ('What does Anthroposophy have to say about Konnersreuth?'),[62] words with which 80 years ago this important pupil of Rudolf Steiner sought to warn anthroposophists against an excessive enthusiasm for such phenomena: 'Spiritual progress [on the true Christian-mystical path] is a step-by-step elevation into ever higher regions of the spiritual world. If certain prerequisites of a mystical, visionary nature meet up with a pathological loosening of the members of a person's being, the situation may arise that spiritual facts which cannot be mastered by the soul thrust their way into the constitution and give rise to a counter-picture of initiation processes, which are brought down to a stage too deep; the processes then unfold not within the astral body but in the etheric body and are imprinted [as permanent stigmata] in the physical body ... It is probably unnecessary to make particular reference to how, at the moment when the sensation of such processes extends its influence more widely, a mutual element of suggestion enters in, the dangers of which should not be underestimated.'

The seriousness and care with which Carl Unger expresses this can be understood from Rudolf Steiner's words when he was referring to the danger of atavistic forces finding their way into the Anthroposophical Society. The danger that Carl Unger has in mind here is indeed particularly great if, through the spread of false imaginations, a person's individual capacity of judgement is limited[63] and, as a result, the foundation for a sensation with a suggestive influence is created. For in this way his free will is limited, increasingly shackled and hence restricted.

Appendix: The Forces of the Phantom and Stigmatization

Rudolf Steiner says in this regard: 'If the tendency to shackle free will and bind it to the realm of visionary clairvoyance becomes evident again and again, this is a sign that opposition is being generated to the aspirations towards clarity within our movement out of a propensity to fetter free will to visionary clairvoyance ... It was not from Blavatsky or from external sources but through our members themselves that breaches were constantly being made in what we are aiming to achieve. This has happened and continues to happen because of the constant admiration that greets what visionary clairvoyants bring to our attention!' (GA 254, 18 October 1915).

Likewise Ita Wegman, in her article entitled 'Wie bewertet geisteswissenschaftlich orientierte Medizin wie die in Konnersreuth?' ('How does anthroposophically orientated medicine evaluate phenomena such as those in Konnersreuth?'), which she wrote after a thorough investigation of the available facts, refers to the dangers associated with such states. For she sees here a phenomenon which stands in obvious contradiction to the path of schooling appropriate for our time, as given in anthroposophically oriented spiritual science. Thus she comes to the following conclusion: 'In—for example—the constantly repeated similar experiences which she [Therese Neumann] does not consciously call forth and which, moreover, she is unable to prevent, thus indicating the passive nature of what is going on here, there lies the pathological and also the dangerous aspect of her condition, which can, moreover, bring her into mortal danger ... What is pathological here is the inability to create a balance between a spiritual occurrence and an earthly effect, which can be explained through the fact that the soul-spiritual [aspect of her being] has not undergone a systematic schooling in the right way. The path into the spiritual world must be trodden consciously and voluntarily today, with a complete control of all phenomena that manifest themselves. The anthroposophy of Rudolf Steiner gives the guidance necessary for this.'

Thus one can arrive at the conviction that these spiritual-scientifically based judgements of both these important pupils and colleagues of Rudolf Steiner were completely in harmony with his intentions.

Afterword

The present work has evolved out of lectures which I have given in various places over a number of years. The theme of the first lecture, 'The Mystery of Golgotha and the Nature of Spiritual Communion', on which I have spoken in many countries, forms the continuation of the last, ninth chapter, 'The Foundation Stone Meditation. Karma and Resurrection', in my book *May Human Beings Hear It! The Mystery of the Christmas Conference.*

The lecture on the event of the Ascension introduced the conference on 'The Christological Foundations of *The Philosophy of Freedom*' that took place at Ascension 2007 at the Goetheanum in Dornach. Its content forms the first part of the second chapter.

Through the sequence of events at the Turning Point of Time, Easter and Ascension form a unity with the ensuing event of Whitsun. In the cycle of the year this comes about through the three festivals forming a living organism, as described in the second chapter. I have also over the years given lectures on this theme.

In the present book, quotations from Rudolf Steiner's work which, because of limitations of time, could only briefly be mentioned in the lectures have been included in full. The reader is therefore enabled to embark upon his own studies, in order to expand and deepen what has been presented here.

The observations about the mystery of Easter Saturday arose out of looking at the events of Good Friday and Easter Saturday together. For if these events are described in the way that was attempted especially in the first chapter, the question arises: What happened in the intervening period, that is, on Easter Saturday, which forms a kind of bridge between the two poles of the Mystery of Golgotha (death and Resurrection)? An attempt to unveil this mystery with the help of anthroposophy was undertaken in the third chapter.

It lies in the nature of things that, in the process of transcribing, the content of the lectures has been further augmented and deepened by new thoughts, in order that—as far as possible—a complete picture of the events under consideration here may be available to the reader. Much of this has lived in my soul for decades (to be precise, since the writing of my book *The Cycle of the Year as a Path of Initiation leading to an Experience of the Christ Being. An esoteric Study of the Festivals*, which first appeared [in German, although originally written in Russian] in 1986). Thus from this time I continued working with this theme; and now it seems to me that this process has matured to the point where I could share in writing some of these thoughts with a larger circle of people who have acquired the necessary prior knowledge.

The Appendix addresses at some length a question that has been coming towards me more often in recent times. It concerns the essential nature of stigmatization and its understanding from an anthroposophical standpoint. By means of an actual example to which Rudolf Steiner has unambiguously referred (even though this is little known), the attempt has been made here to look into the phenomenon so that a certain orientation may be available for the reader to form a judgement of his own.

Addendum: Responses to Questions

After the appearance of this book in German, a number of questions were put to me both orally and in writing which will now briefly be considered here.

The first question concerns the relationship of the phantom to the Resurrection body and whether Rudolf Steiner himself used the term 'Resurrection body'. Rudolf Steiner does not mention the Resurrection body explicitly, although in the cycle *From Jesus to Christ* he speaks of the 'resurrected body', which approximates closely to the term in question (GA 131, 11 October 1911). It would be possible to omit it altogether and to speak only of the second transformation of the phantom in the process of the Resurrection. For the first transformation, the restoring of the phantom to its condition before the Fall took place already on Good Friday as a consequence of the three years of Christ's presence in the physical body of Jesus of Nazareth. In this connection Rudolf Steiner in the cycle referred to uses words such as 'wiedergeben' ('give back' in the sense of 'reproduce') or 'Wiederaufrichtung' ('resuscitation'), where the prefix (suffix) 'wieder' ('back', 're-') clearly refers to how the phantom, which was corrupted by Lucifer's intervention, was restored in its original form. Likewise the verb 'zurückgeben' ('give back'), which Rudolf Steiner also employs, through the prefix (suffix) 'zurück' ('back') points in the same direction. From the word-formation itself the orientation of what occurred towards the past is clearly apparent.

When, on the other hand, Rudolf Steiner speaks with respect to the phantom of the 'birth process of a new member of human nature' (ibid.), what is evidently meant is not something connected with the past but with the future. For every birth opens up a new perspective on the future from out of the present. This is indicative of the future aspect of the phantom, or its second transformation, which could come about only through the Resurrection. Whether or not one calls this doubly transformed phantom the 'Resurrection body' is not of any particular significance. In the one case one could for example speak of the phantom of the *crucified Christ* and in the other of the *resurrected Christ*. In both cases one has to do with the same essential entity which passed through these two stages or metamorphoses at the Turning Point of Time.

In one respect, however, there is a decisive difference between the two events. For the restored phantom was immediately separated from the material components of the body of Jesus of Nazareth. Rudolf Steiner states: 'When it [the body] was taken down from the Cross, its [material] components continued to maintain their integrity, though *without any connection with the phantom*, because the phantom was completely free from them' (GA 131, 12 October 1911). This separation had become possible because the phantom was of supersensible origin and had entered into a connection with matter (above all in its mineral form) only through the Fall. Hence the phantom as restored by Christ was able to rescue man's ego ('the phantom on which the evolution of the ego depends', ibid.), but it could not out of itself as yet spiritualize matter to the extent of its mineral components. This was and is the essential task of the Resurrection body after the Resurrection. Rudolf Steiner describes as follows what this is essentially about: 'It is the spiritualizing of the human body, or, as it is popularly called, the "Resurrection of the Flesh"' (GA 102, 24 March 1908). This has to do no longer with the restoring of the phantom but with the spiritualizing of the matter that permeated the body, indeed, of matter in general. Rudolf Steiner continues: 'Enlightened circles will not be able in any case to understand ... that matter could one day be spiritualized, that is, that some day something will come about which one calls spiritualization, the Resurrection of the Flesh' (ibid.). But through the forces of the Resurrection body this will indeed happen. By forming a connection with them a human individual will with his last incarnation be in a position to spiritualize all the matter of his physical body.

At the end of this aeon something similar, though on a macrocosmic plane, will happen with the Earth itself. It, too, will be completely spiritualized; and the material parts of the physical body of Jesus, which were received by the Earth itself as a great cosmic communion on Good Friday, will serve as a primal seed for this.[1]

Thus at the end of the book *An Outline of Occult Science* one finds these words: 'We see then that "Grail knowledge" [as described in this book] culminates in the highest imaginable ideal of human evolution: that of spiritualization, brought about by man's own efforts' (GA 13). However, these 'own efforts' have a prerequisite: man's conscious connection with the Resurrection body of Christ, which will become accessible to him from our time onwards in the new Christian mysteries through Rudolf Steiner's deed of inauguration.

To conclude the remarks on this theme, it must once more be indicated here that the essential difference between the phantom and the Resurrection body lies merely in their temporal sequence: according to Rudolf Steiner, the restoring of the phantom was already completed on Good Friday, whereas the transformation into the Resurrection body happened in that process which unfolded from Easter Saturday to Easter morning. From a higher point of view, one that transcends the dimension of time, both metamorphoses—that is, the phantom and the Resurrection body—form an inseparable unity. One can also say: they represent two stages of a single, integrated process.

The fact that Rudolf Steiner only hinted at this difference in 1911 is in my view because, in order to characterize the essential nature of the Resurrection body (as he subsequently did in the Foundation Stone Meditation), he needed the fully developed knowledge of the three systems of man's physical body. Almost 30 years were necessary in order for him to have such a clear and unambiguous understanding of this central result of his spiritual research that he could communicate it to the world. The first time he presented it was in the Appendix to the book *Von Seelenrätseln* ('Riddles of the Soul'), which appeared in 1917,[2] six years after the cycle *From Jesus to Christ*.

The sheer difficulty and complexity of Rudolf Steiner's research path to this truth—which is for us today so natural and plausible—can be gauged from the division of the physical body into 21 members which he presented in the cycle *Man in the Light of Occultism, Theosophy and Philosophy* (GA 137), where the structuring of the members into 3 × 7 represents a first recognizable allusion to the three systems of the physical body.

A further question concerned the thoroughly complicated relationship of the Resurrection body to the condensed etheric body of the Risen One. The difficulty here lies in the fact that in earthly life it is the physical body which forms the outer sheath for all supersensible members of man's being, also for the etheric body. With the Risen Christ, however, it was the other way round. In His case the 'etheric body condensing into visibility' (GA 130, 9 January 1912) formed the outer sheath for His Resurrection body. The physical body of earthly man likewise makes manifest his supersensible members (e.g. the etheric body is revealed in the streaming of fluids). Thus the condensed etheric body has the task of bringing the Resurrection body to manifestation in such a way that it can be perceptible by man's rudimentary clairvoyant faculties.

For according to Rudolf Steiner, researching the spiritual foundations of the physical body (that is, researching the phantom) is one of the most difficult aspects of spiritual science. Thus in the cycle *From Jesus to Christ* he introduces his first description of the nature of the phantom with these words: 'The study of the physical human body as such is one of the most difficult clairvoyant problems, indeed the hardest of all!' (GA 131, 10 October 1911). Hence at the initial stages of clairvoyance the spiritual foundations of the physical body are still entirely hidden from view. 'A higher clairvoyance' (ibid.) is needed in order to be able to investigate these and also the phantom.

Likewise in the earlier mysteries, the problem of researching the phantom was one of the greatest challenges and was referred to in the Middle Ages as a 'Mysterium Magnum' (GA 137, 8 June 1912). Rudolf Steiner says of one master of esoteric Christianity, who had from ancient times been particularly initiated in 'the mysteries of the physical body', that he 'lived in deep concealment, withdrawn behind those who had themselves withdrawn and were pupils of [this] great initiate' (GA 113, 31 August 1909).

From this the question arises: what degree of clairvoyance and initiation did Rudolf Steiner himself possess in order to reveal to a public audience the mystery of the Resurrection body and the phantom from his spiritual research?

At least one of the tasks of the condensed etheric body becomes understandable from what has been said. It was necessary for those individuals around Christ who had not as yet developed a higher clairvoyance (other than Lazarus-John) and, hence, needed the help or mediating power of this special etheric body for their meeting with Him after the Resurrection. In this way they were able to come to a perception of the Resurrection body and thus to an experience of the full reality of the Resurrection.

In his article 'Vom Mysterium der Auferstehung' ('Of the Mystery of the Resurrection'), Dietrich Spitta presents this event in a very illuminating way.[3] For without the mediation of the condensed etheric body, not even the apostle Paul would have been in a position to see the Resurrection body, which led him to make the transformation from Saul to Paul: he did not possess the higher clairvoyance necessary for this.[4] Only because the Resurrection body was veiled in the condensed etheric body was Paul able to perceive it supersensibly. Hence he emphasizes himself that Christ appeared to him in the same form as to the other apostles (and to a wider circle of the disciples).[5]

Dietrich Spitta also solves a further problem associated with this, which stems from what Rudolf Steiner says about Paul's Damascus experience. If Paul perceived above all Christ's Resurrection body (phantom) before the gates of Damascus, so that he arrived at the conviction that the Resurrection had indeed taken place, how can one regard his experience as a prophetic premonition of the present appearance of Christ *in the etheric* (as Rudolf Steiner has indicated in a number of places)? For in the one case it was a question of perceiving the phantom of the physical body—and in the other of a purely etheric manifestation. Both indications are, however, possible and justified, because the perception of the resurrected etheric body of Christ—a perception which has an intrinsic relationship with His etheric raiment in the etheric Second Coming—formed part of the beholding of the phantom as Paul saw it.

It is also understandable from what has been said that Thomas, who—like the other disciples—did not as yet possess higher clairvoyant faculties, could only perceive the scars supersensibly on the condensed etheric body. (See GA 130, 9 January 1912.) If, however, he had possessed a higher clairvoyance, he would have arrived at the insight that the scars on the phantom had an altogether different, indeed a future significance (the significance of new spiritual organs), in contrast to the corresponding marks on the condensed etheric body, which were imprinted upon it as a last memory of the sufferings on the Cross. For the etheric body is also the bearer of memory.

A further question concerned the relationship of the Resurrection body to the Spirit Man. If the Resurrection body—already on Earth—represents the condition of the body on Vulcan, must it not be identical with the Spirit Man? Likewise in this case—as with comparing the Resurrection body with the phantom—one can answer both yes and no, depending on the aspect of the event that one is seeking to emphasize.

As a fully developed bodily member the Resurrection body manifests that stage of evolution that man himself will have reached at the end of the Vulcan stage. Thus on Easter morning Christ revealed to all human beings their future ideal, which they will attain only at the end of cosmic evolution. At the same time, however, the Resurrection body is an altogether different entity from the future Spirit Man. Rudolf Steiner refers to this difference in the course on the Book of Revelation that he gave for the priests of the Christian Community: 'There [in the Mystery of Golgotha] we have the being that man will be *as a human being* at the end of the Vulcan condition *as a God*' (GA 346, 7 September 1924).

What man will in the course of evolutionary development have become at the end of Vulcan was made manifest to humanity on the Earth by Christ in the Mystery of Golgotha *as a God*. For Christ did not create the Resurrection body in the course of evolution but brought His Spirit Man as Resurrection body to the Earth through all intermediary stages from Venus and Jupiter out of the eternity that follows Vulcan, out of the inverse, esoteric stream of time,[6] in order in the sign of Mercury to share this Resurrection body with all human beings as a seed for their further, independent evolution towards the Spirit Man.

Following on from this, a few words need to be said about the nature of Theodora's clairvoyance, out of which she proclaimed her vision of the future in the first Mystery Play. What she sees and speaks about is in itself true. On the basis of Theodora's proclamation the possibility exists from our time onwards—through the clairvoyant faculties newly appearing amongst mankind which bring with them 'a clairvoyance' wholly 'illuminated by reason and knowledge'[7]—of beholding Christ in future in the etheric. However, Theodora does *not* herself possess this future clairvoyance, for she is 'a seeress. With her the element of will is transformed into natural seership' (GA 14, list of characters for the third play). That is to say, her clairvoyant faculty has nothing to do with scientific rigour and strictly disciplined thinking. Hence Rudolf Steiner says of her: 'Theodora is a figure who is to be thought of in terms of a relapse into a Moon consciousness.' And '[with her] naive seership does, of course, signify a lunar seership' (GA 164, 19 September 1915).

The atavistic character of Theodora's supersensible faculties is evident from the following quality of her proclamation, which begins with the words: 'I am *impelled* to speak ...' (GA 14, 'The Portal of Initiation', scene I). In this moment a power foreign to her takes hold of her, which she is not able to resist. Moreover, she cannot monitor its effect on her out of the power of her own ego. And it is precisely this quality that will later be her undoing, when she is unable to protect herself against the occult onslaughts of Johannes Thomasius, subsequently leading to her death.[8]

From this it clearly follows that, although Theodora's visions have something entirely right about them, it would be a disastrous error to regard her supersensible experiences as the results of modern spiritual research. This is the essential difference between Theodora—as a representative of 'naive seership'—and Benedictus as a modern spirit-researcher.

That Theodora loses her atavistic clairvoyance in the further course of life—probably through working with spiritual science—must be regarded as a great step forward for her. Because she is conscious of this, she accepts this loss calmly and positively.

★

Further questions have related to certain parts of the Appendix, where the spiritual origins of stigmatization were investigated with the help of spiritual science.

First, there was a question as to the authenticity of Rudolf Steiner's remark about Anna Katharina Emmerich and the records of her sightings deriving from Clemens Brentano. The point at issue here is whether the fact that this remark has not yet appeared in the Complete Works [Gesamtausgabe] reflects the editors' doubt about its genuineness.

The truth of the matter is as follows. The original intention of the editors of the collected works was to publish lectures with the questions relating to them (which Rudolf Steiner acceded to especially in earlier years). Something along these lines has already been done. Thus the answers to the questions posed at the end of the cycle *The Spiritual Hierarchies and their Reflection in the Physical World* were included in the corresponding volume (GA 110). Sometimes answers to questions were published after individual lectures, thus for example in the volume *The Christian Mystery* (GA 97). However, it turned out that very often the questions had no or only a distant connection with the content of the lectures that preceded them. The editors then had the idea of publishing all the answers to questions in a separate volume. The first step in this direction has already been taken. Thus most of these answers to questions in the archive of the Rudolf Steiner-Nachlassverwaltung have been collected in a *single* file divided according to various themes, which anyone can look at. However, none of this material has as yet been published in the collected works.

Rudolf Steiner's remark about Anna Katharina Emmerich and Clemens Brentano[9] that was quoted was made during a time for questions after a lecture from the Leipzig cycle *Egyptian Myths and Mysteries in Relation to the Spiritual Forces Active in the Present* (GA 106). All questions and Rudolf Steiner's answers were recorded by the same stenographer who had taken down the lectures of the cycle. Hence there is no comprehensible reason why this question and answer session as a whole and in particular the specific interchange about Anna Katharina Emmerich's sightings should be called into question. As in other cases, the particular question and its answer form part of the whole form and history of the lecture cycle to which it belongs.

Another portion of the book's Appendix which was questioned concerns my initially tentative supposition that Richard Pollak, in whom the stigmata reappeared several times from his youth onwards and who later lived for a number of years in Dornach, might have had a conversation with Rudolf Steiner about this. After the appearance of my book my attention was drawn to a publication which confirms this. Already in his youth Richard Pollak had—not in Dornach but at an earlier time in Vienna—met 'Master John'[10] near Frankfurt, under whose guidance he intensively followed the path of Christian-mystical schooling. As a result of this—or out of his karmic predisposition—the stigmata then appeared on Richard Pollak's body. Hilde Boos-Hamburger, recalling her meetings with Richard Pollak, later writes: 'The knowledge of a higher life shone from his eyes, which radiated great kindness. The deepest seriousness and feeling of responsibility pervaded all that he endeavoured to do. After some years it came to the point where the stigmata began to emerge and he was confined to his bed because of great weakness. At this time he and his future wife, Hilde Kotanyi, heard of Rudolf Steiner and asked him to visit. He came and said to Pollak: "This is no path for you!" and gave him some guidance leading him to the modern, Rosicrucian path. Pollak himself subsequently told me this. I had often visited him and his wife in the flat in Vienna before 1914 and became friends with them.'

In this sense Richard Pollak probably had the example of Francis of Assisi in mind, who had during his lifetime told only a few monks in his most immediate environment of his stigmatization (and even this with reluctance), thereafter obliging them to keep the strictest silence. Thus until his death hardly anyone in a wider circle knew about it.[11]

At this point a few words need to be said about some monks' and saints' alleged refusal of food. Their intake of food—their vital connection to the earthly world, which arises only through nutrition—could indeed be considerably reduced, but it was *never* completely broken off.[12] Even though ascetics in very rare cases lived only from the communion, they received it more often and sometimes even every day.

It was said in this respect of John the Baptist that during his many years in the wilderness he lived off 'hard fruits and wild honey' (Matthew 3:4, following Emil Bock's translation).[13] And as for Christ Jesus Himself, His fast of 40 days is referred to as follows: 'And He fasted forty days and forty nights, and afterward He was hungry' (Matthew 4:2). These words refer to an important mystery of the earthly existence of every human being: the connection to the Earth through nourishment.[14] Also at the end of His life, as some of the last words spoken by Christ in the earthly world, the cry sounded down from the Cross: 'I thirst' (John 19:28). With this it is clear that, during His life on Earth, Christ never wanted to break off the relationship to it through *substances*, neither at the beginning nor at the end of the three years of His existence on Earth.

Thus between these two statements—by the evangelist, 'He was hungry', and by Christ Himself, 'I thirst'—lies the whole of the divine human being's three years on Earth. It was also the time when the phantom of the physical body was fully restored for the first time since the Fall. However, this could happen only through the intense relationship of Christ with the bodily sheaths of Jesus, a relationship that extended to hunger and thirst. For only on the foundation of this infinitely painful fusion with the body[15] could the transformation of the phantom be accomplished for all human beings. Hence Rudolf Steiner said that Christ, as the Son of God who had become man, in contrast to all initiates of pre-Christian times never 'withdrew from the physical body' during the entirety of His earthly life 'but continued to dwell within it. And what He lived through and gave to the world during these three years *He gave through the physical body*' (GA 138, 26 August 1912; italics Rudolf Steiner).

It follows with full clarity that the Christian path of development leads not to the refusing of food and the estrangement from the physical body that is associated with it but has as its aim the body's transformation including the matter that one receives as nourishment and—with the Christ power within oneself—learns to spiritualize as *cosmic communion*.

The relationship of Christ Jesus to earthly nourishment acquires its full significance above all from the perspective of the Last Supper. After He had, like all other people around Him, taken food during the three years of His earthly life, He showed at the Last Supper how crucially and intimately this process was connected with His own Being and with His deed on Golgotha. Thereafter, through receiving the earthly substances of bread and wine, he gave His own Being to His disciples as the new Spirit of the Earth. (See GA 112, 7 July 1909.) The mystery of the Last Supper has to do not with a renunciation of earthly nourishment but with the transformation of the process of nutrition.

Likewise after the Resurrection, according to St Luke's Gospel He took food in the presence of His pupils: 'And while they still disbelieved for joy, and wondered, He said to them: "Have you anything here to eat?" They gave Him a piece of broiled fish and honey, and He took it and ate before them' (Luke 24:41–3). Above all the expression 'before them' shows that it was not that Christ needed to eat something after His Resurrection but that He wanted to show His disciples something by way of a new future perspective of human evolution. Rudolf Steiner explains to us in connection with the scene in Emmaus what was going on here. This was where the Risen One was first recognized during the meal through the breaking of bread: 'When He was at table with them, He took the bread and blessed, and broke it, and gave it to them. And their eyes were opened and they recognized Him; and He vanished out of their sight' (Luke 24:30–1). Through Christ's blessing of the bread the spiritual eyes of the two disciples were opened, and they were able to *recognize* Him. With this a further evolutionary perspective is indicated, namely that in future Christ Himself will become perceptible in the cosmic communion of human beings (see further below).

According to Rudolf Steiner's spiritual research Christ did not merely break the bread and give it to the others to eat but, as also with His later appearance (see above), ate together with them. By means of this example Rudolf Steiner explains how it was inherently possible for the Risen One to receive earthly nourishment. This happened not through the phantom but through His condensed etheric body. 'This Gospel passage (the scene with 'doubting Thomas') is particularly wonderful from an occult perspective. It in no way contradicts the fact that we have here an etheric body condensed to visibility through the power of Christ, paving the way for the Emmaus scene. This is described in the Gospel not as an ordinary intake of nourishment, but as a dissolution of food directly through the etheric body, through Christ's power, without the involvement of the physical body' (GA 130, 9 January 1912).

It follows from this that as regards the Christian relationship to the process of nutrition there is no question of a renunciation of food but, rather, the transforming and spiritualizing of this process. In the two verses of the mantra with which Rudolf Steiner concluded the last lecture in the First Goetheanum on 31 December 1922 (GA 219), he describes how this becomes to some extent possible for someone who in our time has embarked upon the path of initiation in the sense of the book *Knowledge of the Higher Worlds*. If the refusing of food had been a worthy aim in this respect, the cosmic communion of man—the beginning of the path whereby the Earth can in future be spiritualized—would have no meaning whatsoever. Rudolf Steiner goes on to say about cosmic communion that in it 'man's fundamental relationship to the world rises from knowledge to a world ritual, a cosmic ritual'. This is 'the first beginning of what must come to pass if anthroposophy is to fulfil its mission in the world' (GA 219, 31 December 1922). So what is involved here is nothing less than the most important task of anthroposophy in the world.

In her article about Therese Neumann that has been quoted, Ita Wegman has already explained her view of what can be said about the refusing of food from the spiritual-scientific medical perspective. Even though not all the questions relevant to this theme can be answered by what she writes, this does not alter the fact that these phenomena have no direct connection with true Christian evolution and, hence, cannot be used to furnish a proof of a special relationship with Christ.

For Christ ate in the presence of His disciples also *after* His Resurrection, on the grounds that He wanted to indicate to them their path to the future spiritualizing of the Earth in the sense of cosmic communion. Rudolf Steiner goes on to say in the passage already quoted: 'All these things can nowadays be understood by following the esoteric principles of spiritual science. The Gospels can in a certain sense be taken literally—apart from passages that have been badly translated' (GA 130, 9 January 1912), thus also what they say about Christ's receiving of physical nourishment after His Resurrection.

Thus the crucial question is not how one may explain a phenomenon such as the refusal of food in any particular case but whether it is essentially Christian and is a kind of ideal for people in general to strive towards. For an anthroposophist it is clear that engaging with this phenomenon cannot be regarded as part of our real spiritual tasks either from a spiritual-scientific standpoint or from a generally Christian view. Whether a person takes food or not belongs to his private life and has nothing to do with the path of knowledge given by Rudolf Steiner to the Anthroposophical Society.[16]

A further question is as follows. How should it be understood that a somnambulist fundamentally has a stronger connection with the physical body, although from the passage quoted from the lecture of 14 January 1917 (GA 174) it is apparent that what is going on here is, rather, a loosening of the ego in a person's lower abdomen.

Rudolf Steiner begins the lecture in question with the terse sentence: 'Human nature is complicated.' He repeats this remark again and again during the lecture and in one passage adds the following: 'I must emphasize that pictorial explanations can very easily lead to misunderstandings, because things said earlier seem to contradict other things said later. Look at things more closely, and you will soon notice that such contradictions are, in fact, non-existent' (ibid.).

For not only before, but also after, this lecture Rudolf Steiner refers on several occasions to how a person who is involved with somnambulism and mediumism 'enters into states that are linked far more with his bodily existence than are his senses themselves' (GA 72, 28 November 1917). Similarly in the Appendix from 1918 to the book *Knowledge of the Higher Worlds* he emphasizes: 'But what comes to light through revelations of this [mediumistic] character is not a *supersensible* but a sub-sensible world' (italics Rudolf Steiner), and he continues: 'In visionary experience and mediumistic demonstrations, a person becomes wholly dependent on his body' (ibid.). At every conceivable opportunity he emphasizes again and again that any 'investigation' of the spiritual world through somnambulism and mediumism is contrary to the path of spiritual science, which leads through the experience of pure thinking to a total independence from the physical body. In spiritual-scientific research the soul 'knows itself, in the activity of thinking, to be in a supersensible region, outside the physical body' (ibid.). Accordingly, 'the development of soul-life proceeds in the opposite direction from that of visionary and mediumistic experience' and 'the soul makes itself progressively more independent of the body than it is in the [ordinary] life of perception and will. Through experiencing pure thoughts, it achieves an independence which then extends over a much wider range of soul-activities' (ibid.), namely, for researching the spiritual world.

The 'apparent contradiction' referred to above is immediately resolved if, in accordance with Rudolf Steiner's advice, one 'looks at things more closely'. It then emerges because of this particular complexity of human nature that what is loosened at one pole can be bound at the other all the more strongly to the body and its sensory activities. In Rudolf Steiner's lecture of 7 March 1904 one can even find a special term for this condition. He mentions there 'somnambulistic mediums' (GA 52).[17] These are people in whom somnambulistic and mediumistic qualities are connected and are to a certain degree complementary. One also finds that they manifest the phenomenon described: what is loosened at the lower pole of the body is bound all the more strongly to the body in the upper regions, above all to its sensory organization. This relationship is of course enacted from the inner aspect. Hence the person in question no longer perceives external processes and beings—from which such individuals are as though cut off in states of this kind—but only spiritual ones; however, these are perceived only with bodily senses, as if they were of a physical, sensory nature.

In contrast, the path of schooling of anthroposophy in the light of Michael enables the supersensible to be perceived with the eyes of the spirit and not with physical eyes. Hence on this path above all sense-perceptions (even everything that recalls them in the most distant context) must be completely overcome. Only man's sense-free thinking should be an instrument of perception here and lead to a communion through knowledge with the spiritual world and with its beings.[18]

In this connection, Rudolf Steiner mentions an interesting detail which should not go unmentioned. It has to do with the relationship of somnambulists to good and evil as it unfolds in their sightings. Thus, for example, they can easily have all manner of visions of a seemingly apocalyptic nature which, however—because such individuals do not have them fully consciously under their control—can easily lead them astray. For true imaginations of the future must be derived from Devachan, whereas somnambulists have to do almost exclusively with the Moon sphere, that is, the lower astral world.

Rudolf Steiner says in this regard: 'The astral world has a different good and evil [from human beings on the Earth]. If somnambulists have perceptions in the astral world, their concepts are very easily distorted by good and evil; and that is the reason why somnambulistic mediums, who initially communicate only true information from this somnambulistic state of consciousness, can in time become utterly confused, so that they are subsequently unable to distinguish deception from reality' (GA 52, 7 March 1904). Hence one must treat sightings by somnambulists which relate to the future and take on increasingly apocalyptic features with the greatest caution, as errors and aberrations are a particularly frequent possibility here.

In conclusion, it must also be emphasized that, in forming judgements of sightings that have a somnambulistic source, it is not merely a question as to whether they are true or false. This must be ascertained in each individual case with the help of spiritual science and out of a comparison of these sightings with the results of Rudolf Steiner's research;[19] but something more fundamental needs to be borne in mind. Information about the spiritual world or past, historical events that has a somnambulistic or mediumistic source *has been received on a path that is completely contrary to that of anthroposophy.*[20]

In the book already referred to Tradowsky cites some words from the biography about Therese Neumann in which her visionary states are characterized as follows: 'She [Therese Neumann] knows herself only as a medium whom Christ makes use of ... Thus it is thoroughly possible for her wholly to obliterate herself in a state of elevated peace, to be nothing other than just a medium.' One could understand this attitude to the spiritual world in someone who, like Therese Neumann, because of his or her life-circumstances could know nothing of spiritual science and therefore had no idea that Christ does not want to make use of anyone as a medium. But if these words are adduced to justify the sightings of someone who knows anthroposophy, they merely show that also Judith von Halle's 'time-journeys' are in clear contradiction to Rudolf Steiner's spiritual science. Thus Tradowsky himself provides the strongest proof that here too, as in the case of Therese Neumann and Anna Katharina Emmerich, one has to do merely with somnambulistic mediumism.[21]

Thus we must take the following words of Rudolf Steiner very seriously: 'What can be experienced through these abnormal states of being [such as somnambulism or mediumism], causing a person to be like an automaton, can never represent the substance of a knowledge that truly derives from that supersensible domain to which man belongs with the eternal aspect of his nature' (GA 67, 21 March 1918). While in another context Rudolf Steiner expresses this thought as follows: 'Any instance of somnambulistic clairvoyance lies below waking consciousness, not above it ... Thus if a clairvoyant perception arises automatically, it is best not to say to oneself that one is a divinely gifted person to whom something has been given that one has acquired [through a proper spiritual-scientific schooling]; for that is the best way to promote distrust' (GA 161, I May 1915).

Any anthroposophist who gives his attention or even his trust to such somnambulistic, mediumistic sightings today must face the fact that they merely detract from the real tasks that Rudolf Steiner has placed before us.

Notes

Chapter 1

1. See S.O. Prokofieff, *What is Anthroposophy?*, Temple Lodge, 2006.
2. See S.O. Prokofieff, *May Human Beings Hear It! The Mystery of the Christmas Conference*, ch. 3, 'The Rhythms of the Christmas Conference', Temple Lodge, 2004.
3. Carl Unger, *Was ist Anthroposophie?*, Dornach 1996.
4. See GA 233a, 13 January 1924.
5. Regarding these stages in the development of the anthroposophical movement, see S.O. Prokofieff, *Rudolf Steiner and the Founding of the New Mysteries*, ch. 3, 'The Path of the Teacher of Humanity', Temple Lodge, 1994, and *May Human Beings Hear It! The Mystery of the Christmas Conference*, ch. 1, 'Rudolf Steiner's Course of Life in the Light of the Christmas Conference'.
6. In GA 148; see also GA 114 and GA 117.
7. Rudolf Steiner has described what free deeds signify and how they can arise within man above all in his book *The Philosophy of Freedom*. See in this regard S.O. Prokofieff, *Anthroposophy and The Philosophy of Freedom. Anthroposophy and its Method of Cognition. The Christological and Cosmic-Human Dimension of 'The Philosophy of Freedom'*, Temple Lodge, 2009; furthermore *Der Hüter der Schwelle und 'Die Philosophie der Freiheit'. Über die Beziehung der 'Philosophie der Freiheit' zu dem Fünften Evangelium* (The Guardian of the Threshold and *The Philosophy of Freedom*. On the Relationship of *The Philosophy of Freedom* to the Fifth Gospel), Dornach 2007; and *May Human Beings Hear It! The Mystery of the Christmas Conference*, ch. 7, '*The Philosophy of Freedom* and the Christmas Conference'.
8. John 15:26, 16:13.
9. The Emil Bock German translation uses the word 'verwandeln' ('change' in the sense of 'transform') here, as do the Authorized Version and the Revised Standard Version. The New English Bible, acknowledging the thrust of the original Greek, gives the rendering used here.
10. Emil Bock's German translation states 'durch die hohe Kraft' ('through the high power')—meaning the power of the Resurrection. Jon Madsen's translation of this verse runs as follows: 'He will transform the lowliness of our earthly body and make it of like form as his transfigured body. He can do this through the mighty power by which he can subject all existence to himself.'
11. One of the reasons why Rudolf Steiner does not mention the Resurrection body in the cycle *From Jesus to Christ* is that knowledge of the threefold physical body was necessary in order to characterize it. This spiritual research could, however, be concluded only in 1917.
12. Rudolf Steiner indicated that man's ego will reach its highest stage of development only on Vulcan: 'Our ego is [on Earth] the baby of our human members, it is the youngest. This ego will be formed in the way that the physical body [which is at present at the fourth stage of world evolution] is now only on

Vulcan, that is, after the evolutions of Jupiter and Venus' (GA 157a, 20 November 1915).
13. In his book *Cosmic Memory* Rudolf Steiner writes: 'After the Vulcan stage man will develop yet further, and will then ascend to still higher levels of consciousness ... of which a description is quite impossible' (GA 11, the chapter entitled 'The Life of Saturn').
14. In chapter 2 of this book it is described how there are, in all, three streams of time involved here. The first is the ordinary one, in accordance with which one lives in the everyday world and inscribes the events of history. The second is a purely supersensible one, which flows in the opposite direction and in which the hierarchies live in the spiritual world. This latter stream flows through world evolution, which extends from the future Vulcan to Old Saturn. From the standpoint of this second stream, the Resurrection body contains both the parts described: the one that connects it with the past, that is, with Old Saturn (the phantom in the true sense), and the other that bears within itself the forces of the future whose influence extends to Vulcan. In the history of Christianity the formula 'without confusion and without separation' is generally used in such a case. Then Rudolf Steiner mentions a still higher, third stream, which flows from eternity to eternity. Its origin lies before Saturn or after Vulcan, in the realm of duration. From the standpoint of this third stream of time, the phantom and Resurrection body appear no longer as separate but form a unity.
15. This anthropomorphization is particularly strongly in evidence in those visions of Anna Katharina Emmerich which relate to the events of the Turning Point of Time. (See also the Appendix.)
16. It is significant that the allusion to the relationship with the Father God is to be found only in St Mark's Gospel, where above all the cosmic aspect of the events of the Turning Point of Time is portrayed.
17. How this actually happened will be described later on in this chapter.
18. In a certain respect the phantom was the whole time separated from the material components of the body through the presence of Christ in the body of Jesus: 'Throughout the three years the phantom remained untouched by the material elements' (ibid.).
19. This also enables one to understand why the words from the Cross 'My God, my God, why hast thou forsaken me?' (Mark 15:34, see also GA 139, 23 September 1912) sounded in the spiritual world as: 'My God, my God, how you have glorified, spiritualized the "I" within humanity' (GA 96, 1 April 1907). For these words express the reality that the work on the restoring of the phantom, in which the salvation of the human ego lies, has been completed.
20. Rudolf Steiner calls this stage the 'Over-Sun' (GA 110, 14 April 1909), the prophetic revelation of which is to be found in the scene of the Transfiguration.
21. See Matthew 8:24–5; Mark 4:38; Luke 8:23–4.
22. That this 'world Judgment' is beginning already in our time and will last until the end of the earthly age is indicated by Rudolf Steiner in connection with the beginning of Christ's activity as the Lord of Karma. (See also the Appendix.)
23. See the Appendix.

24. S.O. Prokofieff, *May Human Beings Hear It! The Mystery of the Christmas Conference*, ch. 9, 'The Foundation Stone Meditation. Karma and Resurrection'.
25. In this regard it is also important to point out that, although Rudolf Steiner speaks here of 'physical visibility', what is at issue here is not the physical but the etheric body. Thus he explains this complicated state of affairs in the following way: 'He [the risen Christ] went about in this way and appeared to those to whom He was able to appear. He was *not visible to all*, since it was really only a condensed etheric body that He bore after the Resurrection' (GA 130, 9 January 1912). And then Rudolf Steiner cites in addition the well-known example of Mary Magdalene (John 20), who did not immediately recognize the Christ in His new form (see ibid.).
26. Hence in various pictures showing Him after His Resurrection (e.g. in some Russian icons and frescoes) Christ Jesus is sometimes portrayed with scars and sometimes without them. This is connected with the fact that in the former case attention is directed more to the condensed etheric body and in the latter case more to the Resurrection body. It is significant that the form of the Risen One also frequently appears without wounds in representations of scenes from the Book of Revelation.
27. In the Emmaus scene in St Luke's Gospel it does not say that Christ ate but that He was recognized in the breaking and sharing of bread (24:30–1). Nevertheless, when He appeared to the apostles in Jerusalem he had asked for food and had before them (probably in the manner described) eaten 'a piece of boiled fish' (24:41–3). Peter also subsequently reported that he was among those 'who ate and drank with Him after He rose from the dead' (Acts 10:41). That this was indeed an instance of taking in food through the condensed etheric body is borne out by the fact that Christ had immediately beforehand showed the disciples His hands and feet (Luke 24:40), that is, presumably the marks remaining on them which belong to the condensed etheric body. From this it also becomes understandable why during his last illness Rudolf Steiner struggled to take in earthly substance as food. He wanted to remain faithful to the essential nature of cosmic communion, associated as it is with the process of the spiritualization of the Earth.
28. In this 'etheric eating' all physical substance was directly transubstantiated into the substance of the phantom, as happened with the bread and wine at the Last Supper.
29. From this it is clear that the principle of *cosmic* communion (see further in this chapter), which occupies a central place in the process of the spiritualizing of the Earth and is associated with earthly nutrition, will also retain its full legitimacy in the future.
30. Rudolf Steiner spoke about the rescuing of the etheric body by Christ at the Turning Point of Time in another lecture: 'The Christ impulse has injected life, new life into man's etheric body, after the [old] life had been used up!' (GA 112, 5 July 1909.
31. This is not at variance with the fact that man's ego also works through the blood; for this influence is carried mainly by the warmth element of the blood. The etheric body, on the other hand, comes to expression in the rhythm of its movement.

32. This relates to one part of the blood, for the other part was collected in the Grail chalice.
33. It is of significance in this respect that one of the two people who played a leading part in the Deposition from the Cross was connected with the mystery of blood and body, namely Joseph of Arimathaea; while the other, Nicodemus, was connected only with the body. (See further in S.O. Prokofieff, *The Spiritual Origins of Eastern Europe and the Future Mysteries of the Holy Grail*, part I, ch. 2, 'Scythianos and the Mystery of Golgotha', Temple Lodge, 1993.)
34. Rudolf Steiner does not recount when the receiving of the body through the earthquake took place. However, it follows from what is reported in St Matthew's Gospel that this happened on Easter Saturday. Thus at the end of chapter 27 it says that 'on the morrow', that is, on the day after Good Friday, the 'chief priests and the Pharisees gathered before Pilate' and asked that a guard be placed before the sepulchre, which was granted. Then they sealed the stone that Joseph of Arimathaea had rolled before the entrance of the tomb (66). It follows from this that at this time the body must still have been visible in the tomb. For the reason for setting a guard was that the chief priests and Pharisees thought that the disciples might secretly 'steal away' the body, in order to claim its disappearance as the Resurrection.
35. After the sentence that has been quoted Rudolf Steiner adds the following description: 'The violent trembling caused by the earthquake shook and scattered the cloths as described in St John's Gospel. It is wonderfully described in St John's Gospel' (ibid.). This is a reference to the following passage: 'Peter then went out with the other disciple, and they came to the tomb. They both ran, but the other disciple outran Peter and reached the tomb first; and stooping to look in, he saw the linen cloths lying there, but he did not go in. Then Simon Peter came, following him, and went into the tomb; he saw the linen cloths lying, and the napkin, which had been on his head, not lying with the linen cloths but rolled up in a place by itself. Then the other disciple, who reached the tomb first, also went in, and he saw and believed' (20:3–8).

    This is how the author of St John's Gospel describes from his own experience, from what he saw with his own eyes, how the cloths were lying in the tomb. In the lectures on the Fifth Gospel Rudolf Steiner gives a somewhat different colouring to the description given above. Thus in this latter context the particular way that the cloths lay in the tomb was due not only to the earthquake but also to a powerful 'whirlwind' which accompanied the earthquake: 'Then, when the body of Jesus had been taken down and laid in a grave, a manifestation of nature can actually be observed—like something that may occur in the moral life of a human being. A whirlwind arose, a fissure opened up in the Earth; and into this chasm the body of Jesus was received, while the burial cloths were whirled away from the corpse' (GA 148, 18 December 1913). Rudolf Steiner then at this point refers to the same passage in St John's Gospel and states: 'It is truly a shattering experience to observe with the eye of seership that the burial cloths lay as described in the Gospel of St John' (ibid.). He then recapitulates the sequence of natural events taking place on the hill of Golgotha: 'These two happenings— the darkness over the Earth, together with an earthquake and a powerful whirlwind—show us how at one point in earthly evolution, natural phenomena coincided with spiritual events' (ibid.). For it belongs to the unique nature of the Mystery of Golgotha that, in it, natural events and moral happenings were no longer separate but intermingled, as will be the case in general at the end of Earth evolution as a result of the continuing influence of the Mystery of Golgotha.

36. See GA 112, 6 July 1909; GA 103, 26 May 1908; GA 101, 13 December 1907; GA 96, 25 March 1907, 1 April 1907 and elsewhere.
37. Possibly he was waiting for the end of the third seven-year period in the development of the anthroposophical movement and also for the inner maturity of the human beings associated with it. For the time-span of 21 years (1902–23) is connected with the birth of the ego.
38. See the article 'Das Goetheanum in seinen zehn Jahren' (The Goetheanum in its ten years), chapters 6 and 7 (in GA 36).
39. That what was involved here was indeed a 'spiritual baptism' was indicated by Rudolf Steiner himself, when exactly a year later he spoke of how during his last lecture in the First Goetheanum some of the medieval Rosicrucian Masters were acting supersensibly as godparents: 'Many of the spirits who taught their pupils in the Middle Ages in the manner described just now stood, I know, as godparents at that moment. And an hour after the last word had been spoken I was called to the burning Goetheanum' GA 233, 31 December 1923).
40. Of course, cosmic communion is also spiritual communion. Thus it should not be regarded as a contradiction if what I have referred to as 'cosmic' communion is, in the lecture cited, called by Rudolf Steiner a 'spiritual communion'. What is being spoken of here is a 'cosmic ritual' as opposed to the inner ritual of the human soul which is associated with spiritual communion. In order to be able to emphasize the distinction between these two, I have allowed myself to derive the term from '*cosmic* ritual'.
41. Heinz Müller, *Spuren auf dem Weg. Erinnerungen* (Traces on the Path. Recollections), Stuttgart 1976. The two blackboards on which the mantra of cosmic communion was written were destroyed in the fire.
42. There are, of course, other meanings of this motif. For every true imagination reveals different layers of spiritual reality.
43. And Easter Saturday—see note 36.
44. See chapter 3.
45. At this time (1911) Rudolf Steiner still often used the name 'theosophy' for the spiritual stream that he led.
46. That is, out of the Holy Spirit, which alone makes possible spiritual communion by establishing a direct connection to the Resurrection body and the etheric body of the Risen One. (See further in S.O. Prokofieff, *May Human Beings Hear It! The Mystery of the Christmas Conference*, ch. 9, 'The Foundation Stone Meditation. Karma and Resurrection'.
47. The following description from *Parzival* by Wolfram von Eschenbach refers to the influence of the transformed forces of the etheric body in the Grail mystery: 'There never was a human [being] so ill but that, if he one day sees the stone, he cannot die within the week that follows. And in looks he will not fade. His appearance will stay the same, be it maid or man, as on the day he saw the stone, the same as when

the best years of his life began, and though he should see the stone for two hundred years, it will never change, save that his hair might perhaps turn grey. Such power does the stone give a man that flesh and bones are at once made young again. The stone is also called the *Grail*.' (Wolfram von Eschenbach, *Parzival*, Book IX. Translation by Helen M. Mustard and Charles E. Passage, New York 1961.)

48. Assya Turgeniev, *Reminiscences of Rudolf Steiner and Work on the First Goetheanum*, the chapter entitled 'New Year's Eve 1922' (English translation, Temple Lodge, 2003).
49. See GA 148, 18 December 1913. In this lecture Rudolf Steiner described this as follows: 'I cannot say whether there was an actual eclipse or whether the darkness was due to thick clouds.'
50. M. Voloshin, *Die grüne Schlange. Lebenserinnerungen* (The Green Snake. Recollections), the chapter entitled 'Brennender Busch' (Burning Bush), Stuttgart 1997.
51. The article, 'Das Goetheanum in seinen zehn Jahren', January–March 1924, part VI, GA 36.
52. F.W. Zeylmans van Emmichoven, *The Foundation Stone*, English translation Rudolf Steiner Press, 1963.
53. Hence with a Rosicrucian one does not find any visible stigmata on the physical body. See further regarding the reasons for this in the Appendix.
54. Rudolf Steiner says of the phantom: 'It is a transparent body of force', it 'is itself entirely transparent' (GA 131, 10 October 1911).
55. GA 346, 11 September 1924. See further regarding the theme of karma and transubstantiation in: S.O. Prokofieff, *May Human Beings Hear It! The Mystery of the Christmas Conference*, ch. 9, 'The Foundation Stone Meditation. Karma and Reincarnation'.
56. The wording he used can be found in the lecture of 7 October 1911: 'towards the end of the twentieth century' (GA 131).
57. See GA 116, 25 October 1909. Moreover, in the lecture of 21 September 1911 (GA 130), Rudolf Steiner mentions that after His third revelation as the world-encompassing Ego Christ 'then rises to even higher stages together with all mankind', that is, this evolution will in future be carried further by Christ.
58. Luke 22:19 and 1 Corinthians 11:24 and 25. Quoted in accordance with the lecture of 8 April 1923 (GA 223).
59. Regarding this, see also S.O. Prokofieff, *May Human Beings Hear It! The Mystery of the Christmas Conference*, ch. 1, 'Rudolf Steiner's Course of Life in the Light of the Christmas Conference'.
60. See also S.O. Prokofieff, *The Foundation Stone Meditation. A Key to the New Christian Mysteries*, Appendix entitled 'The Three Kinds of Communion and the Foundation Stone Meditation', Temple Lodge, 2006.
61. See GA 346, 11 September 1924.

Chapter 2

1. Hence the image of the Sun chariot appears again and again in the old mysteries. The prophet Elijah's 'ascension in a fiery chariot' refers to the same reality (2 Kings 2:11).

2. See S.O. Prokofieff, *What is Anthroposophy?*, Temple Lodge, 2006.
3. Of course, this is only an etheric aspect of this central sculptural work by Rudolf Steiner.
4. In *The Philosophy of Freedom* Rudolf Steiner writes: 'Thinking, in its own essential nature, certainly contains the real "ego"' (GA 4, ch. 9).
5. Rudolf Steiner nevertheless writes in his central anthroposophical book *An Outline of Occult Science* that the path of *The Philosophy of Freedom* is a particularly 'sure' one (GA 13).
6. Quoted from the anthology *Christian Morgenstern. Der Sieg des Lebens über den Tod* (Christian Morgenstern. The Victory of Life over Death), Dornach 1935.
7. Etheric processes played a particular part here. This follows from the fact that Rudolf Steiner spoke again and again with regard to Christian Morgenstern's experiences after death of 'beautiful tableaux of cosmic imagination' which covered this soul like a spiritual cloak. (Quoted from the anthology *Christian Morgenstern. Der Sieg des Lebens über den Tod*.) Or in another lecture: 'Our friend ... lives in the immense cosmic tableau that is like a kind of soul-body for him after death' (GA 155, 14 July 1914). Generally speaking, this imaginative tableau—behind which the etheric body of the dead person stands—dissolves a few days after death. With Christian Morgenstern it was different. Through the particular connection of his etheric body with the Ascension forces, it did not dissolve after death but was preserved by higher powers in order that it might become his 'spiritual cloak', thus enabling what is described in the following pages of this chapter to become possible.
8. Quoted from the anthology *Christian Morgenstern. Der Sieg des Lebens über den Tod*.
9. Lecture of 24 April 1915. Quoted from the anthology *Christian Morgenstern. Der Sieg des Lebens über den Tod*.
10. Quoted from the anthology *Christian Morgenstern. Der Sieg des Lebens über den Tod*.
11. Hence Rudolf Steiner said of the mortally ill Christian Morgenstern: 'How healthy, how inwardly strong this soul was in this crumbling body' (ibid.).
12. Christian Morgenstern's soul itself experienced a kind of Ascension after death. For it had a very short time in Kamaloka and was enabled soon afterwards to enter the spirit-land, in order to fulfil the task just described for the souls who were there.
13. At this point reference should be made to the excellent article by Friedwart Husemann 'Freiheit und Gehorsam—Abraham und *Die Philosophie der Freiheit*' (Freedom and Obedience—Abraham and *The Philosophy of Freedom*) (*Das Goetheanum*, no. 6, 3 February 2006), which culminates in the author's insight that there is a direct allusion to the Christ Being in the words from the third part of *The Philosophy of Freedom*: 'Thus each person, in his thinking, lays hold of the *universal primordial Being* who pervades all human beings' (GA 4). If one supplements the quoted words by those that Rudolf Steiner spoke after the second German edition of *The Philosophy of Freedom* appeared in 1918, one can experience a full confirmation of the correctness of what Friedwart Husemann has written. Thus Rudolf Steiner said in the lecture of 1 January 1919: 'Thus if

one views things from the standpoint of our spiritual science, one emphasizes the Christ impulse as frequently as one does because the Christ impulse lies in the direct line of a *formative thinking*' (GA 187). And in the lecture of 26 November 1921 (GA 79) he mentioned that his *Philosophy of Freedom* was written on the foundation of such a 'formative thinking'. Hence the path of 'formative thinking', and thus also of *The Philosophy of Freedom*, indeed leads to 'laying hold of the universal primordial Being' who, as Christ after the Mystery of Golgotha, 'pervades all human beings'.

14. One could gain a fresh understanding of further aspects of *The Philosophy of Freedom* and *Truth and Knowledge* from this point of view, but to enter into this would go beyond the scope of this book. (Thus for example it would be possible to consider the relationship between the 'unconditionality'—the absence of any assumptions or prerequisites—in Rudolf Steiner's theory of knowledge, as described in the latter book, and the forces of the Cosmic Midnight Hour which become apparent in Christ's Ascension. See S.O. Prokofieff, *Anthroposophy and 'The Philosophy of Freedom'. Anthroposophy and its Method of Cognition. The Christological and Cosmic-Human Dimensions of 'The Philosophy of Freedom'*, ch. 9, 'Metaphysical Foundations for Unconditionality in *The Philosophy of Freedom*'.) It is self-evident that only *one* source of *The Philosophy of Freedom* is being referred to here. Further aspects are considered in other publications by the author. See also *Der Hüter der Schwelle und 'Die Philosophie der Freiheit'. Über die Beziehung der 'Philosophie der Freiheit' zu dem Fünften Evangelium* (The Guardian of the Threshold and *The Philosophy of Freedom*. Concerning the Relationship of *The Philosophy of Freedom* to the Fifth Gospel), Dornach 2007.

15. In the letter to Rudolf Ronsperger of 27 July 1881 the 20-year-old Rudolf Steiner wrote: 'August will, I hope, grant me the necessary peace to commit a large part of my beloved freedom philosophy to paper' (GA 38).

16. Friedrich Rittelmeyer, *Rudolf Steiner Enters My Life*, Floris Books, 1982, p. 79.

17. See S.O. Prokofieff, *May Human Beings Hear It! The Mystery of the Christmas Conference*, ch. 1, 'Rudolf Steiner's Course of Life in the Light of the Christmas Conference'.

18. See S.O. Prokofieff, *Rudolf Steiner and the Founding of the New Mysteries*, ch. 2, 'The Great Sun Period', Temple Lodge, 1994.

19. See further in S.O. Prokofieff, *Rudolf Steiner and the Founding of the New Mysteries*, ch. 2, 'The Great Sun Period', and *May Human Beings Hear It! The Mystery of the Christmas Conference*, ch. 1, 'Rudolf Steiner's Course of Life in the Light of the Christmas Conference'.

20. Hence Rudolf Steiner called the lecture cycle (and the book derived from it) which he gave directly after the turn of the century in Berlin *Christianity as Mystical Fact* (GA 8).

21. See GA 109, 28 March 1909.

22. 'Especially the ten days between the event known as the Ascension and that of Whitsun seemed to them [after they awoke on Whitsun morning] to have been a period of the deepest sleep' (GA 148, 2 October 1913).

23. See S.O. Prokofieff, *Rudolf Steiner and the Founding of the New Mysteries*, ch. 2, 'The Great Sun Period'.

24. Cf. GA 127, 30 November 1911.
25. See also S.O. Prokofieff, *What is Anthroposophy?*, Temple Lodge, 2006.
26. The word 'unconsciously' in this quotation relates to the situation of the ordinary human being. For a distinctive feature of modern Christian initiation is that the person being initiated becomes conscious of this presence of Christ in his being.
27. In Russian cultural circles it is prophetically called a 'sobornic' being. The meaning of the Russian word 'sobor' is at once 'cathedral' and 'a gathering of people': specifically a human community that is formed by people themselves as a kind of soul-spiritual temple, so that social life can be permeated by higher beings of the spiritual world. (See S.O. Prokofieff, *The Esoteric Significance of Spiritual Work in Anthroposophical Groups*, Temple Lodge, 2007.) Vladimir Soloviev called such a social form permeated by Christ 'Godmanhood', or 'a state of divine humanity'.
28. Rudolf Steiner mentions in this respect also the qualities of reverence and trust.
29. The full context of these words of Novalis is as follows: 'A tremendous intimation of the creative will, of the boundlessness, of the infinite multiplicity, of the sacred particularity and universal capability of the inner man, seems everywhere to be astir... All these things are still only intimations, incoherent and raw, but to the historical eye they give evidence of a universal individuality, a new history, a new mankind, the sweetest embrace of a young and surprised Church and a loving God, and the fervent reception of a new messiah within its thousand members. Who does not feel the sweet shame of good hope? The newborn child will be the image of its father, a new Golden Age, with dark, infinite eyes, an Age prophetic, wonder-working, miraculously healing, comforting, and kindling eternal life—a great Age of reconciliation, a Saviour who, like a good spirit, is at home among men, believed in though not seen, visible under countless forms to believers, consumed as bread and wine, embraced as a bride, breathed as air, heard as word and song, and with heavenly delight accepted as death into the core of the subsiding body amid the supreme pangs of love.' (Quoted with minor amendments from *Hymns to the Night and Other Selected Writings*, translated by Charles E. Passage, Liberal Arts Press, 1960.) By the 'young Church' Novalis does not mean one of the existing denominations, which in his eyes all belong to the old Churches, but the invisible 'mystical Church' as a symbol of a spiritualized and Christ-imbued mankind. A century later, Vladimir Soloviev also spoke of this.
30. Rudolf Steiner spoke about this in the lecture of 6 July 1909: 'Thus the innocent death on Golgotha furnished the proof, which human beings will gradually comprehend, that death is the ever-living Father!' And then he continues in the same lecture: 'Christ espouses death, which on Earth had become the characteristic expression of the Father Spirit. Christ goes to the Father and unites with His manifestation, death—and the image of death is seen to be false, for death becomes the seed of a new Sun in the universe' (GA 112). Similarly, in a conversation with Friedrich Rittelmeyer, Rudolf Steiner fully confirmed Rittelmeyer's discovery that in the Farewell Discourses in St John's Gospel 'the word "Father" occurs where one would have expected Christ to use the word "death"' (Friedrich Rittelmeyer, *Rudolf Steiner Enters My Life*, p. 52).

31. Rudolf Steiner gave the following information about the relationship of the Trinity to the first three stages of world evolution: 'As the highest Regent of Saturn, the Ego Spirit appears to us as the Father God, the highest God of the Sun, the Sun God, as Christ, so will the Regent of the Moon stage of the Earth appear to us as the Holy Spirit with his hosts, which in Christian esotericism are called the messengers of the Godhead, Angels' (GA 99, 2 June 1907).
32. Rudolf Steiner calls the sphere of independent evil out of which Lucifer and Ahriman are able to work *together* the Eighth Sphere. (See GA 254, 18 October 1915.)
33. Moses and Elijah who appear there represent the cosmic forces of the outer planets (Moses) and the inner planets (Elijah).
34. See note 31.
35. The lecture 'Evolution, Involution, and Creation out of Nothingness', 17 June 1909 (GA 107).
36. Rudolf Steiner says regarding this: 'The karma of the first half of evolution fulfils itself in the second. What was built up in the course of the first half of evolution is gradually broken down [also karmically] in the second. The cosmic process of coming into being is where karma is generated; and the passing away of worlds, in the broadest sense of the word, is ... the dissolution of the karma related to them' (GA 110, 18 April 1909–I).
37. Rudolf Steiner also calls the phantom a 'real thought in the outer world' (GA 131, 10 October 1911), whence arises its similarity in nature to the Resurrection body.
38. See the lecture 'Whitsun and the Festival of the Free Individuality', 15 May 1910 (GA 118).
39. Rudolf Steiner indicates out of his spiritual research that Jesus of Nazareth also bore within himself a part of the primordial being of Adam from before the Fall. (See GA 114.)
40. Lecture of 4 February 1913. Quoted from *Briefe von Rudolf Steiner* (Rudolf Steiner's Letters), vol. 1, Dornach 1955.
41. See GA 262, 'The Barr Manuscript', part I.
42. Rudolf Steiner describes this influence of the Risen Christ in the history of humanity in the lecture of 1 October 1913 (GA 148).
43. It is, moreover, not difficult to formulate at this point the connection that exists between the three streams of time that have been described and the threefold ego-organization of man. Thus the earthly ego corresponds to the ordinary stream of time, the higher ego to the spiritual time-stream and the true ego to that which flows from eternity to eternity. See regarding the three egos of man in S.O. Prokofieff, *Anthroposophy and 'The Philosophy of Freedom'*, Appendix 1, 'Concerning the Nature of the Human Ego'.
44. This new calendar should really have begun with Easter AD 33, an idea which Rudolf Steiner introduced in 1913 with the first edition of the *Calendar of the Soul*.
45. Concerning this see chapter 1.
46. From what was presented before it is clear that what is being spoken of here is not the 'great' eternity, which can be experienced only through a connection with

the Resurrection body, but that which is revealed when one grasps man's essential nature simultaneously in its pre-birth state and its condition after death. This, however, corresponds precisely to the experience of the higher ego.
47. GA 262, 'The Barr Manuscript', part I.
48. See S.O. Prokofieff, *Rudolf Steiner and the Founding of the New Mysteries*, ch. 2, 'The great Sun Period', and *May Human Beings Hear It! The Mystery of the Christmas Conference*, ch. 1, 'Rudolf Steiner's Course of Life in the Light of the Christmas Conference'.
49. See S.O. Prokofieff, *May Human Beings Hear It! The Mystery of the Christmas Conference*, ch. 7, '*The Philosophy of Freedom* and the Christmas Conference', also *Anthroposophy and 'The Philosophy of Freedom'*.
50. The forces of the Son had already been connected from Old Sun onwards with the whole evolution of the Sun. (See GA 99, 2 June 1907.)
51. See GA 114, 26 September 1909.
52. Peter in the words that he spoke at Whitsun (Acts 2:24) and in other places (e.g. Acts 3:15; 4:10 and elsewhere); Paul, likewise in many places (e.g. Acts 13:30; Romans 10:9 and 1 Corinthians 6:14 and elsewhere).
53. One reads, for example, in the lecture of 10 October 1911: 'Here we are shown that ... the being who is designated as the Father acted as hierophant in the raising to life of Christ Jesus' (GA 131); and: 'The Father Himself raised up the Christ' (ibid.).
54. From the Foundation Stone Meditation, too, it follows that the forces of the divine Father work through the mediation of the First Hierarchy above all in the bone, or limb, system of the Resurrection body.
55. See S.O. Prokofieff, *Anthroposophy and 'The Philosophy of Freedom'*, ch. 7, '*The Philosophy of Freedom* in the Light of the Fifth Gospel'.
56. S.O. Prokofieff, *May Human Beings Hear It! The Mystery of the Christmas Conference*, ch. 9, 'The Foundation Stone Meditation. Karma and Resurrection'.
57. At the Midnight Hour the influence of the First Hierarchy is added to what had previously derived from the Third and Second Hierarchies. (See GA 239, 9 June 1924.)
58. That by this 'vertical' ascent the new, 'horizontal' connection to Cosmic Midnight was meant is shown through the fact that in the Ascension Christ did not—as is usually imagined—leave the Earth but was all the more deeply connected to it. (See GA 148, 3 October 1913.)

Chapter 3

1. Here Rudolf Steiner mentions Venus as the planet which astronomically follows the Moon. Viewed esoterically, the name for this planet is Mercury. (See regarding this GA 110, 15 April 1909–II.)
2. In the lecture of 15 April 1909 (GA 110) Rudolf Steiner gives the following correspondence: the Angels work in the Moon sphere, the Archangels in the sphere of Mercury, the Archai in that of Venus; similarly the Exusiai are connected with the Sun, the Dynamis with Mars, the Kyriotetes with Jupiter and the Thrones with Saturn.

3. S.O. Prokofieff, *Rudolf Steiner and the Founding of the New Mysteries*, ch. 5, 'The Christmas Conference of 1923/1924'.
4. In the next section the following lectures by Rudolf Steiner about the interior of the Earth were taken into consideration: 16 April 1906 (GA 96); 21 April 1906 (GA 97); 12 June 1906 (GA 94); 11 July 1906 (GA 94); 4 September 1906 (GA 95); and 1 January 1909 (GA 107).
5. Rudolf Steiner also mentions in this connection two similar symptoms, 'a kind of theoretical materialism', out of which later practical materialism—with which the Asuras seek to tempt human beings—also inevitably follows with all its social-Darwinistic tendencies; and 'wild orgies of purposeless sensuality' (ibid.).
6. GA 104, 29 June 1908. In the same lecture Rudolf Steiner calls it the 'frightful marriage, or rather the concubinage, between man and the forces of deteriorated matter', which appears in the Book of Revelation in the imagination of the 'great Babylon'.
7. Whereas the three counter-forces previously mentioned (Lucifer, Ahriman and the Asuras) still belong to earthly evolution (Lucifer remained behind on Old Moon, Ahriman on Old Sun and the Asuras on Old Saturn), Sorath belongs to an evolution that derives from other worlds and had originally nothing to do with the Earth. (See GA 104, 30 June 1908, and also S.O. Prokofieff, *The Encounter with Evil and its Overcoming through Spiritual Science*, Temple Lodge, 1999.)
8. See further in S.O. Prokofieff, *May Human beings hear It! The Mystery of the Christmas Conference*, ch. 9, 'The Foundation Stone Meditation, Karma and Resurrection'.
9. In the lecture of 9 January 1912 Rudolf Steiner mentions that at the end of the three years of Christ's life the separation of the phantom from the material body had advanced to the point where its mineral components were held together only by Christ's Ego. 'For, beginning already before the Baptism, this life of Christ in the body of Jesus of Nazareth was a slow process of dying. With every advancing stage during these three years, one can say that something of the bodily sheaths of Jesus of Nazareth died. Gradually these sheaths died away, so that after three years the whole body of Jesus of Nazareth was close to being a corpse, and was only held together by the power of the macrocosmic Christ Being' (GA 130).
10. This is what this layer was called in the Pythagorean School, on the grounds that in it everything connected with it was multiplied into many copies in accordance with the law of number.
11. In the lecture Rudolf Steiner traces this process through the example of the 'fragmented' phantom body of Pliny the Elder, who perished in AD 79 in the eruption of Vesuvius.
12. Emil Bock, *The Three Years*, ch. 10, 'The Events in Holy Week: Saturday in Holy Week', Floris Books, 1980.
13. One can find an earthly reflection of this in the two crosses of the thieves on the Hill of Golgotha, one of whom shows no remorse and remains connected with the depths of the Earth, whereas the other experiences Christ's promise that he will enter into 'paradise' (Luke 23:43), that is, after his death into a connection with the forces of the cosmic cross.

14. See Friedrich Hiebel, *Time of Decision with Rudolf Steiner. Experience and Encounter*, ch. 14, 'Laying of the Foundation Stone', Anthroposophic Press, 1989, and S.O. Prokofieff, *May Human Beings Hear It! The Mystery of the Christmas Conference*, ch. 2, 'The Mystery Act of the Foundation Stone Laying on 25 December 1923'.
15. A year later, in the cycle on *The Gospel of St Mark*, Rudolf Steiner likewise mentions this process. (See GA 139, 24 September 1912.)
16. See also S.O. Prokofieff, *What is Anthroposophy?*, Temple Lodge, 2006.
17. See further regarding the three egos of man in Rudolf Steiner, *The Threshold of the Spiritual World* (GA 17) and in S.O. Prokofieff, *Anthroposophy and 'The Philosophy of Freedom'*, Addendum I, 'About the Inner Being of the Human "I"'.
18. In the lectures about the Fifth Gospel Rudolf Steiner says that the stage of the historical Whitsun corresponded to the sixth stage of initiation of the pre-Christian mysteries, namely to that of the 'Sun Hero' (GA 148, 3 October 1913). Of course, the Whitsun consciousness of the apostles was of a quite different nature from the pre-Christian stage of initiation; but it did not as yet extend to the seventh stage, to say nothing of a still higher one.
19. One can also say that this higher stage is like a continuation of the Whitsun event at the Turning Point of Time.
20. As this stage makes possible the deepest knowledge of the Earth's core itself and, hence, a knowledge of the origin of evil on our planet, it is also understandable that Mani (Manes) became the greatest authority on the forces of evil in the evolution of mankind. These deepest mysteries of evil are, however, not to be sought in exoteric teachings, which have hitherto been contained only in certain old traditional texts (and for the most part in a distorted form). For the true mysteries of evil, which from the outset have been connected with the mystery of the Earth's core as their background, and also the overcoming of evil through the purifying of the interior of the Earth, have not appeared anywhere in the outward history of mankind but exist to this day only in the most intimate circle of the highest initiates of the Earth, strictly guarded by them and in complete seclusion. What is meant by this becomes clear from the following esoteric communication by Rudolf Steiner: 'Within this whole stream, the initiation of *Mani*, who also initiated Christian Rosenkreutz in 1459, is considered to be of a "higher degree"; it consists of the true understanding of the nature of evil. This initiation and all that it entails will have to remain completely hidden from the majority for a long time to come' (GA 262, 'The Barr Manuscript' II, 1907; italics Rudolf Steiner).
21. Regarding Rudolf Steiner's relationship to this stage of initiation, see the book *The Birth of a New Agriculture: Koberwitz 1924*, Temple Lodge, 1999.
22. Rudolf Steiner does indeed refer to such factors with respect to the Turning Point of Time in the lecture of 2 October 1913 (GA 148).
23. It is in this respect of significance that the earthquake at this point is mentioned only in St Matthew's Gospel. Mark only reports the tearing of the curtain (15:38), an event which Luke places immediately before the onset of death (23:45).
24. It is, moreover, striking that Luke does not only speak of a darkness that came over the whole region between the sixth and ninth hours (23:44; Matthew also

tells of this, 27:45) but he adds: 'the Sun was darkened' (23:45, following Emil Bock's translation). This darkening of the natural Sun is at the same time associated with the illumining of the spiritual Sun, which according to Rudolf Steiner began at the moment when the blood flowed into the Earth from the wounds of the Redeemer. This is a testimony in the context of world history to the fact that the spiritual centre of the solar system can since then be found no longer on the Sun but on the Earth. 'The first impetus towards our Earth becoming a sun was given when the blood flowed from the wounds of our Redeemer on Golgotha' (GA 112, 6 July 1909).

25. This is a further reason (compare also chapter 1) why the words on the Cross from St Mark's Gospel (15:34) sounded forth in the spiritual world as 'My God, my God, how you have glorified, spiritualized the ego within humanity' (GA 96, 1 April 1907). For at this moment the Christ Being became visible for the first time in the aura of the Earth as the 'higher Ego of mankind' (GA 112, 24 June 1909).
26. Interestingly, three Gospels report that the women came to the grave *after* the earthquake which had flung the stone aside, for they found it already rolled away when they arrived. See Mark 16:4; Luke 24:2; John 20:1.
27. The rising of the Sun on Easter morning has a direct relationship to its darkening on Good Friday (Luke 23:45). It is now the image of the future Sun which will eventually replace the 'old' Sun in the cosmos.
28. In one of the descriptions he refers explicitly to the account in St Matthew's Gospel. See GA 130, 9 January 1912.
29. Hence the Gospels testify that the tearing of the curtain in the temple (the temple is always an image of the human body) came about as a sign of the Christ Spirit's merging into the aura of the Earth (according to Luke, *before* the death on the Cross, according to Matthew and Mark, *after* death).
30. What has been said here is not at variance with Christ's struggle with death in the garden of Gethsemane (see chapter 1). For there the ahrimanic powers were trying to wrest Christ out of the physical body of Jesus before the restoration of the phantom was fully completed. Only on the Hill of Golgotha, once the phantom had been completely restored, could the distancing of the cosmic Christ from the man Jesus come about.
31. Further consideration of the theme of the redemption of Lucifer, which began as a consequence of the Mystery of Golgotha—for it was luciferic powers that corrupted the phantom at the beginning of Earth evolution—and is likewise depicted in the sketch, lies beyond the scope of the present book.
32. As described at the end of chapter 2, man's soul comes in contact with the direct influence of the Holy Spirit during Cosmic Midnight and, hence, becomes associated with the Holy Trinity. In order to be able to act out its impulses, Christ had to take hold of the forces of Cosmic Midnight from the Earth and bring them to the Earth.
33. In earlier lectures Rudolf Steiner still used the term 'theosophical movement'.
34. Not everything from the core of the Earth will be rescued, for one part will remain behind at the time of the Earth's transition to the Jupiter condition and form the first rudiments of the depraved planet which Rudolf Steiner calls the

'irreclaimable' or 'irredeemable Moon' (GA 13), which will finally fall away from the good path of evolution on Venus.

35. See S.O. Prokofieff, *May Human Beings Hear It! The Mystery of the Christmas Conference*, ch. 7, '*The Philosophy of Freedom* and the Christmas Conference'.
36. In no. 3 of the Statutes Rudolf Steiner writes that the result of the anthroposophy cultivated at the Goetheanum can 'lead to a social life that is truly founded on brotherly love' (GA 260a, 13 January 1924). Likewise in no. 2 he mentions its fruits 'for brotherliness in human intercourse' (ibid.).
37. See further in S.O. Prokofieff, *The Esoteric Significance of Spiritual Work in Anthroposophical Groups and the Future of the Anthroposophical Society*, Temple Lodge, 2007.
38. It follows from this that Jesus had no part in the actual 'Descent into Hell', for it would not have been possible for any human being to accompany Christ's deed at the centre of the Earth.
39. Regarding the 'second death', see GA 104, 30 June 1908.
40. Rudolf Steiner says regarding the further path of the individuality of Jesus of Nazareth that Christ 'adopted him' in the spiritual world 'as His own *soul-sheath*, through which He then proceeds to work' (GA 142, 1 January 1913). See also S.O. Prokofieff, *The Cycle of the Year as a Path of Initiation*, Temple Lodge, 1995, where this question is considered at greater length in note 83 to part XII.
41. In the same lecture Rudolf Steiner indicates that this contracting of the etheric body referred above all to the scars. It was in itself the consequence of the suffering on the Cross.
42. First, however, Rudolf Steiner speaks about those forces of the etheric body that are present in every human body and associated with the future destruction of the physical Earth. Such forces were no longer present in the etheric body of Jesus of Nazareth. For they arise as a consequence of the earthly karma which had been overcome in him through the three years of Christ's life.
43. Rudolf Steiner speaks at this point only of one 'part of the blood' because the other part was collected by Joseph of Arimathaea in the Grail chalice and so did not flow into the Earth.
44. This observation is not in contradiction with Rudolf Steiner's indications that this beast is at the same time an image of those people who will succumb to the power of Sorath in the future. (See GA 104, 27 June 1908.)
45. As the first death is associated with the disintegration of the phantom of the physical body, so the second death has to do with the disintegration of man's etheric body. (See GA 104, 30 June 1908.)
46. This also means that the opposing forces of Lucifer, Ahriman and the Asuras are, with the help of Christ, banished from the interior of the Earth. Otherwise, the future union of the Earth with the Sun could not take place.
47. In the lecture of 19 December 1920 (GA 202) Rudolf Steiner mentions that the destruction of matter (which is the original task of the focus of destruction within man) is mainly concentrated in the limbs and metabolic region. Similarly, he writes in the letter 'Memory and Conscience' (GA 26, February–March 1925) how 'in the will-organization of man's limbs there lives the chaos of the Earth', which has its origin in the interior of the Earth, as reflected in earthquakes and

volcanic eruptions (ibid.). In the same letter Rudolf Steiner also considers the origin of conscience, which in a spiritual respect is rooted in man's limb system. This location of conscience within man accords with the influence of the First Hierarchy, which works out of the centre of the Earth, as was described earlier in this chapter.

48. It is an entirely different matter if the forces of the Earth's interior are disseminated in the world as evil by *human beings*.
49. See earlier in this chapter. In the same lecture Rudolf Steiner also says: 'In certain occult teachings the hosts of Ahriman are also called Asuras.' It follows from these words that the Asuras are primarily those ahrimanic beings who possess the power to draw their forces from the last three layers of the Earth.
50. The problem of evil is, however, preceded by that of death (see GA 185, 25 October 1918). Only by solving this latter problem, which entails a conscious relationship to the Resurrection body, can evil, too, be overcome. Otherwise there is the constant danger that evil gains power over death and uses it for its own purposes. The history of the twentieth century has shown that the power of evil takes human beings in its grip especially where the fear of death is used as a means of power.
51. It is above all those forces of good which can be attained through moral intuitions and their practical fulfilment, as described in the second part of *The Philosophy of Freedom*, that lead to the transforming of the interior of the Earth. For every free deed that man accomplishes out of moral intuition brings about the redemption of the Earth to its very core. The further development of this important theme would go beyond the limits of the present book.
52. Something similar also happens at the centre of the Earth. Matter is constantly disappearing there. Rudolf Steiner says in this connection: 'Matter is constantly being thrust towards the centre [of the planetary body of the Earth], and, remarkably, disappears into the middle point,' so that every 'piece of matter ... is not being thrust through to the other side; it actually disappears at the centre into nothingness!' (GA 110, 18 April 1909–II).

Appendix: The Forces of the Phantom and Stigmatization

1. It is in this connection of significance that in almost two thousand years of historical development in Eastern Christendom, where above all in earlier centuries a particularly large number of hermits and monks pursued the Christian mystical path very intensively, *no single instance* of lasting stigmatization has been reported. (The Protestant Churches likewise have hardly any knowledge of this phenomenon.) On the other hand, several hundred stigmatics are known within the Catholic Church. Hence the Eastern Church even today regards the appearance of such phenomena within Roman Catholicism with great suspicion. It views phenomena of this kind not as part of the common property of Christianity but considers them to be 'typically Catholic' and perceives their origin to be in the strongly overemphasized interest of Roman Catholicism in the earthly, sense-perceptible aspect of the events of the Turning Point of Time. For according to the conception of Eastern Christianity purely spiritual processes,

which are involved in any true initiation, should *not* manifest themselves outwardly in the physical domain *in a lasting way*, on the grounds that physicality should—and this was also the endeavour of the Rosicrucians—be transformed (spiritualized) from within. This is why we find no lasting examples of stigmatization in either the apostles or in the great Christian saints (with the sole exception of Francis of Assisi, who will be spoken about later on).
2. Only if this entire path is associated with the element of freedom does it remain in accordance with the consciousness soul of contemporary humanity and with the Michaelic character of our time. This cannot, however, be said of Anna Katharina Emmerich and Therese Neumann—if one reads the reports of their soul and bodily states.
3. Elsewhere Rudolf Steiner formulates his description thus: 'At the time of meditation *red stigmata-like points* appear just in the places associated with the holy wounds' (GA 95, 3 September 1906).
4. 'Thus in the course of his meditation the pupil can call forth the stigmata on his skin. This is then a sign that he is ready for the fifth stage, where in a flash of illumination mystical death is revealed to him' (GA 94, 1 June 1906). In other words, the stigmata only play a temporary role in preparation for the next stage of initiation. This follows from another context: 'These exercises [of the fourth stage] lead to the vision that the pupil sees himself being crucified. And *this* stage of initiation manifests itself outwardly through the arising of the so-called wounds' (GA 94, 11 July 1906). The word 'this' refers in this context to the association of the wounds *only* with this stage of initiation. Rudolf Steiner expresses himself even more clearly in the lecture of 19 May 1907: 'The voluntary bringing about of the so-called "trial by blood" is the symptomatic expression of the fourth stage of initiation' (GA 284/285).
5. The apostle Paul bore the stigmata in this invisible way, and said of himself: 'For I bear on my body the marks of Jesus' (Galatians 6:17). Many other saints were also bearers of such invisible marks.
6. The objective is actually reached only at the final stage, which Rudolf Steiner calls the seventh, that of the 'Resurrection'. (See, for example, GA 95, 3 September 1906; GA 96, 16 April 1906 or GA 131, 14 October 1911.)
7. This description, in various formulations, refers as much to the stage of the 'Resurrection' as to that of the 'Ascension'.
8. Thus, for example, Rudolf Steiner says in the lecture of 30 November 1906 (GA 97) just before the beginning of his description of the seven stages of the Christian-mystical path: 'The Christian teacher must guide the pupil's feelings and sensations... It is best if we characterize these seven steps in such a way that we describe how the relationship between teacher and pupil unfolds. The teacher says something like the following to the pupil...' Then follows the description of the first stage and also the further ones. And in another context he observes: 'Hence the Christian master demands of his pupil a higher degree of humility and devotion' (GA 94, 1 June 1906). Moreover, in the lecture of 19 May 1907 Rudolf Steiner says: 'Then he [the spirit-pupil] was received by his master of Christian initiation.' And then he adds: 'Anyone who seeks to do this without the advice of a teacher is certainly in danger' (GA 284/285).

9. *Prager Erinnerungen aus den Jahren 1920–1929 an Stadt und Menschen, Vorträge und Studien. Funde und Veröffentlichen von Walter Kühne*, Radolfzell am Bodensee ('Prague Memories from the Years 1920–1929 of City and People, Lectures and Studies. Discoveries and Publications by Walter Kühne').
10. See the observations by Carl Unger and Ita Wegman at the end of this Appendix.
11. During his life only very few monks intimately associated with him knew of it, and they had undertaken to say absolutely nothing. Only after his death did his stigmatization become generally known.
12. The significance of the latter becomes immediately apparent in comparing Francis of Assisi with Thomas Aquinas.
13. Hence there were never reports of individuals who reached the higher stages of this initiation in the times before Francis of Assisi that they received the stigmata, although according to Rudolf Steiner 'hundreds and hundreds of people underwent this initiation. It became an actual experience for thousands' (GA 97, 22 February 1907). For if this kind of initiation is rightly followed through, the stigmata appear at the fourth stage of the path in the form described above and, moreover, only temporarily (because called forth solely by meditation). With the attainment of the higher stages, however, they disappear again.
14. This is a reference to the council of the highest initiates of the Earth which took place in the fourth century. (See GA 113, 31 August 1909.)
15. See GA 131, 5 October 1911.
16. The following description by Rudolf Steiner may serve as one example among many of such an *indirect* influence upon the physical body: 'The Greater Guardian is encountered when this sundering of connections [between thinking, feeling and will] extends also to the physical parts of the body (primarily the brain)' (GA 10). So that 'the brain of the higher clairvoyant divides into three independently active entities: the thinking-brain, the feeling-brain and the willing-brain' (ibid.). But because this transformation of the physical body is brought about by conscious inner work, it 'is not physically perceptible in the ordinary way' (ibid.).
17. In the ninth chapter of *The Philosophy of Freedom* Rudolf Steiner indicates that the activity of ordinary thinking is possible only if the organic processes of the body are held back. Similarly, thinking can achieve a sense-free condition—which alone makes it possible for man to gain conscious entry to the spiritual world— only through being separated from all sense-impressions. Rudolf Steiner says in this regard: 'Spiritual science shows us how man evolves in the course of time. What spiritual science regards as the aim of this evolution is the achievement of the spirit-researcher, the scientist of the spirit, in freeing himself from everything that is connected with outer nature, with outward physicality' (lecture of 13 June 1910, published in *Beiträge zur Rudolf Steiner Gesamtausgabe*, no. 106).
18. And in an earlier lecture from the same cycle Rudolf Steiner mentions how the Rosicrucian alchemists worked with the problem of how the phantom can pass over into human beings. They were able to do this only because they '[felt] in their hearts ... a connection with Christ' (GA 131, 12 October 1911).
19. This question and answer session has not as yet been published in the Collected Works (Gesamtausgabe).

20. From the lecture entitled 'Manifestations of the Unconscious from the Standpoint of Spiritual Science' (GA 67, 21 March 1918). In the same lecture Rudolf Steiner describes how hallucinations and visions have their origin within man in the unconscious relationship of the life of the imagination to the physical body. In the case of somnambulistic 'sightings', on the other hand, it is more a question of the bodily relationship of the will, which can even bring about changes in the physical organism.
21. In Anna Katharina Emmerich's principal work, *Das bittersüsse Leiden unsers Herrn Jesu Christi* (The Bitter-sweet Suffering of Our Lord Jesus Christ) the thoroughly naturalistic description of Jesus' martyrdom takes up over 100 pages, whereas the description of the Resurrection occupies only a few.
22. In this connection one can also describe Mel Gibson's film *The Passion of Christ* as a Hollywood production of the 'Gospel' according to Anna Katharina Emmerich.
23. Furthermore, in the detailed accounts that Anna Katharina Emmerich gives of the early years of Jesus and the life of Mary nothing can be found about the two Jesus children or the two Marys. Nor does she have any awareness that Lazarus and John the Evangelist are the same individuality.
24. This alien spirit is manifested above all in the erroneous balance between earthly and spiritual events. The excessive emphasis upon the purely earthly aspect of what happened, together with the blatant stirring of the reader's emotions through the accumulation of gruesome details, create a gloomy atmosphere which is altogether foreign to the purity of the all-illumining Christ Spirit. As a result, the reader is diverted from what is essential and focused solely upon the sense-perceptible aspect. Through such sightings one does not reach beyond the limits of the sense-perceptible world but remains all the more strongly ensnared within it by the fascination of such images.
25. One must of course bear in mind with such a hypothesis that in the case of every human being the etheric body dissolves within three days after death. Only with high initiates, who are able to work on their Life Spirit, does the etheric body remain largely intact and works in the further course of evolution as a source of inspiration from the spiritual world. It happens even more rarely that such an initiate is reborn with the same etheric body. As examples of this phenomenon Rudolf Steiner names individualities such as Christian Rosenkreutz and the Master Jesus. It goes without saying that their stage of development cannot be compared to that of Anna Katharina Emmerich or Therese Neumann. Moreover, it is necessary to recall that immediately after death, when the etheric body is freed from the physical body, time at once becomes space in the former, so that the person concerned for three days sees the panorama of his past life unfolding before him in one single picture, which would scarcely be possible with sensory organs. This shows that the memories in the etheric body are not preserved in the form of sense-perceptions.
26. In early lectures Rudolf Steiner still used the word 'theosophy' instead of 'anthroposophy', which is what he actually meant.
27. 'Theosophie und Somnambulismus', lecture of 7 March 1904 (GA 52). The danger of error is especially great with sightings that are perceived with the

senses. For the luciferic and ahrimanic powers have a great interest in sensory representations of this kind. 'They [Lucifer and Ahriman] always have an interest in things being conceived far too spatially and temporally' (GA 286, 7 March 1914).

28. Herein lies what is most problematic about this condition. For a person who has *visions* of the spiritual world may possibly ask himself whether they are indeed true. But it is very difficult to doubt what one sees with one's own eyes as sightings of events on the *physical* plane (in this case the events of the Turning Point of Time). And yet everything that one beholds in the form of sense-perceptions is not free from the consequences of the Fall and is therefore 'impure' (or, to use the old-fashioned word, 'unchaste'). This is, after all, one of the main consequences of the Fall: 'And the eyes of them both were opened, and they knew that they were naked' (Genesis 3:17).

29. A first publication in this direction appeared several years ago.

30. See S.O. Prokofieff, *Eternal Individuality. A Karmic Biography of Novalis*, Temple Lodge 1992.

31. If it had been otherwise, one might well imagine that Rudolf Steiner would have recommended the writings of Anna Katharina Emmerich, for example, for religion lessons in Waldorf schools or for the Christian Community. Probably for the reasons mentioned, Rudolf Steiner determined against this. On the other hand, he gave Emil Bock the task of developing a new theology on the basis of anthroposophical Christology, which Bock implemented in his seven-volume life's work *Beiträge zur Geistesgeschichte der Menschheit* ('Contributions to the Cultural History of Humanity'), Stuttgart 1978–1981 (available in English under separate titles).

32. Rudolf Steiner had already given an exact description of Christ's countenance from his inner perception three years previously, first in the lecture of 8 May 1912 (GA 143) and then in greater detail in the lecture of 14 May 1912 (GA 133).

33. Friedrich Rittelmeyer, *Rudolf Steiner Enters My Life*, p. 73 (English translation 1929).

34. See A. Fant, A. Klingborg, A.J. Wilkes, *Rudolf Steiner's Sculpture in Dornach* (English translation 1975). If one compares these three works executed personally by Rudolf Steiner with many other models and studies that Edith Maryon helped him with, it is immediately evident that she brought into her work a style completely different to that of Rudolf Steiner. If one contemplates her work today, it belongs—for all its beauty and originality—to the artistic productions of its time. The three works by Rudolf Steiner that have been mentioned do, however, have a timeless quality. The following episode shows how difficult it was even for Rudolf Steiner's most gifted pupils to understand his spiritual impulses, never mind carry them out. When Rudolf Steiner had returned to Dornach after a lengthy journey and saw the figure of the Representative of Humanity executed by Edith Maryon he said of it: 'This English Lord is not my Christ, however' (Assya Turgeniev, *Reminiscences of Rudolf Steiner and the Work on the First Goetheanum*, the chapter entitled 'The Statue of the "Group"', English translation 2003). Nevertheless, it was a mark of Edith

Maryon's inner greatness that such a critical remark from her teacher did not evoke in her the slightest indignation, for 'it came as a matter of course to her, with all her artistic gifts, to be merely a pupil, the hand which was there to serve Rudolf Steiner' (ibid.). See also Peter Selg, *The Figure of Christ. Rudolf Steiner and the Spiritual Intention behind the Goetheanum's Central Work of Art*, Eng. tr. 2009.

35. The author learnt of this personally from Marjorie Spock (1904–2008), who visited Rudolf Steiner in his studio and had heard him speak these words. Without any external help and solely out of the strength of his own ego, Rudolf Steiner arrived at this direct perception of Christ in the spiritual world and portrayed this supersensible perception of his in plasticine and then in wood. To think otherwise would mean failing to recognize Rudolf Steiner's stage of initiation and, hence, questioning the whole of anthroposophy.

36. Quoted from *The Architectural Conception of the Goetheanum* (GA 290).

37. The *present* experience of Christ signifies, in an occult sense, that in His figure the past events of the Turning Point of Time flow together with the future stages of human evolution. Hence Rudolf Steiner says regarding the painted Christ figure in the First Goetheanum that He appears between Lucifer and Ahriman 'in His Jupiter majesty, in His future splendour' (GA 161, 3 April 1915).

38. Heinz Müller, *Spuren auf dem Weg. Erinnerungen* ('Traces on the Path. Recollections'), Stuttgart 1976, p. 40.

39. Friedrich Rittelmeyer, *Rudolf Steiner Enters My Life*. See also Andrei Byeli, *Verwandeln des Lebens* ('Transforming Life'), ch. IV, 'Rudolf Steiner und das Thema Christus' ('Rudolf Steiner and the Theme of Christ'), Basel 1975.

40. Rudolf Steiner was then able to descend from thus experiencing the Mystery of Golgotha in Intuition through the stage of Inspiration to that of Imagination, in order to come to the experience of it which he describes as follows: 'Yes indeed, it is possible to attain to the Imagination of the mount on which the Cross was raised, that Cross on which a God hung in a human body' (GA 131, 14 October 1911). It is clear that if one beholds such imaginations as are imbued with the corresponding intuition, the countenance of Christ can be experienced in the smallest details.

41. Hence in another context I described the whole of anthroposophy with this in view as a 'Resurrection science'. See S.O. Prokofieff, *What is Anthroposophy?*

42. See GA 95, 23 August 1906.

43. Rudolf Steiner refers in this connection to how in the case of a somnambulist those forces of the ego that in normal life are bound by the 'abdominal organs' achieve an ever greater independence (GA 174, 14 January 1917). These forces of the ego which have unconsciously become free feel attracted by the Moon sphere and, together with the astral body, take a portion of the etheric forces with them also. Thus somnambulists such as Anna Katharina Emmerich and Therese Neumann were by the end hardly able to leave their beds, for their bodily organs were increasingly deprived of the supportive and nurturing forces of the etheric body.

44. Rudolf Steiner additionally mentions that 'somnambulistic states ... are very complicated' (GA 52, 7 March 1904), and also that the experiences of somnambulists can be distorted through 'quite definite combinations and connections', a point on which he does not elaborate further (GA 67, 21 March 1918).

45. What has been said here is connected with a further property of the Moon, namely that it has the task of leading souls into the physical world of the senses. This is why all experiences of this sphere inherently have the character of sense-perceptions which in themselves are illusory, because one is not dealing with a physical reality here.
46. The many outward cultural details, such as Jewish customs, language, clothes, habits and so forth which Anna Katharina Emmerich perceives to a considerable degree in her sightings fit in with this picture.
47. See the description of such states on the part of Therese Neumann in the testimonies of Dr E. Schickler, which Dr Wegman published in her article 'Wie bewertet geisteswissenschaftlich orientierte Medizin Erscheinungen wie die in Konnersreuth?' ('How does anthroposophically orientated medicine evaluate phenomena such as those in Konnersreuth?'). See the anthology *Im Anbruch des Wirkens für eine Erweiterung der Heilkunst* ('At the dawn of the work devoted to an extending of the art of healing'), Arlesheim 1974. One can observe a limitation of freedom in all somnambulistic phenomena of this kind, even though not in so extreme a form as in the case of Therese Neumann.
48. Regarding the connection of the Sun forces with freedom and the Moon forces with necessity, see GA 240, 25 January 1924.
49. See GA 26, the article entitled 'The Sense and Thought Systems of Man in relation to the World'.
50. See GA 26, the article entitled 'Second Study (continued). Hindrances and Help to the Michael Forces in the Dawn of the Age of the Consciousness Soul'.
51. Perceptions that are purified by a cultic service or a Goetheanistic manner of observation form an exception here.
52. See GA 99, 1 June 1907.
53. What has been said here should not be confused with what Rudolf Steiner has said about the relationship to the Moon sphere in the old mysteries, for example in the lecture of 21 April 1924 (GA 233a). For the aim of these mysteries was to behold the spiritual Sun—which was at that time the dwelling-place of Christ—from the Moon sphere. One cannot, however, follow this path today, since Christ is no longer to be found on the Sun.
54. Rudolf Steiner writes concerning this: 'No soul which, with its thinking, is still tied to a physical body should reflect about Vulcan and its life' (GA 11, the chapter entitled 'The Earth and its Future').
55. Or in other words: where the perceptions of past events (as in 'time-journeys') retain their sensory character, there can be no question of an influence of the phantom or the Resurrection body.
56. See GA 260, 25 December 1923 and also S.O. Prokofieff, *May Human Beings Hear It! The Mystery of the Christmas Conference*, ch. 2, 'The Mystery Act of the Foundation Stone Laying on 25 December 1923'.
57. See S.O. Prokofieff, *The Twelve Holy Nights and the Spiritual Hierarchies*, part I, ch. 2, 'The Starry Script as a Key to Anthroposophical Christology'.
58. As is known historically, such bodily features bring about in people who see them a state of total unfreedom, because they are confronted by something which apparently contravenes natural laws. This unfree situation is fundamen-

tally at variance with the only path into the spiritual world that is appropriate today, which is based upon pure knowledge and, hence, upon the complete recognition of human freedom. Moreover, as already mentioned, the admiration of stigmata promotes occult materialism, for one falls prey to the illusion that one might see the spirit with the visual senses.
59. See S.O. Prokofieff, *What is Anthroposophy?*
60. See GA 152, 2 May 1913.
61. Rudolf Steiner says concerning the seventh stage of this initiation: 'It signifies being fully received into the spiritual world' (GA 94, 26 February 1906).
62. Carl Unger, *Schriften* ('Writings'), vol. 2, Stuttgart 1966.
63. Rudolf Steiner says for example in the lecture of 28 March 1913 that 'false imaginations then infect the soul to such an extent that they stifle healthy human reason and intelligence... And it might very well be that, whereas a person who disseminates intellectual absurdities easily invites criticism, anyone who spreads false imaginations takes away from those who believe in him the possibility of criticism, that is, he blinds them to the need to reject the imaginations in question' (GA 145).

Addendum

1. See chapter 1 of this book, 'The Mystery of Golgotha and Spiritual Communion'.
2. GA 21, 'Commentary Notes', part 6: 'Principles of Psychosomatic Physiology'. See chapter VII of *A Case for Anthroposophy*, ed. Owen Barfield, RSP, 1970.
3. Published in *Anthroposophie. Vierteljahrschrift zur anthroposophischen Arbeit in Deutschland*, Easter 1/2009.
4. This follows, for example, from the fact that, during the second decisive spiritual experience of his life, Paul was unable to determine precisely whether this occurred within or outside the body. See 2 Corinthians 12:3–4.
5. See GA 112, 7 July 1909.
6. See chapter 2 of the present book, 'Easter, Ascension and Whitsun in the Light of Anthroposophy'.
7. GA 121, 17 June 1910. In the same lecture Rudolf Steiner describes the Archangel Vidar as the inspirer and guardian of this new clairvoyance.
8. See GA 14, the third play 'The Guardian of the Threshold'.
9. That Rudolf Steiner was well aware of Clemens Brentano follows from his remark about the inclination of some Romantics towards Roman Catholicism, which he described as unhealthy. (Clemens Brentano, who converted to Roman Catholicism, was one of them.) Referring to an example of the contrary, he says that spirits such as Novalis were 'healthy enough by nature to guard against converting to Catholicism' (GA 184, 13 October 1918). Rudolf Steiner's wellnigh lifelong association with Clemens Brentano's nephew, the philosopher Franz Brentano (1838–1917), whose lectures at Vienna University he had attended from time to time and whom he greatly valued as a sensitive and subtle thinker and specialist in the philosophy of Aristotle, points in the same direction. (See GA 21.) In contrast to his uncle, Franz Brentano—who had already become

a Catholic priest in his youth—came out in protest against the dogma of the infallibility of the Pope and was thenceforth active only as a free philosopher.
10. His real name was Alois Mailänder (1844–1905). See regarding him in Emil Bock, *Rudolf Steiner. Studien zu seinem Lebensgang und Lebenswerk*, lecture of 17 October 1956, 'Von den okkulten Bewegungen in Deutschland am Ende des 19. Jahrhunderts' ('Concerning Occult Movements in Germany at the End of the 19th Century'), Stuttgart 1967.
11. Thomas von Celano (*c*. 1190–*c*. 1260), the first biographer of Francis of Assisi, who was himself a Franciscan and had known the saint very well personally, writes about this. His book became the foundation for all later descriptions of Francis of Assisi's life.
12. For example, nothing is known from his immediate environment about Francis of Assisi's refusal of food. For such a state was certainly not an aim that either he or his pupils aspired towards; even though—in common with all ascetics—they were modest in their intake of food, they never renounced it altogether. The reduction of physical nourishment was never an aim that ascetics set themselves but was one of the means whereby they controlled their bodily desires in order to attain a greater moral perfection. One can also find remarkable testimonies along these lines in descriptions of the lives of Eastern yogis.
13. In Christian tradition John is regarded as a strict ascetic. Hence Christ Jesus said about him and of Himself to the people: 'For John came neither eating nor drinking, and they say: "He has a demon"; the Son of Man came eating and drinking, and they say: "Behold, a glutton and a drunkard, a friend of tax collectors and sinners!"' (Matthew 11:18–19). Thus Christ testifies that He did not refuse food during the three years of His life on Earth (apart from the 40-day fast in the wilderness). Even after His Resurrection he gave His disciples a comparable example (see below).
14. In Eastern Europe, one speaks of eating as a communion with the Earth.
15. See GA 148, 3 October 1913.
16. Thus the booklet on this theme by Peter Tradowsky, *The Stigmata, Destiny as a Question of Knowledge* (Temple Lodge Publishing, 2010), is from an anthroposophical standpoint completely misconstrued. For the details cited there from someone's private life are none of anyone else's business. They cannot, therefore, in isolation provide the basis for a public discussion. Moreover, the reference to the visions of Anna Katharina Emmerich and Therese Neumann in Tradowsky's publication and also in the previously appearing publication by W. Garvelmann, *Sie sehen Christus. Anna Katharina Emmerich, Therese Neumann, Judith von Halle. Erlebnisberichte von der Passion und der Auferstehung Christi. Ein Konkordanz* ('They see Christ. Anna Katharina Emmerich, Therese Neumann, Judith von Halle. Reports of Experiences of the Passion and Resurrection of Christ. A Concordance'), Dornach 2008, is indicative of the unmistakable connection of this kind of sensory vision—as manifest in all three stigmatics—to a specifically Catholic 'mysticism'.
17. Likewise in another lecture Rudolf Steiner speaks about 'somnambulism ... which is related to mediumistic phenomena' (GA 67, 21 March 1918).
18. The foundation for this—which is at the same time indicative of the whole

orientation of spiritual science—was expressed by Rudolf Steiner in the familiar words: 'Becoming aware of the idea in reality is the true communion of man' (GA 1, ch. VI). This is also the basis for the modern path into the spiritual world.

19. On pages 146–148 four examples of Anna Katharina Emmerich's sightings are given which are clearly at variance with the fruits of Rudolf Steiner's research. With no more than minor differences, all four can likewise be found in the books of Judith von Halle.
20. Probably for this reason, in the entirety of his work Steiner never mentions the content of Anna Katharina Emmerich's sightings, although Clemens Brentano's publications of them were well known at the time.
21. In his book *Sie sehen Christus. Erlebnisberichte von der Passion und der Auferstehung Christi. Ein Konkordanz* (Dornach 2008), W. Garvelmann has already shown that Judith von Halle's sightings belong—also as regards their content—quite clearly to the kind of visions experienced by Anna Katharina Emmerich and Therese Neumann (and they incorporate the same errors).

Bibliography

The following list of Rudolf Steiner's works includes the writings and lectures referred to in the present book and is given in accordance with the bibliographical numbers of the volumes in the collected works.

GA

1	*Goethean Science*
4	*The Philosophy of Freedom*
8	*Christianity as Mystical Fact*
9	*Theosophy*
10	*Knowledge of the Higher Worlds*
11	*Cosmic Memory*
12	*The Stages of Higher Knowledge*
13	*Occult Science*
14	*The Four Mystery Plays*
15	*The Spiritual Guidance of Humanity*
21	*Von Seelenrätseln* (part of this volume is available in English under the title *The Case for Anthroposophy*)
26	*Anthroposophical Leading Thoughts*
28	*The Course of My Life*
36	*Der Goetheanum-gedanke inmitten der Kulturkrisis der Gegenwort*
38	*Briefe Band I: 1881–1890*
52	*History of Spiritism / The History of Hypnotism and Somnambulism*
67	*Das Ewige in der Menschenseele. Unsterblichkeit und Freiheit* The lecture of 21 March 1918 was published in the *Anthroposophical Quarterly* 14:2, 3 under the title 'Manifestations of the Unconscious: Dreams, Hallucinations, Visions/Sleep and Dreams'
72	*Freiheit—Unsterblichkeit—Soziales Leben*
79	*Paths to Knowledge of Higher Worlds*
94	*An Esoteric Cosmology*
95	*At the Gates of Spiritual Science / Founding a Science of the Spirit*
96	*Original Impulses for the Science of the Spirit*
97	*The Christian Mystery*
99	*Theosophy of the Rosicrucian / Rosicrucian Wisdom*
100	*Menschheitsentwicklung und Christus-Erkenntnis* The lecture of 27 June 1907 is included in *Theosophy and Rosicrucianism*
101	*Occult Signs and Symbols*
102	*The Influence of Spiritual Beings upon Man*
103	*The Gospel of St John*
104	*The Apocalypse of St John*
105	*Universe, Earth and Man*
106	*Egyptian Myths and Mysteries*

107	*Geisteswissenschaftliche Menschenkunde*
	The lectures of 1 January and 22 March 1909 are published under the title *The Deed of Christ and the Opposing Spiritual Powers*)
	The lecture of 17 June 1909 is included in *The Being of Man and his Future Evolution*
109/111	*The Principle of Spiritual Economy/Rosicrucian Esotericism*
110	*The Spiritual Hierarchies and their Reflection in the Physical World*
112	*The Gospel of St John in its Relation to the Other Gospels*
113	*The East in the Light of the West*
114	*The Gospel of St Luke*
116	*The Christ Impulse and the Development of Ego Consciousness*
117	*Deeper Secrets of Human History in the Light of the Gospel of St Matthew* (does not include all the lectures in this GA volume)
118	*The Reappearance of Christ in the Etheric*
	The lecture of 15 May 1910 is included in *The Festivals and their Meaning*
121	*The Mission of Folk Souls*
123	*The Gospel of St Matthew*
127	*Die Mission der neuen Geistesoffenbarung*
	The lecture of 30 November 1911 is available in typescript Z437 under the title 'The Threefold Call from the Spiritual World'
129	*Wonders of the World, Ordeals of the Soul, Revelations of the Spirit*
130	*Esoteric Christianity*
131	*From Jesus to Christ*
132	*The Inner Realities of Evolution*
133	*Earthly and Cosmic Man*
136	*The Spiritual Beings in the Heavenly Bodies and in the Kingdoms of Nature*
137	*Man in the Light of Occultism, Theosophy and Philosophy*
138	*Initiation, Eternity and the Passing Moment*
139	*The Gospel of St Mark*
142	*The Bhagavad Gita and the Epistles of St Paul*
143	*Erfahrungen des Übersinnlichen. Die drei Wege der Seele zu Christus*
	The lecture of 17 April 1912 is included in *Three Paths of the Soul to Christ*
	The lecture of 8 May 1912 is included in *Artistic Representation of Christ*
	The lecture of 17 December 1912 is published under the title *Love and its Meaning in the World*
145	*The Effects of Spiritual Development*
147	*Secrets of the Threshold*
148	*The Fifth Gospel* (does not include all lectures in this volume)
152	*Approaching the Mystery of Golgotha*
153	*The Inner Nature of Man and the Life between Death and a new Birth*
155	*Christ and the Human Soul/The Spiritual Foundation of Morality*
157a	*The Forming of Destiny and the Life after Death*
159/160	*Das Geheimnis des Todes*
161	*Wege der geistigen Erkenntnis und der Erneuerung künstlerischer Weltanschauung*
	The lecture of 10 January 1915 is available in typescript Z273, 'Perception of the Nature of Thought'

The lecture of 1 May 1915 is included in typescript Z346, 'Meditation and Thought Training'
The lecture of 3 April 1915 is included in *Festival of the Seasons*
164 *Der Wert des Denkens für eine den Menschen befriedigende Erkenntnis*
The lecture of 19 September 1915 is included in typescript R77, 'Value of Thinking for a Knowledge Satisfying to Man'
168 *Die Verbindung zwischen Lebenden und Toten*
The lecture of 18 February 1916 is available in typescript NSL217, 'Concerning the Life between Death and a new Birth'
172 *The Karma of Vocation*
174 *The Karma of Untruthfulness*, vol. 2
175 *Bausteine zu einer Erkenntnis des Mysteriums von Golgotha*
180 *Ancient Myths—their Meaning and Connection with Evolution*
181 *Earthly Death and Cosmic Life*
182 *Der Tod als Lebenswandlung*
185 *From Symptom to Reality in Modern History*
186 *The Challenge of the Times*
187 *How can Mankind find the Christ again?/The Birth of Christ in the Human Soul*
193 *The Inner Aspect of the Social Question/Influences of Lucifer and Ahriman*
194 *Mission of the Archangel Michael/Archangel Michael: His Mission and Ours*
202 *Die Brücke zwischen der Weltgeistigkeit und dem Physischen des Menschen: die Suche nach der neuen Isis, der göttlichen Sophia*
The lectures of 18 and 19 December 1920 are included in *The Bridge between Universal Spirituality and the Physical Constitution of Man*
207 *Cosmosophy*, vol. I
208 *Cosmosophy*, vol. II
212 *Menschliches Seelenleben und Geistesstreben im Zusammenhang mit Welt-und Erdenentwicklung*
214 *The Mystery of the Trinity*
216 *Supersensible Influences in the History of Mankind*
219 *Man and the World of Stars*
223 *The Cycle of the Year/Michaelmas and the Soul Forces of Man*
224 *Die menschliche Seele in ihrem Zusammenhang mit göttlich-geistigen Individualitäten*
The lecture of 7 May 1923 is included in *The Festivals and their Meaning*
225 *Drei Perspective der Anthroposophie*
The lecture of 23 September 1923 is available in typescript Z244, 'Jacob Boehme, Paracelsus, Swedenborg'
226 *Man's Being, his Destiny and World Evolution*
229 *The Four Seasons and the Archangels*
233 *World History in the Light of Anthroposophy*
233a *Rosicrucianism and Modern Initiation/The Easter Festival in the Evolution of the Mysteries*
236 *Karmic Relationships*, vol. II
237 *Karmic Relationships*, vol. III
238 *Karmic Relationships*, vol. IV (lecture of 28 September 1924 also published separately as *The Last Address*)

239   *Karmic Relationships*, vols. V and VII
240   *Karmic Relationships*, vols. VI and VIII
254   *Occult Movements in the Nineteenth Century*
257   *Awakening to Community*
260   *The Christmas Conference*
260a *The Constitution of the School of Spiritual Science/The Life, Nature and Cultivation of Anthroposophy*
262   *Correspondence and Documents*
264   *From the History and Contents of the First Esoteric School, 1904–1914*
284/285   *Rosicrucianism Renewed*
286   *Architecture as a Synthesis of the Arts*
346   *The Book of Revelation and the Work of the Priest*

A note from the publisher

For more than a quarter of a century, **Temple Lodge Publishing** has made available new thought, ideas and research in the field of spiritual science.

Anthroposophy, as founded by Rudolf Steiner (1861-1925), is commonly known today through its practical applications, principally in education (Steiner-Waldorf schools) and agriculture (biodynamic food and wine). But behind this outer activity stands the core discipline of spiritual science, which continues to be developed and updated. True science can never be static and anthroposophy is living knowledge.

Our list features some of the best contemporary spiritual-scientific work available today, as well as introductory titles. So, visit us online at **www.templelodge.com** and join our emailing list for news on new titles.

If you feel like supporting our work, you can do so by buying our books or making a direct donation (we are a non-profit/ charitable organisation).

office@templelodge.com